OPEN SHELF

T4-ACZ-692

Illinois Library
at Urbana-Champaign

THE TAXATION OF CORPORATE INCOME IN INDIA

BY THE SAME AUTHOR
A Grammar of Indian Planning
Malthus and Classical Economics

THE TAXATION OF CORPORATE INCOME IN INDIA

S. AMBIRAJAN

ASIA PUBLISHING HOUSE
NEW YORK

© 1964 by S. AMBIRAJAN

PRINTED IN INDIA

By D. D. Karkaria at Leaders Press Private Limited, Bombay and Published by P. S. Jayasinghe, Asia Publishing House, 119 West 57th Street, New York

To
P. A. SESHAN
with affection & gratitude

PREFACE

THE aim of this monograph is to study the evolution, structure, administration, effects and future prospects of the taxation of corporate income in India in the context of the changing ideas and concepts that are influencing our tax policy. The subject, important enough at any time, is of particular significance now, since Indian economy, being Plan-conscious and Plan-directed, is in a transitionary stage, when efforts are being channelled towards the rapid economic development of the country. One unmistakable sign of this is the growing industrialisation, the definite shift in emphasis from agriculture to industry ; and it is through the steady expansion of corporate activity that much of this development is being achieved. For several decades in the past, corporations have been playing no negligible part in the economic life of India ; but their role has greatly increased during the last 20 years, and more especially during the last 10 years.

On the other hand, this steady expansion of the corporate form of industry and business has materialised under peculiar conditions, not all of them favourable to such expansion. The possibility of reaping profits has coaxed corporate expansion, but profits have also called forth taxes, and there has accordingly been a race between increasing profits and higher taxation. In the result, an elaborate and complicated structure of corporate taxation has come into being, almost in a haphazard manner. Compelled to steer between the long-term need to help the corporate sector to grow (and with its growth to advance the nation's economy) and the short-term need to secure funds for the manifold tasks of the administration (including the feeding of the 'public sector' enterprises), corporate taxation in recent years has had to make compromises of all sorts, now offering tax incentives to promote corporate investment and expansion, now drastically increasing the tax load on the corporations. Corporate taxation has had, besides, to reflect, now in greater now in lesser measure, the socio-economic policies of the Ruling Party. It is an absorbing subject, if also, at times, a most exasperating one ; and I was attracted to it both on account of its intrinsic interest and on account of its immediate relevance to the problem of India's economic development.

A study of the taxation of corporate income in India necessarily involves also the exploration of the appropriate backgrounds: namely, the economics of corporate taxation in general, the history of corporate activity in India, and the volume and variety of the legislation relating to companies and corporate taxation in India. Corporate activity and corporate taxation have many features that cut across national barriers, while there are other features that have a recognisable local colour. Underdeveloped countries, for example, have problems of their own, and corporate activity and corporate taxation in such countries may have to meet special needs in a special way. While trying, therefore, to fix my gaze steadily on the problem of corporate taxation in the present Indian context, I have not wholly ignored the wider backgrounds either. For example, in the Appendix I have briefly tried to compare the rates and incidence of corporate taxation in various countries. Again, I have tried in the first chapter to give a resume of the economics of corporate taxation to serve as a theoretical framework to my study. For writing this chapter I found the works of authorities like J. R. and Ursula K. Hicks, Richard Goode, Nicholas Kaldor, J. R. Petrie and R. A. Musgrave very instructive and enlightening. Likewise, for writing the third chapter, in which I have tried to see my way through the tropical jungle of income-tax legislation and case-law, I found the standard treatises of V. S. Sundaram, A. C. Sampath Iyengar and G. C. Sharma both invaluable and indispensable.

This book is a revised version of the thesis for which the Andhra University, on the unanimous recommendation of a Board of Examiners consisting of Mrs. Ursula K. Hicks (Oxford), Mrs. Vera Anstey (LSE, London) and Dr. A. R. Prest (Cambridge) awarded me the degree of Doctor of Philosophy in July 1961. The original draft was read by, and profited from the comments of, my Professor, Dr. K. K. Das, President of the Faculty of Commerce, Andhra University, and Mr. P. A. Seshan, Financial Editor of *The Hindu* (Madras). Mr. William Peters, Lecturer in Economics at the University of Manchester, read the thesis at a later stage and offered useful suggestions. I am, besides, deeply grateful to my three examiners for their approbation and helpful comments. I should also make special mention of the advice and assistance I had at every stage from my father, Prof. K. R. Srinivasa Iyengar, who helped me particularly to improve my expression; and but for the way my parents sustained me with sympathy and encouragement during my periods of disappointment and gloom, I might not have successfully persevered in my career of research.

While engaged in writing the book, I received kindness and help from many, and in particular from Prof. B. B. Deshpande, Mr. S. Jagannathan, Mr. K. S. Sunderrajan, Mr. A. K. Jauhar and Mr. V. N. Murty. My thanks are also due to the librarians and staff of the following libraries in which I collected the materials for this book : Andhra University Library, Madras University Library, Library of the Department of Economics and Sociology of the Bombay University, Sir Ratan Tata Library at the Delhi University, the *Hindu* Office Library at Madras, and the India House Library at London.

Lastly, I thank my sister, Dr. (Mrs.) Prema Nandakumar, for help in the arduous task of proof-reading as also the preparation of the Index.

S. AMBIRAJAN

Faculty of Economic & Social Studies
University of Manchester
Manchester-13
7 *March* 1964

CONTENTS

Preface ... vii

I THE ECONOMICS OF CORPORATE TAXATION ... 1

Introduction: Pre-Independence and Post-Independence policies, 1. What are Corporations? 3: Early History, 3; The Corporate 'Personality' 4. Why Should Corporations be Taxed? 7: The 'Cynical' Financial Plea, 7; The 'Privilege' Theory, 8; The 'Social Costs' Theory, 11; The 'Socio-Political' Theory, 14; 'Functional Finance', 14; The 'Ability to Pay' Theory, 17; Conclusion, 19. How Should Corporations be Taxed? 20: Tax on Gross Sales, 21; Tax on Capital Stock, 22; Capital Levy, 23; Tax on Income, 25; What is Income? 25; Excess Profits, 32; Undistributed Profits, 33; Partnership Method, 35; Dividend-Credit at the Corporate Level, 36; Dividend-Credit at the Individual Level, 36; The Withholding Scheme, 37; Capital Gains, 38; Bonus Shares, 41; Intercorporate Dividends and Consolidated Returns, 42; Justice in Taxation, 43. Effects of Corporate Taxation, 46: Shifting and Incidence, 46; Economic Consequences, 50; Retardation of Risk-Taking, 53.

II THE CORPORATE SECTOR IN INDIA ... 58

Introduction, 58: The Managing Agency System, 59; 'Public' and 'Private' Companies, 61. Corporation Finance, 62: Financing Corporations, 62; Capital, 63; Share Capital, 64; Share Distribution, 66; Company Legislation in India, 69: The Act of 1956, 71; Holding and Subsidiary Companies, 72. History of the Corporate Sector in India, 76: The Beginnings: The Nineteenth Century, 76; The Twentieth Century, 78; The First World War and After, 79; The Second World War Period, 81; The Post-War Period, 82; The Private and Public Corporations: Their Relative Growth, 85; The New Companies and the Old, 87; Profits, 89; Business Cycles, 97; Nature and Extent of Demand, 97; Controls, 98; Competitive Conditions, 99; Corporate Saving, 99; The Dividend Policy, 100; Role of Retained Profits in the Corporate Sector, 102; Dangers of Excessive Ploughing-Back of Retained Profits, 110; Corporate Investment, 111; Capital Formation, 113; Size of Corporate Investment, 116; Relation of Corporate Profits to the National Income, 117; Conclusion, 118.

III THE EVOLUTION AND STRUCTURE OF THE TAXATION OF CORPORATE INCOME ... 119

Introduction, 119: Corporate Taxation in India, 119; Jurisdiction of the Central Government, 119. Income-tax Legislation in India, 120: The

Beginnings, 120; The Act of 1886, 122; Period of Integration: 1886-1916, 123; The Act of 1916, 123; Supertax, 125; The Act of 1922, 125; Amending Acts, 126; Status of Companies, 127; Division by Dichotomy, 128; Classification of Companies, 129; Section 23A of the Act, 130; Companies in which the Public is Substantially Interested, 131; Non-Indian Companies, 132; Companies with non-resident Shareholders, 133; Companies with a Low Income, 134; Refunds to Shareholders, 134; Supertax or Corporation Tax, 135; The Exemption Limit, 136; Summary, 137. Rate Structure of Company Taxes, 138: Rate Structure of Company Income-tax, 138; Surcharge on Income-tax, 138; Post-war Amalgamation and After, 139; Rate Structure of Corporation Tax, 140; Total Tax Burden, 140; Formal Rates and Real Rates, 141; Rebates on Income-tax, 142; Rebates on Corporate Tax, 144; Post-Independence Rate and Rebate Structure, 145; Excess Dividends and Bonus Shares, 147; Section 23A Companies, 148; Reforms under the Finance Act of 1955, 150; Definition of 'Dividsnd', 152; Are Bonus Shares 'Dividends'? 155; Kaldor's Views, 156; Views of the Royal Commission (1955), 157. Tax on Bonus Shares, 157; Bonus Shares and 23A Companies, 158. Computation of Income, 159: What is Net Income? 159; Heads of Income, 161; Permissible Deductions, 162; Depreciation Allowances, 163; Development Rebate, 165; Deposits, 166; Capital Gains and Losses, 167; Tax Holiday, 167. Other Taxes, 168: The Excess Profits Tax, 169; Method of Computation, 169; Compulsory Saving, 170; The End of the Tax, 172; The Business Profits Tax, 173; The Tax on Capital Gains, 174; Abolition of the Tax, 175; Re-introduction in 1956, 176; The Wealth Tax, 177; The Gift Tax, 179. Conclusion, 180; A Vicious Circle, 181; Evils of Hasty Legislation, 182.

IV EFFECTS OF CORPORATE TAXATION 184

Introduction, 184. Changing Structure of the Tax System in India, 185; Pre-War Preponderance of Indirect over Direct Taxes, 185; Wartime Shift to Increasing Direct Taxation, 187; Wartime Shift from Customs to Excise Duties, 189; Post-War Developments, 189. Pattern of Corporate Taxation in India, 191: Income and Corporate Taxes, 191; The Principle of 'Grossing', 195; Growth of the Corporate Sector, 197; Corporate Profits, 197; Higher Tax Rates in the Post-War Period, 199. Effects of Corporate Taxation in India, 202. Psychological Effects, 203; Trend of Security Prices, 204; Physical Effects, 220; The Problem of 'Shifting', 220; Cutting Down Wages and Shifting to Labour, 221; Raising Prices and Shifting to Consumer, 224; The First Phase, 1939–51: A Sellers' Market, 225; The Second Phase, 1951–59, 227; Slashing Dividends and Shifting to the Shareholders, 229; Impact of Company Taxation on the Level of Corporate Savings, 229; Vicissitudes of Corporate Savings: First Phase, 1939–51, 230; Vicissitudes of Corporate Savings: Second Phase, 1951–59, 235; Effects of Company Taxation on the Growth of the Corporate Sector, 240; Supply of Capital for Investment, 241; Depreciation Allowances, 241; Deleterious Effects of Corporate Taxation, 243; Investment Risks, 246; Who are the Investors? 250; Investment for Capital Gains, 253; Socio-Political Effects of Corporate Taxation, 254; The Corporate Tax System Progressive as a Whole, 255. Conclusion, 256.

V CORPORATE TAXATION AND ECONOMIC DEVELOPMENT IN INDIA 259

Introduction, 259. Economic Development and Underdeveloped Countries, 259: Determinants of Economic Progress, 259; The Problem of Population, 260; The State of Technology, 261; Capital Accumulation, 262; Income and Investment in India, 263; A 'Vicious' Circle in the Underdeveloped Economies, 264; The Problem of Industrialisation, 265; Political Freedom and the Urge Towards Economic Development, 266; Mixed Economy in the Free Underdeveloped Countries, 267; Role of Taxation, 268. Corporate Taxation and India's Economic Development, 269: Direct and Indirect Taxes, 269; The Growth and Role of the Corporate Sector, 270; Corporate Taxation in an Underdeveloped Country, 272; Taxation as a Means of Reducing Inequalities in Income, 274; Taxation as a Tool for Encouraging Investment, 275; The Case for a Reduction of Corporate Taxes, 280; Incentive Taxation, 283. Tax Reform, 287: Improvement in Administration, 287; Prevention of Evasion, 288; Kaldor's Reform Proposals, 289; Need for Simplicity in the Tax Structure, 291; Elimination of 'Nuisance' Taxes, 293; Security for Investors, 296; Need for Continuity, 297. Conclusion: The Future of the Corporate Sector in India, 298.

Appendix

A Comparative Note on Corporate Taxation 301

Select Bibliography 304

Index 313

LIST OF TABLES

CHAPTER II

I	Issues of Fresh capital	68
II	Number and Paid-up Capital of Joint-stock Companies (1882-1900)	77
III	Number and Paid-up Capital of Joint-stock Companies (1939-45)	81
IV	Number and Paid-up Capital of Companies Incorporated (1945-51)	83
V	Number and Paid-up Capital of Companies Incorporated (1951-61)	84
VI	Number and Paid-up Capital of Public and Private Companies	86
VII	Joint-stock Companies Registered Newly Year by Year	88
VIII	Profits of Indian Joint-stock Companies and Unregistered Firms and Associations of Persons	92
IX	Index of Profits (Base 1939=100)	94
X	Index of Profits (Profits after taxes: Base year 1950=100)	96
XI	Uses of Net Corporate Income	103
XII	Corporate Profits and Savings	105
XIII	Net Profits and Retained Profits	106
XIV	Rise in Paid-up Capital	112
XV	Estimate of Capital Formation in the Corporate Sector in India	114
XVI	Estimate of the Capital Formation in the Indian Corporate Sector Based on the Gross Capital Formation in Six Major Industries	115

CHAPTER III

I	Tax Collected from Business as percentage of Total Tax Collection	124
II	Rates of Company Taxation	142

CHAPTER IV

I	Percentage Revenue of Some Important Heads	185
II	Taxes on Income as Percentage Share of Union Revenues	186
III	The Growth of Central Tax Revenue	188
IV	Customs and Central Excise as Percentage Shares in Total Revenue	189
V	Indices of Industrial Production	190
VI	Import of Machinery and of Iron and Steel	191
VII	The Relative Importance of the Corporation Tax	192

LIST OF TABLES

VIII	Corporate Contribution to the Treasury	194
IX	Growth of the Corporate Sector	198
X	Percentage of Corporate Taxes on Corporate Profits	200
XI	Corporate Tax Liability of Certain Income Groups	201
XII	Indices of Variable Dividend Securities	206
XIII	Average Earnings of Factory Labour in India	222
XIV	All India Consumer Price Index	223
XV	Index of Wholesale Prices of Manufactured Goods in India	225
XVI	Indices of Labour Earnings and Cost of Raw Materials	226
XVII	Indices of Industrial Production and Price of Manufactured Goods and Money Supply	228
XVIII	Company Finances and Capital Formation in Six Indian Industries	231
XIX	Gross Profits, Taxation, Dividends and Retained Profits + Depreciation as Percentages of the Total Gross Income	232
XX	Net Company Savings	234
XXI	Percentage Shares of Various Items in Total Gross Income of Corporate Sector	236
XXII	Dividends as Percentage of Net Worth	237
XXIII	Tax as Percentage of Gross and Net Trading Profits	238
XXIV	Gross Receipts and Payments of the Corporate Sector	239
XXV	Annual Consents of Capital Issues (1948–1959)	245
XXVI	Paid-up Capital and Difference between Net Receipts and Net Payments of the Corporate Sector	246
XXVII	Loan Capital as Percentage of Total Capital Used	247
XXVIII	The Risk Factor in the Corporate Sector	249
XXIX	Table of Income Assessed	251
XXX	Market Value of Shares Held by Certain Income Ranges	252
XXXI	Effect of Capital Gains Tax on Capital Issues	253
XXXII	Relative Shares of Dividend Income	255

CHAPTER V

I	Paid-up Capital of Indian Companies	271
II	Corporate Securities in the Savings of Household Sector	276
III	Share of Dividend Income	277
IV	Ownership of Corporate Securities	278
V	Industrial Production and Excise Duty	282
VI	Excise Duties and Direct Taxes as Percentage of Total Receipts	283
VII	Number of Assessees, Cost of Tax Collection and Actual Tax Collection	288
VIII	Ratios of Gross Profits to Total Capital and Profits after Tax to Net Income	292
IX	Growth of Government Companies	299

CHAPTER I

THE ECONOMICS OF CORPORATE TAXATION

Like many other good things in life, the corporate tax came into being through error and deception.

Gerhard Colm

Introduction

OVER the past few decades, there has grown in India a fairly elaborate and complicated structure of taxation affecting the corporate form of enterprise. As it stands now, this tax structure is marked by the absence of any formal coherence, and is also somewhat inconsistent with the principles underlying corporate taxation. The 'structure' is, in fact, no structure at all, and could be described rather as a shapeless product, the result of recurrent financial need and promiscuous piecemeal legislation. In its present configuration, it is no more than an accidental grouping of laws enacted at different times for different purposes and applied to different types of business according to the exigencies of the moment. Such a miscellany must reflect, not the translation of a uniform principle, but only the haphazard expression of a whole host of divergent ideas as to what constitutes or should constitute a really fair basis for the taxation of corporations.

PRE-INDEPENDENCE AND POST-INDEPENDENCE POLICIES

So long as the British were in India as our rulers, the basic criterion of the tax policy was, understandably enough, the need to raise funds for running the Government. In other words, the Government, requiring finances of a certain magnitude, tried to collect the amount in as simple and easy a manner as was possible. However, after the achievement of independence, there was a radical change in the national Government's attitude towards the tax structure and policy. Professedly, the dominant feature of our economic policy was the maximisation of social welfare. Not only revenue was to be collected, but such collection was also to conform to certain socio-economic policies aimed at achieving maximum social good. Thus the redistribution of income through taxation became one of the determinants of the economic policy of the Government. More recently, the feeling of urgency to find resources for the Five Year Plans has given a decisive twist to our taxation policy and tax structure. In this way new ideas and new forces are emerging, and these in their turn are influencing our tax policy and structure.

It is proposed in this monograph to study the evolution, working, effects, and future prospects of the taxation of corporations in India. This subject, interesting in itself, is of particular significance in the present context of our economy which is at a transitionary or so-called 'take-off' stage, when every effort must be centred on economic growth. One wrong step at this crucial stage may well precipitate a series of chain reactions leading to a grave set-back, if not disaster, to our economy.

In the past, corporations have played no mean part in the economic life of our country. Whatever economic development has been achieved in India, the credit for it must undoubtedly go in large measure to the various joint stock companies that have been functioning here, on the whole with vigour and fruitfulness. Taxes being a major factor that affects the working of the corporations, it is a *sine qua non* of their future success that corporate taxation should be so conceived and applied as to cause the minimum ill-effects on the functioning of the corporations. In other words, it is necessary—it is both prudence and justice—that these taxes on corporations should be based on sound economic principles so that they may serve the purpose of raising the needed 'golden eggs' without actually killing the 'goose' herself. Our task in this monograph is primarily to examine whether the Government of India has consistently been following a rational policy of taxing corporations or whether it has merely been following the fatally easy, but really unwise, 'Principle of Expediency' and fabricating a hotch-potch of taxes which accentuates certain fundamental weaknesses in the economy and which renders even the administration of the taxes both ponderous and infructuous. In this opening chapter, an attempt is made to seek answers to the following questions, generally from the economists' point of view: What are corporations ? Why should corporations be taxed ? How should corporations be taxed ? What results flow from the imposition of taxes on corporations ?

What are Corporations ?

The word 'corporation' comes from the Latin *corporare*, ultimately based on a Sanskrit root meaning 'to form into a body'. A 'corporation' has been defined by the *Encyclopaedia of Social Sciences* as "a form of organisation which enables a group of individuals to act under a common name in carrying on one or more related enterprises, holding and managing property and distributing the profits or beneficial interests in such enterprises or property among the associates ... its shares are transferable ; its life independent of the lives of the individuals ; its debts do not usually create a liability for the latter". This is, of course, more than a mere definition ; it is almost a complete description of a corporation, which is really a voluntary association of certain people who pool their resources together and undertake some type of activity—generally business or trading—for the express purpose of making profits. If the members of a corporation choose to function thus, it is because of the many benefits that this form of organisation confers on them. The foremost of such benefits, no doubt, is the principle of limited liability and the comparative immunity deriving therefrom. It is, perhaps, for this reason that the corporate form of organisation has become so popular a feature of the world of business, and in all countries with a 'free' economy the corporation is almost the dominant type—the 'archetype' as it were—of the business structure. Apart from this specific economic role, the corporation, because of its general currency and wide popularity, brings in its wake numerous social problems as well. Hence it is not surprising that Adolf Berle and Gardner Means should declare : "The corporation has become more than a method of doing business; it has assumed the aspect of an institution of social organisation comparable to the State itself".[1]

EARLY HISTORY

While it is clear that corporations came to be organised during the eighteenth and nineteenth centuries, the early origins of

[1] Article on 'Corporations' in the *Encyclopaedia of Social Sciences*.

corporations are lost in remote antiquity. A. B. Levy, however, traces the origins of the corporate form of organisation to the *Code of Hammurabi* (2075-2025 B.C.).[2] But it was only during the period of the Industrial Revolution in England that the vast potentialities of this form of organisation were noticed, and corporations have accordingly played a greater part in galvanising the economy during the eighteenth and nineteenth centuries, thus leading to the phenomenal expansion of the corporate sector in our own times.

THE CORPORATE 'PERSONALITY'

If we are to account for the undoubted popularity of the corporate form of public enterprise, we can only point to the 'mystique' of the corporate 'personality'. We have seen already that the principle of limited liability has been responsible for the vogue of the corporations. Once a corporation is established, it ceases to be the absolute property of any one individual. If a person owns only a few shares, he has rights over the corporation and duties towards it only to the extent proportionate to his possession of those shares. Numerous individuals can jointly own the corporation, but individually they can claim ownership of only an infinitesimal part of the whole. This is how a corporation becomes a separate 'artificial' or 'fictitious' entity or individual. In this artificial-legal form, the corporation is entitled to be treated as if it were a person indeed. Actually, however, it would be more appropriate if the corporation were described, in Richard Goode's words, as a "mere conduit through which legal and economic relations flow between shareholders and others".[3] Thus a corporation has the right to purchase and sell property and to prosecute or defend itself in

[2] See for a detailed history of the corporate form of business organisation, A. B. Levy, *Private Corporations and Their Control*, Vol. I, Chapter I. Justice Blackstone categorically states: "The honour of originally inventing these political constitutions entirely belongs to the Romans. They were introduced, as Plutarch says, by Numa; who finding, upon his accession, the city torn to pieces by the two rival factions of Sabines and Romans, thought it a prudent and politic measure to subdivide these two into many smaller ones, by instituting separate societies of every manual trade and profession." *Commentaries on the Laws of England*, Vol. I, p. 498.

[3] *The Corporation Income Tax*, p. 12.

a court of law, as if it were an ordinary human being. But it is a person in the legal sense, as distinct from its shareholders, managers, or employees. The corporation is also in itself a deathless entity, for it can cease to exist only if the people who own its shares 'will' its death and take the necessary legal measures. Even though the present owners of the stock may not be the same as those who were the original owners, still the corporation is supposed to retain its essential identity. It is sometimes compared to a river because, just as a river is the same river "though the parts which compose it are changing every instant"[4], so also a corporation is the same corporation, though the people who own it may change from time to time. However, even though the corporation is a legal though fictitious person, it is subject to certain limitations of action. Though artificially created and owning but a fictitious existence, a corporation is nevertheless a person in the eyes of law, and it enjoys certain rights and discharges certain duties. Yet, as Norman S. Buchanan rightly points out, "to say that a corporation is a legal person, an 'artificial' person, need not imply that it is capable of all those legal relationships open to 'natural' persons; while a corporation may not marry or make a will, it is yet true that for a vast number of legal situations it makes no difference whether the relationship involves two corporations, a corporation and a man, or merely two men: the legal principle is the same".[5]

Numerous theories have been put forward which seek to justify the existence of corporations and at the same time to sound the origins from which sprang the idea of the corporation. According to the 'sovereignty' theory, if a company is regarded legally as a fictitious person, it is because the State or the sovereign authority has allowed such an assumption. Hence corporations exist because the State authorises their existence. However, Otto von Gierke feels that, when a few persons join in a contract, this creates a unity of purpose, an organism possessing a common will or determination. Thus, according to this view, corporations are but *groups* of persons, and not individual persons however unreal or fictional; the corporation is really no more than a method of cooperative

[4] Sir William Blackstone, *Commentaries on the Laws of England*, Vol. I, p. 498.
[5] *The Economics of Corporate Enterprise*, pp. 38-9.

effort.[6] Another view holds that the corporate personality is just a convenient short-hand expression to convey certain attributes of these associations of persons. For example, from the commercial viewpoint, it is specified that the members of a company are limited in their personal liability ; and from the legal point of view, actions can be taken only against the corporation as a whole, and not against the component shareholders. Yet another connotative relevance in calling the corporation a 'person' is to emphasise the fact that "it is a financial and accounting unit : that is to say, it is a unit for the purpose of computing cost and measuring income. Indeed, in terms of the social consequences, the significance of the corporation as a unit for computing costs and income doubtless exceeds the limited liability feature."[7] Whatever, then, may be the precise justification, it is obvious that the corporate personality is at once similar to and distinct from the individual personality ; just as the individual earns and pays taxes, the corporation also earns and has to pay taxes, but there are things the individual does—a whole complex of emotional or other reactions—which the corporation cannot do. Moreover, the foremost trait of the modern corporation, according to Berle and Means, is the separation of ownership and control.[8] Even though the actual owners are the shareholders, the real power is vested in the hands of the paid managers and executives. In such a situation, the owners are inevitably relegated to the position of mere lenders of money to the corporations, with alas ! the added risk of losing the principal itself should the business fail to prosper. While the limited liability principle seems to enable the shareholder to have the best of both worlds, the loss of effective control makes him often really have the worst of both worlds. Such a situation has definitely an important connection with the tax policy of the State, because on the one hand there is no justification for merely inflating the returns to the management and on the other it is not necessary to divert

---

[6] See *Political Theories of the Middle Ages*, edited by F. W. Maitland, pp. 96 ff.

[7] Norman S. Buchanan, *The Economics of Corporate Enterprise*, pp. 44-5.

[8] See *The Modern Corporation and Private Property*, especially Part II, Chapter VIII, and Part IV. See also A. A. Berle, Jr., *Power Without Prosperity*, pp. 64, 164 *et seq*.

to the idle investors more than what is necessary to attract their savings.[9]

Why Should Corporations be Taxed?

A corporation tax is a tax paid by the corporation from its resources, income or capital. As we saw earlier, the corporation is but a comparatively recent form of business organisation, and hence it will be a rewarding task to examine the basis on which corporations are taxed. In other words, the cardinal question here is: Why should the corporations be taxed? Several answers have been formulated, though none of them is completely satisfactory.

THE 'CYNICAL' FINANCIAL PLEA

The question-begging reason usually given for taxing the corporations is the already established nature of the corporation tax. It is there, it has been there, and therefore it should be there. The corporation tax has somehow come to be established, and let us not now upset it; besides, since it is easily productive of substantial revenue to the Government, there is no reason why it should be scrapped. In modern countries, the corporation as a form of business organisation occupies a dominant position in the economy, and hence a tax on the incorporated enterprise will naturally have a wide coverage. In many advanced countries, the corporation tax brings in a sizeable share of the total revenue as compared with the other taxes. When such is indeed the case, it is surely superfluous to look too curiously for the justification of so productive a tax. However, following Gerhard Colm, Richard Goode rightly describes this sort of reasoning as merely 'cynical', and proceeds to examine the various attempts that have been made at a more positive justification of a corporation income-tax.

Like the 'cynical' financial plea, the plea of administrative convenience too is hardly worth serious consideration. It is said that the corporation is taxed, not only because it produces a large amount of revenue, but also because it entails comparatively little administrative inconvenience and expenditure. By virtue of the fact that the corporations are in the organised sector of the economy,

---

[9] R. Goode, *The Corporation Income Tax*, p. 23. See also Berle & Means, *The Modern Corporation and Private Property*, pp. 340-4.

the Government will have no great difficulty in enforcing any tax measures on them. The Government, to be able to discharge its functions, requires a certain volume of finance to carry on its day-to-day affairs or to embark on any special adventures ; and if it finds that much of the needed revenue could be got with the minimum inconvenience from the flourishing corporations, it will certainly take the line of least resistance and decide accordingly, that is to say, tax the corporations. Moreover, corporation taxes, unlike other taxes—direct as well as indirect—that fall on individuals, are unlikely to evoke much opposition from the large mass of the people, except when the increased taxes come to be clearly reflected in the higher price levels of the products of the corporations.

Another reason offered in justification of the corporation income-tax is that it gives variety to the tax structure. The more widely distributed, the more diversified the incidence of taxation, the less intensively is it likely to be felt at any one point.

There is, then, the ethical plea that the corporation tax tends to reduce inequalities in the distribution of wealth. But there is little substance in this plea for, if the State were really seized by the ethical motive of redistribution of wealth through taxation, income-tax on individuals would serve the purpose more obviously and more adequately than corporation taxes. The corporation tax hits almost alike the rich and the poor shareholder, whereas income-tax on individuals will be directly in relation to their wealth or income. Besides, because of their very 'impersonal' nature, corporations cannot, after all, 'enjoy' their wealth as rich individuals can. Thus it would appear that if corporations are being taxed, it is only to augment the revenues of the State ; necessity and opportunity, rather than administrative convenience or ethical plausibility, seem to govern such taxation. The conclusion, therefore, seems to be unescapable that the main, if not sole, objective of corporate taxation is financial, and not social or administrative or ethical. The corporation tax is an effective means of increasing the volume of revenue, and that is all that we know for certain and all that we need to know about it ! Such broadly is the 'cynical' financial plea.

THE 'PRIVILEGE' THEORY

Another theory, originally formulated by Thomas Adams in

1917, which is being commonly advanced in defence of the corporation tax is the 'privilege' or 'benefits' theory. It is but reasonable, so runs the theory, that the corporation should pay a price for the privilege of being allowed to exist and to function under the corporate form with its unique advantages. Taxes in general are sometimes sought to be justified on the ground of benefits received by the taxpayers, and more often than not the argument is negatived by pointing out that such benefits do not subject themselves to objective measurement, without which there can be no solid basis for taxation. Moreover, in the case of corporations, certain special privileges come into the picture : the liability of the shareholders is limited, the corporations have a lease of almost perpetual life, transfers of ownership can be effected with easy facility, the sources of financing can be very diffused, and the possibilities of intercorporate affiliation are endless.[10] These privileges are quite apart from and in addition to the other services which the Government renders, like the maintenance of law and order, the assurance of security of property, etc., which corporations need as much as mere individuals. Such benefits and special privileges enable corporations to function smoothly and effectively, to grow in size, and to reap large profits from business. Big Business in the form of corporations thrives in modern times mainly as a result of the special benefits and privileges extended to it by the Government. Thus the possession of such privileges as a juristic personality and the enjoyment of limited liability make a corporation rather distinct from other accretions of property and render it capable of being taxed. Accepting this line of argument, Mr. Justice Day of the Supreme Court of the United States of America has categorically stated that the corporation tax is not a direct tax at all but only an 'excise' on the privilege of doing business in a corporate capacity.[11]

The 'privilege' theory is not quite convincing because there are unprofitable corporations which pay no taxes at all, but still enjoy all the privileges of a corporation that actually pays taxes. The successful Peters are thus to be apparently 'robbed' so that the luckless Pauls may be the beneficiaries ! Studenski, however, while conceding that the corporations are admitted to certain privileges

[10] Goode, p. 28.
[11] Flint *vs.* Stone Tracey Co. (220. U.S. 107) ; cited by Goode, p. 27.

in the public—rather than in their own special—interest, nevertheless argues that, whatever the Government's intention, the corporations *are* benefited as a matter of fact, and are hence "proper subjects for special taxation".[12] In other words, taxes are collected only from those corporations that benefit from the enjoyment of the given privileges, and not from those that are unfortunately unable to exploit successfully the various privileges of corporate existence to increase their profits or capital value.

Apart from all this, it is not possible, as already pointed out, to evaluate the benefits received by the corporations from Government recognition, and thus the 'benefits' theory fails to offer any guidance whatsoever regarding the manner in which they should be taxed. There is no calculus to measure the value of the 'benefits' conferred on corporations, for these are only one of the many factors that render possible the profits that corporations make. However, as we saw earlier, the special benefits which corporations take advantage of are doubtless a factor—though not a strictly commensurable one—that influences the conduct of their business. If this much is admitted, and if there *are* profits, there is no reason why a tax should not be paid to the Government.

Sometimes it is argued ingeniously that, since the privileges of incorporation are available almost for the mere asking, they should not be considered as special privileges at all. Against this Richard Goode argues as follows: "The argument that the availability of the privileges of incorporation to all destroys their economic value seems to confuse 'benefit' with exchange value. In examining the benefit theory we are considering the social justification for taxation, not appraising a marketable commodity".[13] The fact that some capitalise these privileges and some do not (or cannot) clearly indicates that, for some people at least, these privileges are really profitable in spite of the taxes. In other words, according to Edwin Seligman, "it is the indefinite something which gives vitality to the enterprise and makes its business worth having";[14] some make use of the corporate form to seize the 'indefinite something' that makes the business a great success while, for the others,

[12] 'Towards a Theory of Business Taxation', *J. P. E.*, October 1940, p. 625.
[13] *The Corporation Income Tax*, p. 29.
[14] *Essays in Taxation*, p. 223.

the corporate form is not productive of gain. Thus it could be reasonably assumed that profits have some causal connection with the benefits received, and could therefore be justifiably taxed.

However, it should not be stressed too often that the connection between the benefits received and the profit that ensues is essentially vague. If the value of the rights given to a company is to be measured by the income, dividends, shares or bonds, and taxed accordingly, these corporate taxes become in no way different from the income-tax or dividend tax or a tax on shares or bonds, etc. If, on the other hand, in the words of Seligman again, "an attempt is made to reach the capital value of the franchise by a method of appraisal, without resort to any specific criterion, it becomes mere guess work".[15]

This, then, is the crux of the matter : Are we taxing because of the fact of incorporation or the fact of accrued profits ? If the tax is to be based on the benefits of incorporation, then it should be levied on all firms, irrespective of whether they are profit-making or running at a loss. In such a context, the tax should, perhaps, more properly be called a 'fee'. If, however, the tax is to be related to the profits alone, it could be broken down under different heads, and the name 'corporate tax' would become a misnomer.

It is thus hardly possible to advance strictly logical grounds for the levy of the corporate tax. Custom, expediency, and necessity call the tune, and the theorist of public finance must do what he can to interpret it and even, if possible, to justify it. All that can be said therefore is that there is some sort of pragmatic justification for the tax on corporations, depending no doubt upon their special circumstances, though the benefit principle by itself is inadequate to justify or guide the taxation policy.

THE 'SOCIAL COSTS' THEORY

There are certain items in the cost structure of a corporation which cannot be accounted for through the usual procedure. These are the various social costs which cannot be individually paid for. There are many governmental services which are essential for the conduct of business ; if the Government failed to provide them, these services will have to be organised by the corporations them-

[15] Ibid., pp. 231-2.

selves. To vary the language, the relationship between the Government and the corporation is that of an external agent supplying services to the corporation and being thus entitled to receive fees from it, irrespective of whether the business enterprise in which the corporation is engaged is profitable or not. But, in actuality, no such payment is asked for or made for a good many of the services thus performed. For example, the Government spends vast sums on technical and professional education—and education generally—and trains hordes of technicians and administrators, and the various businesses thus get trained personnel without their having to train them at their own cost from the beginning. Public health and sanitation programmes undertaken by the Government are no less essential. For these and other services, the Government hardly charges any special fee. As Goode puts it, "Although this does not alter the economic nature of the services, it means that their costs are not reflected in the accounts of private producers".[16]

A variation of the above viewpoint is that the Government is really a partner in all business, participating "in the work of every enterprise and having a claim on its profits, which it enforces through taxation".[17] But it may be added, however, that the Government is only an incidental partner; the main object of the Government in helping the private producers is not profit-making and profit-sharing, but social benefit. In the process of benefiting society, the Government partners with the companies and draws its own share of the profits whenever such profits have accrued; this share takes the shape of corporate taxes.

There is another side to the shield too: just as the invisible benefits received from the Government are not recorded in the company's books, the damage caused by the company to society, however unwittingly, is not also recorded. Many types of business activity incidentally cause considerable damage to the physical and human resources of the community. Such damage includes deforestation, pollution of rivers, overcrowding in urban areas, smoke in the industrial towns, disintegration of traditional kinship solidarities, etc. These give rise to various problems, and these have to be tackled by measures like public health programmes, social

[16] *The Corporation Income Tax*, p. 30.
[17] P. Studenski, 'Towards a Theory of Business Taxation', *J. P. E.*, October 1940, p. 630.

insurance and slum clearance schemes, etc. by the Government. Naturally, the companies must bear at least a proportion of the costs of these measures, and thus corporate taxes may be sought to be justified on grounds both of equity and necessity.

These two sets of costs, then, one indicating positive gain to the company and another indicating responsibility for loss to the community, cannot be found in the books of the company. But if these costs too are properly taken into account, there would be found a significant change in the cost structure of the corporations. On both counts, therefore, the Government is entitled to claim a share in the profits made by the companies. Such broadly is the plea made by the apologists of the social costs theory in defence of corporation taxes.

Even so, this theory, however seemingly plausible, could only establish a vague and remote justification for corporate taxation because, not only corporations, but also all types of economic activity raise this problem of social costs. Theoretically, all forms of business deserve to be charged a share in the social costs, though it is felt in practice that it might be expedient to have the tax limited only to the corporations. This theory also justifies a special tax or fee on corporations which are responsible for any specific damage to the community.

The parable of the cistern and the feeding and the outlet pipes will illustrate the difficulty of relating meaningfully as well as accurately the social costs (positive as well as negative) on the one hand and the profits made by the corporations on the other. If a cistern is fed with water by three pipes, A, B and C, and if water from the cistern finds outlet through three other pipes, D, E and F; while it is clear that without the first set of pipes, the second set could not take out water, it would still be impossible to determine how much of the water brought in by one particular pipe, say A, went out by one of the second set of pipes, say D. And suppose, quite apart from D, E and F, stray people also take out water from the cistern in their buckets; this must make for more complexity still. So it is with corporations, with business generally, the social costs and the Governmental benefits on the one side, and the corporate profits on the other. There is some obvious relation between the two sets of factors, but it is not mathematically measurable.

THE 'SOCIO-POLITICAL' THEORY

Adolf Wagner has propounded a doctrine of public finance known as the 'socio-political' theory. According to him, there is a persistent tendency on the part of the Government to extend its functions both intensively and extensively. The main economic function of the Government should be to bring about equality of incomes, that is to say, to level down the rich Peters so that the poor Pauls may be levelled up. This egalitarian or socialistic approach is sometimes made also with regard to the taxation of corporations. Generally speaking, corporations are likely to have large accumulated reserves, and they also usually possess considerable economic power. According to the socio-political theory, the corporations should be taxed so as effectively to reduce this heavy concentration of wealth and to spend the revenue derived from the taxation of corporations on the upliftment of the poorer sections of the community with a view to raising their economic status. But this approach does not take into account the variable economic status of the individual shareholders, as distinct from the total economic status of the corporation as a whole. Even though the corporation itself may be rich, if the individual shareholders (most of them at any rate) are far from being rich, then any tax on the corporation will tend to be regressive and the whole socio-political purpose of such taxation will be frustrated.

'FUNCTIONAL FINANCE'

Economists likte Abba P. Lerner feel that public finance must be 'functional finance' and that the prime objective must be that of the maintenance of an adequate level of national income. Taxation, according to him, is "important not as a means of raising money but as a means of cutting down private spending", because, after all, "the Government can raise all the money it needs by printing it if the raising of the money is the only consideration".[18] In other words, Lerner feels that the tax system should be used as a vital tool of fiscal policy aimed at controlling the economy so as to keep it stable at a high level of production, employment and national income. More than its utility as a means of raising revenue, the tax is a method of persuading or compelling the society to vary the distribution of its expenditure and thus influence its

[18] *The Economics of Control*, pp. 307-8.

propensity to earn and save. A similar argument is offered by W. L. Thorp who says that "the power to tax is the power to define the character of our economic system".[19] As against this view, Harold M. Groves feels that "an economy run by its tax system would indeed be the tail wagging the dog".[20]

These are extreme views, though there is doubtless some justification for both. Certainly, it is very much to be desired that taxes should guide the economy into the avenues of stability and growth. Taxes produce certain effects which at times are crucial to the stability of the economy. When taxes are being formulated, these various possible effects should be taken into account so that from the tax system may issue beneficial results. Corporate taxation, for example, could be the means of encouraging new and small units, stimulating healthy competition, influencing innovation, and encouraging the taking of reasonable business risks. Further, corporate taxation could be used to check the abuse of power by the corporations and to exercise control over them. According to the exponents of this social control theory, corporations, despite their notable contribution to the satisfaction of human wants, have certain grave disadvantages as well. With the passage of time, corporations tend to develop anti-social features, the most glaring of these being the growth of monopolistic forms, the massive concentration of economic power in the hands of the few, and the excessive complexity and intricacy of the corporate financial structure.

It is, of course, necessary that monopoly power should be effectively curbed so that monopolists may not exploit the large body of consumers. "The corporation tax and the monopoly problem are closely allied", writes Henry C. Adams, "and no satisfactory adjustment of corporate taxation can be expected except it be made under the influence of some general theory respecting the solution of the monopoly problem".[21] However, it is highly problematic if the monopoly problem could be solved by higher taxation alone because as Petrie, following Kimmel, argues: "If monopoly profit results in exploitation of consumers, as it surely must, the consumer is not relieved of his exploitation simply because the

---

[19] *Taxation of Corporate Enterprise* (T.N.E.C. Monograph), p. xi.
[20] *Post-War Taxation and Economic Progress*, p. 14.
[21] *The Science of Finance*, p. 453.

State prevents the monopolist from keeping that part of his net earnings deemed to be derived from his monopolistic position".[22] On the other hand, it can also be argued that the monopolist, finding that anyhow he is unable to reap the monopoly profit, might reduce the prices after all, both in order to earn the goodwill of the consumers and to increase the sales of his products.

The problem of the menace of massive concentration of economic power is essentially a problem of social justice. The concentration of economic power in the hands of the corporations need not by itself lead to inequality, for the corporations are only fictional persons. Such concentration becomes harmful only when the size of the corporation directly reflects an unfair price structure and a monopsonistic attitude towards labour. Even in these cases, measures other than taxation might prove adequate to deal effectively with the evil.

It has been suggested by Harold M. Groves that the objective of the taxation of corporations must be the simplification of the corporate structure.[23] He waxes eloquent, especially on the various dubious methods adopted by the corporations to evade taxes. However, more often than not, such intricacies in the corporate structure are themselves the result of complicated tax laws: it is indeed a never-ending process, like an irate kitten chasing its own tail. Again, the reason for corporate taxation given by Groves is not convincing, for complexities in the company organisation could more easily be remedied by appropriate legislative action than by a resort to corporate taxation. It is equally possible, as already pointed out, that the complicated tax laws, far from remedying the disease of a complicated business structure, have rather been responsible for aggravating the malady still further. If this be indeed the case, then it follows that the tax structure itself should be subjected to a complete overhaul with a view to drastic rationalisation and simplification.

There are many anti-social features which develop in the economic system from time to time. The tax structure is only one of the many weapons that are used against anti-social malpractices found in the economy. It must also be realised that taxation is, not only

[22] *The Taxation of Corporate Income in Canada*, pp. 107-8.
[23] Article on 'Equity and Expediency in Business Taxation' in *How Shall Business be Taxed?*, pp. 39-44.

an edged, but also a double-edged weapon. If it is used unwisely, it may lead to reduced production with the attendant consequences; and hence taxation as a measure of social control should be given no more than a subsidiary place in the formulation of fiscal policies.

THE 'ABILITY TO PAY' THEORY

Another doctrine often advanced in defence of corporate taxation is the so-called 'ability to pay' theory. According to Seligman, this theory teaches that "the measure of general obligation to the support of Government is, in the state as in the family, the capacity on the part of the individual to contribute to that support".[24] Corporations ought to be taxed because, being affluent, they can afford to pay the taxes; such of them as are affluent, at least, can. The ability to pay, generally speaking, derives from the economic condition of the individual or the corporation. But however deceptively simple this may look, no two interpretations of the concept of the ability to pay quite agree with each other.

One view is that the corporation may have an individuality in the eyes of the law; it may even reveal certain features of transacting business not generally found in other types of business units. But essentially the corporation is a form of business organisation in which individuals join together and do business as a collectivity with a view to earning profits. The ability to pay is a subjective concept which does not take into account numerous personal feelings and predilections like the readiness to make sacrifices, the sense of utility, and the desire for security. As stated already, the modern corporations are largely impersonal in character; though made up of individuals, the corporation itself is an impersonal aggregate, even something of an abstraction. Each corporation will thus have two factors of ability to pay, viz. the ability to pay of the corporation as a whole taking into account only *its* income and expenditure, and the ability to pay of the individual shareholders, depending upon each individual shareholder's total income and expenditure, not to mention his unique psychological set-up. The personal 'abilities' of the individual shareholders are different from one another and also different from the ability of the corporation to pay. It is thus argued that the distinction between corporations and the shareholders who constitute them is only a

[24] *Essays in Taxation*, p. 338.

legal fiction. Taxes imposed on the corporations are not borne by them; it is the shareholders who feel the pinch. Nay more; actually, as Kimmel feels,[25] the taxes are borne by the shareholders in the shape of decreased dividends, the consumers in the shape of increased prices, and by labour as decreased wages.

This too is special pleading, for it ignores the fact that, in some corporations at least, the situation is somewhat different. In these there is an effective divorce of ownership from the management, so much so the latter is in a position to "formulate policy for the good of the corporation itself, rather than for the shareholders, who often receive only a small fraction of the net earnings".[26] Paul Studenski also opposes the unitary view on the score that it is based on the false associations of business enterprises with the owners thereof.[27] According to Hobson, again, the 'ability to pay' is synonymous with surplus.[28]

Richard Goode interprets the ability to pay concept as "the capacity of paying with minimum interference with socially approved aims"; the ability to pay thus signifies, according to him, "possession of income or wealth that has in its probable origin and use a lower order of social priority, which is socially less useful than other private income or wealth".[29] In other words, according to this concept, the State should tax away the socially least useful kinds and parts of corporate and even individual economic resources. The ability to pay of a person or a corporation would thus be a function of both the needs of the State and the economic condition of the others. All this, however, is extremely vague; there is no measuring rod to differentiate objectively between varying degrees of usefulness from the social point of view; and Goode himself is sceptical about this interpretation of the ability to pay concept, for he says: "Whether the social-usefulness criterion is identified with 'ability to pay' is largely a matter of convenience ... ability to pay, socially interpreted, cannot be definitely applied to the corporate income tax".[30]

---

[25] *Postwar Tax Policy and Business Expansion*, p. 9.
[26] J. R. Petrie, *The Taxation of Corporate Income in Canada*, p. 103.
[27] 'Towards a Theory of Business Taxation', *J. P. E.*, October 1940, p. 633.
[28] See J. C. Stamp, *The Fundamental Principles of Taxation*, p. 75.
[29] *The Corporation Income Tax*, p. 34.   [30] Ibid., pp. 36-7.

Ultimately all discussion of the concept of the ability to pay as applied to corporate taxation tends to become misty or gets lost in a metaphysical and ethical quagmire. As William Vickrey points out, "More often than not, ability to pay turns out to mean just about what the user wants it to mean.... Indeed one finds serious discussion of the ability to pay of corporations as such; at such a point one suspects that the concept of ability to pay has degenerated to a notion very close to 'inability to squawk' or at least inability to vote."[31]

CONCLUSION

After considering the various grounds on which corporations are supposed to be taxed—financial, 'benefit', social costs, social control, and 'ability to pay'—we have necessarily to come to the conclusion that not one of the above pleas can exclusively form the basis for corporate taxation. Economists about half a century ago shuddered at the thought of corporate taxation.[32] But now that the taxation of corporations has become a regular, universal and an almost indispensable feature of the tax system, economists are trying to find a rational basis for it. Corporate taxation in all modern countries originally arose out of financial necessity on the State's part. Having come into the tax structure, it has remained there; even though revenue could be raised in other ways, still corporate taxation is being retained because the modern State, with its endless extension of functions, can never have too much finance. Economists have tried to discover the motives behind this continuance of a tax for which no rational justification other than the merely pragmatic is available. But, then, like Iago's soliloquies, these discussions also too often tend to approximate to the "motive-hunting of a motiveless" tax whose main justification is that it brings in money to the State's coffers. None of the various grounds discussed in the preceding pages satisfies fully. It is also somewhat unwise to attempt to look for any single motive to justify corporate taxation, for there can always be more than one motive behind an action. For example, as Seligman says, "A business tax is none the less based upon ability to pay because the predominant criterion may consist in the profits derived in part from the privileges due to

[31] *Agenda for Progressive Taxation*, p. 375.
[32] See Petrie, *The Taxation of Corporate Income in Canada*, p. 51.

the general economic or legal environment".[33] In practice, all taxes are motivated variously and have diverse and mixed objectives.

The foregoing discussion about the basis of corporate taxation has centred around the question whether the corporations should pay a separate tax as a corporation or not. If it is made to pay an independent tax without taking into account the assets, the sales, or the profits made, it becomes no more than a fee, which will be just an item in the cost of production. It will be more appropriate if, in levying the various taxes that are paid by the corporations, care is taken to see that the taxes have a proper relation to particular objectives. It may thus be that a special tax on some corporations will have a clear justification on account of some particular benefit received, each individual tax levied on the corporation thus having some objective. And on the whole, the ends—be they financial, social, economic, or political—should justify the imposition of the various taxes.

Finally, the economic policy of the Government will inevitably influence to a considerable extent the objectives of the tax system. If the Government is planning for economic development through a widening of the public sector, the motive in taxing will be mainly financial. On the other hand, if the Government is not specially interested in expanding the public sector but rather in maintaining the stability of the present economic system, then the tax system will be used, as Lerner and others visualise, only to regulate the flow of money into the hands of the public.

How Should Corporations be Taxed ?

Let us grant —tardily, and without much conviction, perhaps— that the corporations are to be taxed. But the question now arises : How ? What should be the *modus operandi* ? How is the taxable capacity or the ability to pay of the corporations to be assessed ? On what basis are the taxes to be levied ?

Now, apart from a fixed tax (or fee) on the corporations as such, taxes could be levied on the gross sales, on the capital stock, or on the profits of the corporations. The last mentioned is the tax base most commonly adopted ; but the other two bases are also used, though not very often.

[33] *Essays in Taxation*, p. 702.

TAX ON GROSS SALES

Not seldom a tax on gross sales is described as the most equitable form of corporate taxation. In this connection, Seligman says emphatically: "The value of the franchise from the economic point of view consists in the earning capacity of the corporation. That is the real basis of all taxation and can best be gauged by the amount of business done."[34] Such a tax would be akin to a tax on the gross earnings of the corporations. In other words, the tax could be levied on the total earnings from the business without deducting the cost elements incurred in earning the income. Ordinarily such taxes will be low flat rates ranging from 0.1 to 2.0 per cent. Public utility corporations are usually subject to this type of tax on the gross sales.

The principal merit of such a tax is that it is 'certain', and evasion would be very difficult. But this tax, although it has an immediate appeal, is not without its drawbacks. It does not take into account the costs involved in the production of the particular commodity. The business might be large in volume, but the profit margin could yet be very small due to the costs involved and also due to the prevalence of stiff competition. Even though Seligman considers the tax on the total business done as equitable in theory, he is extremely sceptical about the validity of the tax in practice. "The business transacted", he says, "is an exceedingly rough way of ascertaining the prosperity of a corporation. It affords no test of profits, and fails to take into account the personal equation which may make all the difference between good and bad management."[35] It comes to this: If a corporation is doing good business owing to efficient management or the operation of any other factor, it will be liable to be penalised for just that reason. The expectation of an increased net income is a worthy incentive, but if a tax is imposed on gross profits, then the incentive loses its edge. Hence it is plain that a tax on gross sales will largely be a tax on initiative and enterprise, and will tend to help those corporations that are comparatively inefficient and inactive.

Yet another aspect of the problem of gross sales is that they are largely determined by turnover of capital more than anything else. This, in turn, varies from industry to industry, and enterprise to

---

[34] Ibid., p. 237.   [35] Ibid., p. 243.

enterprise. Accordingly, an enterprise may earn as little as 4 per cent on the sales but as much as 20 per cent on the invested capital, as is alleged to be the case in the Oil industries. Thus a tax on gross sales would be a tax on the turnover of capital, ignoring the inventory aspect.

Another criticism that could be levelled against the imposition of a tax measured by the volume of sales is that such imposition must add directly to the costs of production. In its incidence it will be identical with that of a sales tax. The net result, then, of a tax based upon the gross sales will be a shifting of the tax to the consumer. Such a tax must therefore be inevitably regressive in character.

TAX ON CAPITAL STOCK

There are two varieties of taxes based on the capital stock of a company: an annual capital tax and an occasional capital levy. While income, no doubt, has been accepted till recently as the most important indicator of an individual's ability to pay, of late capital levy too is being viewed as a supplementary, if not as an alternative, indicator to measure the ability of people (or corporations) to pay taxes. Actually, it is a matter of doubt whether there is any justification at all for a tax on the capital of companies. Very often a tax on the capital of the companies proves to be an extension of a similar tax—property tax or wealth tax—on individuals. The mere possession of wealth enables individuals to derive a certain amount of pleasure and prestige, but companies cannot so contemplate the mere existence of capital when there is no monetary income from it. In fact, the income itself is the source of capital value; for, as Seligman neatly puts it, "Physically, the fruit is the product of a tree; economically the tree has a value only because the fruit has a value".[36]

An annual capital tax is like a fee, though it will vary annually as per the capital stock owned by the companies. Moreover, the annual capital tax must come from the profits of the company because it is a regular annual charge based on the capital worth of the company. One cannot expect the company to go on paying the tax indefinitely without making a profit.

It is true that an annual capital tax is much less damaging to incentives than an equivalent income tax. Not being based upon

[36] *Studies in Public Finance*, p. 103.

income, an annual capital tax cannot discriminate against high-return risky investment.[37] But as Hicks, Hicks and Rostas say, the method of tax assessment will determine the favourable effects produced by the tax. They say that collection at source would ruin the capital tax. The corporation pays an income-tax if it gains a profit; if there is no profit, there is no income-tax either. But a capital tax will have to be paid irrespective of whether the corporation makes a profit or not. As they put it, "unless the firm had some means of recovering the tax from its shareholders—which does not look feasible—the tax would be a direct addition to overhead costs".[38] This means that the tax will have to be shifted of necessity to the consumers in case the firm fails to make a large enough profit and doesn't know how to recover the amount from the individual shareholders. Hence Hicks, Hicks and Rostas conclude: "The only sort of capital tax which can establish a good case for itself on economic grounds is one . . . laid on individual holdings of capital, and collected from individual capitalists".[39]

CAPITAL LEVY

A tax is generally an annual imposition, but a levy may be an occasional demand. Capital levy is resorted to only once in a way, depending upon the prevailing financial climate. This levy is imposed on the capital base, and generally it will not be repeated in the near future. Indeed, as urged by J. C. Stamp, "a capital levy, once it has been imposed, should not be repeated for at least another twenty-five years".[40]

The important characteristics of the levy are that it is large, and hence it cannot normally be paid out of the current income; it must, therefore, necessarily make inroads into the capital stock as well. A capital levy is really rather like a big slice cut out of a cake; so much the worse for the cake, for it cannot be whole now —for, here as elsewhere, one cannot both eat the cake and have it. Since the levy abridges the capital stock, it goes without saying that the future production capacity too will be correspondingly reduced. In view of these obvious defects, a capital levy will be imposed only in times of grave emergency. To quote Hicks, Hicks

[37] See I.S. Gulati, *Capital Taxation*, p. 36.
[38] *The Taxation of War Wealth*, pp. 206-7.   [39] Ibid., p. 207.
[40] *Studies in Current Problems in Finance and Government*, p. 235.

and Rostas again, "A capital levy is not capable of being adopted as a regular part of the fiscal system ; and it is only suitable for use in emergencies".[41] And the emergencies that call for the imposition of such capital levies are, firstly, financing wars, and secondly, liquidating war debts.

The problem of capital levy is that it taxes only the physical capital and not the earning capital, otherwise known as 'brain capital'.[42] As with the annual capital tax, the opinion of the economists is that the capital levy must also be confined only to the individual shareholders. However, in actual practice we find invariably, in the words of Hicks, Hicks and Rostas, "that the levies were laid upon business capital ; indeed in many cases the greater part of the levy was collected, not from private individuals, but from firms".[43]

In any scheme of taxing the capital stock, the main problem will be one of the valuation of business assets. This problem springs from the fact that there is no agreed definition of 'capital'. For our working purposes, capital could be supposed to comprise the money and the stock of goods at any given moment. In ordinary life, the individual's capital consists of (a) physical goods—land, buildings, etc.,—whether held for personal use or rent or investment, (b) securities, Government bonds, etc., and (c) liquid cash ; and it is the valuation of the first item that presents most of the difficulties. However, for corporations, the value of the assets would be included in the value of the shares. But the problem still remains for certain classes of securities "which change hands so seldom that their quotations are more or less fictitious".[44] Seligman also feels that to tax corporations on the basis of the capital stock at its market value is open to serious objections. He feels that "heavily bonded corporations would in this way escape taxation ; because in such cases—and they are the great majority—the capital stock alone would not represent the value of the property".[45] If a corporation that has no bonded debt distributes

---

[41] *The Taxation of War Wealth*, p. 180.

[42] See A. C. Pigou, *A Study in Public Finance*, p. 134.

[43] *The Taxation of War Wealth*, p. 185.

[44] A. C. Pigou (*The Economic Journal*, 1918), quoted in I. S. Gulati, *Capital Taxation*, p. 39.

[45] *Essays in Taxation*, p. 239.

dividends, then the value of the stock would be a fair index to its earning capacity. But if the corporation distributes no dividends, how is the value of the capital stock to be determined? It would be "wholly uncertain and largely speculative, depending on the manipulations of the stock exchange".[46]

Taxes based on capital will have essentially—or, at least, psychologically—a distinct disincentive effect. As we saw earlier, an annual capital tax, collected from individual capitalists, could be better defended, and would be better than an individual income-tax. But, in practice, the income-tax is too firmly entrenched in the fiscal system to be replaced now by an annual capital tax.

TAX ON INCOME

By far the most common form of corporate taxation is the one based on income. Yet, although income has generally been accepted as the best conceivable measure of the ability to pay, it is also realised that income cannot be a perfect indicator of ability because of the inherent difficulties in the computation of income for tax purposes. The measurement of income for the assessment of personal income-tax is difficult enough, but the calculation of corporate income for the purpose of taxation is a far more difficult problem owing to the complications involved in the deduction of permissible expenses.

WHAT IS INCOME?

In spite of the considerable thinking that has been bestowed on the subject, a perfect definition of 'income' is yet to be evolved. There is no dearth of definitions, of course, but none of them is entirely satisfactory. The most common definition of income is that given by Robert Murray Haig : "Income is the money value of the net accretion to one's economic power between two points of time".[47] However, this definition limits income to money income alone, and therefore a more comprehensive definition is very much to be preferred. The problem of the income concept lies in its exact relationship to capital, for capital in its broadest sense generates income. According to J. R. Hicks, a man's income is the amount

[46] Ibid., p. 239.
[47] Article on 'The Concept of Income—Economic and Legal Aspects,' included in *Readings in the Economics of Taxation*, p. 59.

which he can consume away in a given period of time without impairing the productive ability of his capital.[48] Perhaps Hicks does not take into account the factor of saving, for it is not necessary that all income should be consumed away. In Hicks's approach, says Kaldor, "Capital appears only as the capitalised value of a certain future prospect and Income as the 'Standard stream equivalent' of that prospect".[49] Thus capital and income become one and the same thing, though expressed in two different ways! However plausible this reasoning may look, it actually involves circular reasoning.[50]

Irving Fisher and, recently, Nicholas Kaldor have defined income as the value of a given flow of services. This flow which is taken into account is the net flow emanating from all one's property; thus "it follows that saving and appreciation in capital value are always capital, not income. They are saved from being invested".[51] This definition tries to solve the vexed problem of capital gains by intimately linking up savings and appreciation in capital value with capital.

From the definitions given above, we may attempt to summarise the characteristics of income as follows:

1. Income is a flow which could be measured only as between two points of time, and it is distinct from capital, which is the reservoir—or stock—at any given moment;

2. Income is a flow which takes place without hurt to the capital;

3. Sometimes, however, capital may rise in value, thus leaving a gap between the present value and the past value; it becomes necessary therefore, while computing income, to take also into account the invisible gains in the value of capital. From the purely economist's point of view, income is a net accretion in real terms.

---

[48] *Value and Capital*, pp. 172-4.   [49] *An Expenditure Tax*, pp. 64-5.

[50] See Kaldor: "We cannot first define Income as what is left after maintaining Capital intact and then define the latter as what is required to maintain Income intact, without getting involved in circular reasoning" (*An Expenditure Tax*, p. 66).

[51] Irving Fisher, quoted in Magill, *Taxable Income*, p. 17.

The Minority Report (G. Woodcock, H.L. Bullock & N. Kaldor) of the Royal Commission held that identifying income with expenditure for tax purposes alone satisfies "Society's prevailing sense of fairness and equity". *Final Report of the Royal Commission on the Taxation of Profits and Income* (1955), p. 355.

As J. R. Petrie says, "the economic concept of business profit involves matching current replacement costs against sales income".[52] Accretion in the value of capital, caused only by changes in the general price level, is not income for this in no way increases the net gain in real terms.

As far as a business or a corporation is concerned, the income or profit is the residue from the gross income after deducting every expenditure item incurred to achieve the gross earnings without impairing the value of the capital stock, *plus* the accretion in the value of the capital. However deceptively simple it may look, the practical application of the concept to tax purposes is beset with innumerable difficulties.

As opposed to the economist's concept of real income, the accountant's concept takes note of the money income only. For example, an economist will give importance to items like imputed interest on equity capital and imputed price to scarce factors of production in order to determine the real net income. However, in a broad view of the matter, accounting ideas of income are not, after all, very different from the economist's concept. Hatfield refers to "the increase in proprietorship which has taken place during that period, making due allowances for any part of such increment as may have been distributed", and adds: "This is the broadest use of the terms, but is one which is occasionally employed by both accountants and economists".[53] But, in a somewhat narrower sense, accountants limit income only to realised money gains. Since the accounting concept uses money as the standard of measurement, sometimes it has to include unrealised increments in value. As Petrie puts it, "In essence, conventional accounting practice sets up a balance sheet which is a statement of costs (prudently adjusted for anticipated returns), not a statement of values".[54] In the practical affairs of business, the economist's concept cannot be used; for example, it excludes withdrawals and new investments in computing income, because it is a net concept. So much so, as Charles John Gaa says, in the accountant's concept, "in order to face practical difficulties and to gather information in the most convenient and economical manner, theoretically correct ideas

---

[52] *The Taxation of Corporate Income in Canada*, p. 217.
[53] Quoted in C. J. Gaa, *The Taxation of Corporate Income*, p. 10.
[54] *The Taxation of Corporate Income in Canada*, p. 214.

regarding income calculation are often deliberately side-tracked for more expedient methods".[55]

The definition of income or profit for tax purposes is mainly based on the accounting practice on the one hand and the administrative limitations on the other. As far as the corporation is concerned, the problem is the presentation of the net profit, which, as we saw before, is the gross earning *minus* the costs *plus* the capital gains. Thus the essential idea behind taxation is, not only the severance of current costs, but also the separation of capital from the total gains.

The determination of costs, then, is the most important problem in the calculation of the total taxable income. There can be no two opinions, of course, about wages, raw materials, salaries, rent, etc., which inevitably go into the cost of production. Even so, interest on debts constitutes something of a problem. Sometimes, owing to the dividends being taxed twice, at the corporate as well as the individual level, corporations might resort to bond-financing.[56] Interest could be treated as a cost of production, whereas dividends could not be. Richard Goode rightly considers as 'illogical' this difference in the tax treatment of corporate earnings used to pay interest and corporate earnings available for dividend declaration. Yet he too comes to the conclusion that, "in view of the practical difficulties and probable economic repercussions, it seems that expansion of the corporate tax base to include interest and net rent paid would be undesirable".[57]

The problem of the ultimate taxable income could be solved only by the valuation of the current assets and the fixed assets. The valuation of the opening and closing inventories of a firm is the determinant of the cost of goods sold and thus of the net income. Usually inventories will be valued at the lower cost of market value method. However, this method tends to exaggerate the profit or loss in times of sudden or sharp shifts in the price level. Even though from a long run point of view the imaginary profits and losses will cancel out one another, they will nevertheless create special problems during the short run period. Alternatively, the

[55] *The Taxation of Corporate Income*, p. 12.
[56] This was so in the U.S.A. See Donald C. Miller, "Corporate Taxation and Methods of Financing", *A.E.R.*, December 1952.
[57] *The Corporation Income Tax*, p. 180.

base-stock method and the 'last-in-first-out' method are used in inventory valuation. But no perfect method is available that would meet the various needs of the different types of business. Ultimately, however, the inventory problem arises solely due to changes in the price level. If only a stable price level could be maintained, then inventory valuation would not present so much difficulty.

The capital goods used in the production of commodities naturally wear out. Invariably, owing to the passage of time, the equipment used becomes obsolete. Moreover, in industries like mining, forestry, etc., the marketable materials such as oil deposits, coal, and timber come to be completely used up in course of time. Income from such industries is actually derived from the sales of the capital itself, though in infinitesimal parts. This creates the problem of the wearing out or depletion of capital. It may be a slow process, but one can visualise the end all the same.

Such being the case, the extent of wearing out, obsolescence and depletion should also be included in the current costs of production, and such costs should be deducted from the gross earnings. As William Vickrey correctly says, "Depreciation is deducted in order to permit the tax payer to recover intact and free from income-tax his capital investment in plant and equipment. In principle depreciation should reflect the decrease in the value of the capital arising from weathering, wear and tear, exhaustion of useful life and obsolescence."[58] Ultimately, the sum of all depreciation deductions *plus* the scrap value will equal the cost of replacing the same asset when its useful life has been exhausted. In theory, if depreciation is correctly calculated, there could never be any capital gain or loss, since "the cost or basis of the property, adjusted by such a depreciation allowance, would always equal the works value".[59]

But, then, this doesn't happen in every case. For one thing, the main difficulty here is the inadequacy of our tools to measure the amount of destruction and also to provide the norm. In calculating depreciation allowances, many estimates have to be made, like the life of the asset and the cost of replacing the asset in the future. Groves, describing the depreciation estimates, has remarked: "The process involves so many variables and imponderables that it may be closer to guess work than to estimating".[60] Apart from

---

[58] *Agenda for Progressive Taxation*, pp. 100-1.   [59] Ibid., p. 101.
[60] *Post-War Taxation and Economic Progress*, p. 156.

these, changing price levels create a host of other problems. Sometimes, again, overstatement of profits and understatement of depreciation allowances occur owing to a price rise.[61] As a general rule, conditions of inflation or deflation tend to distort profit and loss reports, because of their effects on depreciation, inventory valuation, etc. It is also possible that considerable amounts have been set aside for the maintenance of the capital equipment, and this must reflect in the depreciation allowances. If even larger amounts are spent for the upkeep of the machinery, naturally the value will decline less rapidly, and consequently less should be deducted for depreciation.

Apart from such normal depreciation, accelerated depreciation allowances also will be allowed with a view to stimulating investment. In the words of E. Carry Brown, accelerated depreciation, "broadly viewed, means an increase in the speed with which the historic cost of an asset is written off through depreciation deductions".[62] The main advantages of accelerated depreciation are, first, reduction of risk in investment, and, second, speeding up of replacement of plant and machinery and promotion of new and more economical processes; on the debit side, accelerated depreciation may sometimes be instrumental in companies discarding much useful equipment. It is, however, held by some people that accelerated depreciation is not a gain to the taxpayer; as Ralph Brown writes, "After all, the entire outlay is in any event deductible from income over some period of time".[63] The advantage is that reduced taxes immediately mean availability of more working capital (this, even though, ultimately, increased taxes are inevitable), and thus Ralph Brown equates this extra working capital with a tax-free loan from the treasury. Psychologically, the scheme of accelerated depreciation has a great value. It provides the incentive for companies to embark on new investment.

Many factors being involved in it, some of them imponderable, business of necessity is subject to fluctuating fortunes. In one year the company may register a huge profit, but in the very next

---

[61] See Goode, *The Corporation Income Tax*, p. 173.

[62] *Effects of Taxation : Depreciation Adjustment for Price Changes*, p. 155.

[63] *Income Stabilisation for a Developing Democracy*, Ed. by M. Millikan, p. 419. But, in the words of Musgrave, "Over a period during

year it may suffer serious loss. In such circumstances, the taxation at a high rate of the profit that accrued in the first year without taking into account the company's losses in subsequent years would be unfair. On the other hand, a uniform levy for all years will work as a damper to risky types of enterprise. Basically, then, the problem of losses is linked with the total accounting period. Such fluctuations in profits and losses generally affect small businesses more than large companies, because the larger concerns will have diversified their activities; profits in one are likely to cancel out losses in another. Again, large corporations usually maintain huge reserves to tide over periods of loss. Yet, whether it is a large or a small corporation, the problem of fluctuating fortunes is real; and discrimination is possible because one firm with a fluctuating income will be paying more to the treasury than another which also nets the same aggregate income but evenly distributed over the period. Further, this situation is apt to be even worse under progressive tax rates. As far as the United States of America is concerned, J. K. Butters and H. M. Groves have independently shown that a definite and marked discrimination between corporations does in fact take place, and the greatest discrimination is against those most sensitive to business cycle fluctuations.[64] Not only more taxes are paid by such corporations, but they also get less than full income-tax credit for the wear and tear of the capital. Thus, as Norris Darrel says correctly, "it is inevitable that any system of income taxation which puts on binders and looks only at a particular twelve month period will not always work equitably".[65] Apart from such equity considerations, lack of provision for offsetting losses can adversely affect risk-taking and the growth of new enterprises. A corporation earns a net income in a profit-year only after it has reinvested the erosion in capital during the loss-year. So the net income of the company in a profit-

which the tax payer expects fluctuations in tax rates, flexibility in the timing of depreciation charges permits him (investor) to take depreciation during times of high rates and thus reduce his tax-liability for the period as a whole". For a list of advantages of accelerated depreciation see R. A. Musgrave, *The Theory of Public Finance*, p. 337.

[64] J. K. Butters,'Discriminating Effects of the Annual Computation of the Income Tax', *Q. J. E.*, November 1939; and H. M. Groves, *Post-war Taxation and Economic Progress*, pp. 135-8.

[65] *How Should Corporations be Taxed? A Symposium*, p. 135.

year is not in actuality the real net income if the company had sustained losses in the preceding years; the good harvesting of one year has been made possible by the hard investment-sowing of the earlier years. Moreover, a newly started corporation will not be earning any profits at all (and it will thus be eroding into the capital) during the infant years. A twelve-month accounting year can thus markedly accentuate business instability.

In order to remedy this situation a longer accounting period than the conventional twelve-month period suggests itself. But this, too, is not an ideally desirable procedure because it is not good for the corporations to have tax liabilities unsettled for long periods. Another method of assessing the annual tax payment would be to base it upon the average annual profit and loss over a period of years. Many methods of averaging are put forward, but again none is entirely acceptable or satisfactory, for there is no system which achieves equity and at the same time is not so complicated as to create confusion in accounting as well as in administration.

By far the best approach to the problem seems to be the carry-over system of business losses. Carry-over and/or carry-back systems fall under this category. The carry-over system is preferable to the carry-back system, for the latter makes it imperative to reopen accounts long since closed. The usual range of the carry-forward period is anywhere from five to ten years; even an unlimited carry-forward period is sometimes suggested.

Apart from the taxation of the normal profits of corporations which we have so far examined, other taxes also are levied on special types of income earned by the corporations or their shareholders. There is, however, very little unanimity of opinion regarding the taxation of these items, namely, excess profits, undistributed profits, capital gains, bonus shares, intercorporate dividends and consolidated returns.

EXCESS PROFITS

Taxes on excess profits are levied to siphon off the unusually high profits earned during a war period. The reasons given in defence of the tax on excess profits have been too often repeated to merit any detailed discussion here. Suffice to say that in war-time companies are able to amass colossal profits, mainly because of heavy expenditure by the Government; hence the Government feels that it is entitled to a share in the extra profits. Moreover, it is rather unfair that excessive profits should be earned by one section of the community in times of war when the vast bulk of the people is struggling for very survival. The excess profits tax is a sort of corrective to this, and it is supposed to be the most efficient way of taxing the war-time gains.

Ordinarily, two methods are adopted to calculate the excess profits : the base period method and the invested capital method. Under the base period method, the profits of the pre-tax period are considered as the base or normal, and the present taxable excess is calculated with reference to the pre-tax period normal profits. Under the invested capital method, profits above a certain per cent of the capital will be declared excess and taxed accordingly. It has also been suggested that the tax could be levied in peace-time as well. Here the idea is to tax those profits of a firm which "represent a higher rate of return on capital than is common in industry or more than what is generally supposed to be a reasonable rate."[66] If it is decided to have a peace-time excess profits tax, the invested capital method will be preferable, for, if it is to be, not an emergency but a continuing tax, no base will be valid, while the invested capital method will have the merit of simplicity and uniformity. An excess profits tax during peace-time is advocated mainly to control monopoly, act as a stabilising force during boom periods, and check excessive income inequality. But it is no less true that an excess profits tax during 'normal' periods may tend to curb initiative and encourage wasteful expenditure on the part of the companies, not to mention innumerable administrative problems involved in the imposition and collection of a permanent excess profits tax. It would thus be, on the whole, advisable for the Government not to levy an excess profits tax in peace-time. If huge profits are earned by some corporations for long stretches of time, then the remedy would lie in appropriate anti-monopoly laws.

UNDISTRIBUTED PROFITS

More often than not, the treatment of undistributed profits

[66] J. R. Hicks, U. K. Hicks, and L. Rostas, *The Taxation of War Wealth*, p. 35.

presents difficulties. It is customary for the corporations not to distribute by way of dividends all the profits earned by them. The amount thus kept back from the shareholders is utilised mainly for the expansion of the business. Such ploughing back of profits into the business is a *sine qua non* for the healthy growth of the corporate sector. But sometimes profits are left undistributed for quite another reason. The dividends are taxed as per the personal income-tax rates, but that part of the company's profits which is not distributed as dividends is left untaxed, even though this also is the shareholder's income. Whereas the savings of individuals and partnerships are taxed, the savings of shareholders in the shape of undistributed profits are left out of the purview of taxation. The shareholders thus enjoy a tax free income in the shape of capital gains. This may be said to constitute a clear case of discrimination against individual proprietors and partnerships. If, on the other hand, such undistributed profits are taxed at a uniform rate, even then discrimination takes place, though of another kind; now the discrimination is between different shareholders, for the tax does not take into account their individual total income.[67]

When undistributed profits are not taxed, there is not only some discrimination as above indicated, but there may also result misallocation of investment of resources. A. S. Dewing thinks that corporate savings tend to encourage the ever-growing expansion of factory equipment, thus leading to booms and depressions.[68] The favoured treatment accorded to dividend income has adverse effects on investment in risk capital, and thus only large and well established corporations will be able to secure new capital for the requirements of expansion. The problem of undistributed profits is thus created by the taxing of corporate income and dividends separately. To solve the problem of undistributed profits, the remedy can only be the integration of the corporate and personal income taxes. Any such integration scheme must treat the dividend income shareholders of all income groups equitably and at the same time prevent undue tax avoidance through corporate retention. The important means suggested to achieve such inte-

[67] See A. G. Buehler, *The Undistributed Profits Tax*, p. 57
[68] See H. M. Groves, *Post-war Taxation and Economic Progress*, pp. 46-7.

gration are the Partnership method, Dividend-credit at the corporate level, Dividend-credit at the individual level, and the withholding approach.

PARTNERSHIP METHOD

In the partnership method, the corporation income-tax is not levied. For purposes of taxation the corporation is treated as a partnership firm. The profits of a corporation—whether distributed or not—are divided among the owners of the corporation, and these owners are taxed accordingly. Stockholders show their share of the corporate profits and losses on their income-tax returns, just as they show any other items of income or loss. As far as the capital gains taxation is concerned, "the basis of stock would be increased by the amount of undistributed profits taxed to stockholders and would be decreased by the amount of losses allocated to stockholders".[69]

On paper, this method appears to be sound and logical. For practical application, however, the scheme presents many difficulties. Moreover, the scheme doesn't take into account the personality of the corporations as such, which is real in its own way. But apart from this objection, the difficulties inherent in this method make its application next to impossible. As a general rule, corporations have hundreds or even thousands of shareholders, and it would be a terribly complicated task to allocate the profits and losses between them all. Besides, some listed stocks pass from hand to hand too often to permit the fixation of ownership for a given year on one person. Further, not all investors and shareholders are of the same type. "If all corporations were thoroughly solvent," says H. S. Simons, "and if their security issues were uniformly restricted to three or four standard contract forms, the task would not be altogether forbidding.... On the other hand, where companies have a great variety of contracts with their investors, and where some classes of securities represent no clear equity at all, apportionment is almost out of the question."[70]

One writer, H. M. Bowen, has argued in favour of partnership

[69] Goode, *The Corporation Income Tax*, p. 184.
[70] See his paper on 'Optional Partnership Treatment of Corporate Earnings' in *How Should Corporations be Taxed? A Symposium*, pp. 61-71.

option to small corporations. According to him, this method would reduce discrimination against corporate, as compared with non-corporate, business. Under this scheme, small businesses could operate under the corporate form and thus obtain the needed relief without unduly jeopardising the interests of the treasury. However, J. K. Butters feels that this method will not really be of much help to the small corporations.[71] This is because a tax saving would arise only if the marginal rate of tax of the shareholder was lower than the corporate rate. If the shareholder had a large income from other sources, then he would actually be required to pay more by way of taxes.

DIVIDEND-CREDIT AT THE CORPORATE LEVEL

In the dividend-credit at the corporate level method, the corporate and personal income-taxes are retained. But the corporation is granted a deduction for the dividends actually disbursed, and the dividends are taxed only at the hands of the shareholders : thus 'double taxation' of distributed profits is completely eliminated. This method will also ensure lesser tax avoidance through undistributed profits. Moreover, less reliance will be placed by corporations on borrowed capital. If the tax reduction leads to the declaration of bigger dividends, individuals will have more incentive to invest, which is certainly very desirable.

The difficulty with this scheme is its bias against small and expanding corporations because, whereas big and established concerns will be able to distribute large dividends, smaller concerns will have to depend upon the ploughing back of profits for expansion. This method of taxation is different from a tax on undistributed profits only 'semantically', and hence it suffers from most of the defects of an undistributed profits tax.

DIVIDEND-CREDIT AT THE INDIVIDUAL LEVEL

According to this approach, the corporate income-tax will be retained, but an exemption or tax-credit will be given to dividends received by the shareholders. This could be done in three ways : (1) Imposing a tax on all profits of the corporation, but treating a part or the whole of it as a withholding tax when dividends are

[71] See his paper on 'Should the Profits of Small Corporations be Taxed like Partnership Earnings ? ' in the same *Symposium*.

distributed; (2) Exempting dividends from an individual top-bracket rate; (3) Excluding a part of the dividends received from the taxable income of the shareholders.[72]

The main objection to this approach is that it offers substantial advantages only to shareholders with high incomes. Moreover, there is another problem to be solved in the application of this scheme, namely the determination of the type of dividends to which a credit is to be attached. For example, the law may confine itself to the most junior class of shareholders, leaving out the preferred shareholders. In essence, however, this scheme looks somewhat like the withholding approach, which we shall examine presently.

THE WITHHOLDING SCHEME

Under this scheme, a tax is levied on all corporate profits. This tax is, besides, regarded as having been paid by the corporation on behalf of its shareholders. When presenting their income-tax returns, the shareholders will include, not only the dividends distributed, but also the tax paid by the corporation on their behalf. The shareholder is then allowed to deduct from his tax the amount of the tax paid on the dividends by the corporations. If the corporation has paid tax at a higher rate than the shareholder's individual tax liability, then he would be entitled to a refund from the Government.

The withholding method reduces the double taxation of distributed profits because it sets off all or part of the tax paid by the corporation on such profits against the tax liability of the shareholders. The advantage to the shareholder is that he is not required to pay a tax on the dividends unless his individual tax liability exceeds the amount which the corporation has paid.

Tax rates are a problem for the withholding approach. If tax avoidance through the accumulation of undistributed profits is to be prevented, then a high withholding tax (equal to the top-bracket personal income-tax) is a necessity. But this is sure to produce deleterious effects on corporate enterprise. Accordingly, there must be a correlation between the individual income-tax rate and the corporate tax rate for the successful application of this approach.

[72] Randolph E. Paul, *Taxation for Prosperity*, p. 364.

CAPITAL GAINS

The treatment of capital gains and losses in the field of corporate taxation is important for two reasons : (1) the capital gains tax is related to the problem of the integration of corporate and personal income taxes, (2) the main problem of income-tax is to make a clear distinction between income and capital receipts. If the ability to pay concept alone is applied strictly, taking into consideration only the receipts, then capital gains have to be taxed; and the problem here is one of deciding whether capital gains should be deemed ordinary income or as a special kind of income.

Capital gains in the ordinary sense are the profit that one makes in selling any of one's assets which are not offered for sale in the usual way of business. In the same way, capital losses are the decline in the market value of such assets. The main sources of such gains and losses are those capital assets which are owned mainly for making an income rather than for consumption purposes. Such assets include corporation securities, real estate, Government bonds, and interests in partnerships, leases and contracts. Capital gains and losses are the result of the same factors which cause unexpected gains or losses from the exchange of goods. These factors are :

1. A change in the absolute value due to natural growth ;
2. A change in the value of a particular property in comparison with the value of other properties due to external causes ;
3. A change in the money value of property due to appreciation or depreciation of currency ; and
4. Accumulated errors in asset amortisation of prior periods.[73]

From the tax-gatherer's point of view, the gain or loss *must* be realised ; here increases or decreases in the value of the capital assets are not to be included in the income-tax returns. The reason is that it is impossible to get at the unrealised capital gains ; and this aspect of the capital gains taxation provides the major loophole. Wealthy tax payers could easily evade such taxation by delaying the realisation, and when they die, the property, inclusive of capital gains, will automatically pass on to their heirs.

Capital gains represent a real increment in one's economic posi-

[73] See C. J. Gaa, *The Taxation of Corporate Income*, p. 92.

tion when there is an absolute change of value. In the four factors listed above, all except the third mean a real increase in one's economic power.

Opinion is not unanimous regarding the tax treatment of capital gains and losses. Those who favour a tax on the capital gains argue that these are not different from ordinary income, for these capital gains also increase the economic power of the individual, even as capital losses reduce his economic power ; and hence there is every reason to add the former and deduct the latter from the ordinary income. But most of the authorities who favour the tax stress that only realised gains and losses should be taken into account. Before the gain or loss is realised, the gain or loss exists only as capital. The point where the capital gain separates itself from the capital is the actual sale. In the words of Seligman, "the real point is the separation of the increment from the capital. The separation is necessary in order to constitute income. The increment when separated is income ; the increment unseparated remains capital."[74] In other words, an unrealised capital increment cannot be considered as income, but only as an accretion in the value of the capital. Only when the idea of an increment in economic power and its actual realisation are fused does the ability to pay emerge as a positive conclusion. But capital gains and losses have other characteristics which distinguish them from ordinary income, and in these one finds the objection to taxing capital gains as ordinary income.

Firstly, capital gains are occasional and irregular, and hence they cannot be considered as current disposable income. It is unfair to tax capital gains as the income of the year in which they are realised, because this discriminates in favour of regularly coming ordinary income. Moreover it is but natural for a person to suffer sporadic losses also, even as he enjoys sporadic gains, and it is possible that capital gains and losses will after all cancel each other out over a long period.

Secondly, capital assets are valuable because of the incomes that are expected of them and, of course, it is such derived income that is taxed. Such being the case, a rise in the value of capital reflects only an anticipation of increased income from it. Taxing both the increase in income and the rise in the value of capital

[74] *Studies in Public Finance*, pp. 114-5.

(that is, capital gains) from which the increase in income derives is thus a case of taxing the same thing twice.[75]

If a strictly economic interpretation is sought, then capital gains cannot be considered as income. From the standpoint of general economic theory, "the essential element in a capital gain or loss is its unexpected character. An expected rise in the price of *any* asset is ordinary income; an unexpected rise, a capital gain".[76] Moreover, capital gains do not meet the definition of income as the money value of the gross income which could be used up without destroying the prospect of equal gross income in any future period. However, our immediate concern is not to inquire into the pros and cons of capital gains taxation, but rather to see whether the exclusion of capital gains from the tax base will occasion any injustice so far as the treatment of undistributed profits is concerned.

H. C. Simons, Nicholas Kaldor and many others have advocated that business should be left untaxed, but that the realised capital gains from holding corporate stock should be treated as taxable personal income. Under the proposal of Simons, realised capital gains from holding corporate stock would be taxed at the same rates as other personal income.[77] Kaldor too makes this point explicitly: "If capital gains were taxed, in the same manner as ordinary income, and at the same time as they accrue, there would be no logical justification for taxing company profits as such—the benefits derived from these profits would be adequately and far more appropriately taxed in the hands of the individual property owner".[78] It is true that, for administrative reasons, only realised gains will be taken into account. But, then, transfer of property through inheritance or gifts should also be reckoned as realisation. Vickrey also supports this method: "Full taxation of capital gains would substantially reduce the opportunities for avoidance through reinvestment of earnings, for then all such earnings would eventually be taxed at full rates".[79]

---

[75] See Lawrence H. Seltzer, *The Nature and Tax Treatment of Capital Gains and Losses*, p. 10.
[76] Ibid., p. 47.
[77] See H. M. Groves, *Production, Jobs and Taxes*, pp. 25-6, 40.
[78] *An Expenditure Tax*, p. 146.
[79] *Agenda for Progressive Taxation*, p. 151.

However, this approach too is not without its drawbacks. In the first place, this involves the postponement of tax collection till the appreciated stock is actually sold or passed on to the inheritors. Groves makes this point clear when he says: "The timing of taxation is exceedingly important, and it is doubtful if any burdens imposed upon the dead can make up for immunities allowed the living".[80] Even though Kaldor argues in favour of a capital gains tax, he is not blind to its deficiencies, especially the facility it gives to individual capitalists to indulge in irrational and antisocial behaviour.[81] Actually, however, Kaldor advocates an expenditure tax at the personal level as a remedy for all the problems created by corporate taxation. "The justification for company taxation would disappear", he says, "if the principle of taxing income were abandoned in favour of taxing expenditure. For under an expenditure tax, all capital gains would automatically be brought into charge in so far as they were spent, while in so far as they were saved, they would be no more liable to tax than any other form of saving."[82] But the introduction of an expenditure tax raises its own crop of difficulties, though we are not concerned with them here. As for the capital gains taxation, a majority of the economists favour it in theory, though a like unanimity does not prevail regarding the manner in which capital gains should be computed and taxed.[83]

BONUS SHARES

Otherwise called also stock dividends, bonus shares are an interesting method of distributing the accumulated earnings of the corporations without, however, actually distributing them. What

[80] *Post-war Taxation and Economic Progress*, p. 61.
[81] *An Expenditure Tax*, p. 171.
[82] Ibid., p. 146.
[83] It is interesting to see what the Royal Commission on the Taxation of Profits and Income has to say on this subject:

"The propriety of the tax has received some support on economic grounds, the view being advanced that the absence of a tax on capital gains contributes to the course of inflation. The premise is that the capital gain forms a resource that is peculiarly likely to be withdrawn from investment and expended in consumption".

Even such a defence being hardly convincing, the majority observes: "No sound conclusion could be arrived at, one way or the other, on this theme". (*Report*, p. 36).

is done is that new shares of stock are issued to the shareholder in proportion to their present holding; this issue of bonus shares to the existing shareholders does not, of course, confer any extra privilege on them; actually what happens is that a part of the reserves is converted into fresh paid-up capital. In the result, even though the earning capacity of the company remains the same, there will be a proportionate decrease in the dividend per share.

Sometimes these bonus shares are taxed as current income on the ground that this is a method of tax-avoidance. Theoretically such tax-avoidance is possible, for, as Anderson says, "receivers can immediately sell their share and be taxed only on the capital gains dating from the purchase of the original shares, rather than at full income-tax rates on the market value of the dividend".[84] However, shareholders as a general rule tend to treat their stock dividends as capital rather than as income. Moreover, the brokers' commission charges make the sale of a few shares of stock relatively expensive, and hence the stockholder, in a majority of cases, will not sell his stock. Economists like Seligman have held the opinion that stock dividends are not income. The test for current income is 'separation' and 'realisation'. Applying these two criteria, Seligman comes to the conclusion that the stock dividends are *not* current income.[85] But this view, plausible as it sounds, cannot be accepted without demur. If accumulation by corporations in the form of undistributed profits could be considered as an accretion in the economic power of the shareholders (through the rises in the value of the shares), why should the stock dividends also not be considered as a method of increasing the economic power of the shareholders?

INTERCORPORATE DIVIDENDS AND CONSOLIDATED RETURNS

If ever the system of intercorporate holding of shares and preparation of consolidated returns is resorted to, the result may very well be the emergence of monopoly. Corporations sometimes hold shares of other corporations, which likewise hold shares of still other corporations, leading to a chain reaction of control from one end, thereby inevitably attracting monopolistic attitudes and

[84] *Taxation and the American Economy*, p. 219.
[85] *Studies in Public Finance*, pp. 22-3.

practices. On the other hand, consolidated returns are a device to reduce or avoid taxes. For example, if a particular concern is prosperous and nets in a high income, it may have to pay a higher tax rate than a concern that is less prosperous and is earning little if not actually losing. In such a situation, two or more concerns can join and present a consolidated income-tax return. The high profits earned by one corporation will be cancelled out by the losses sustained by another. Ordinarily a special tax may be levied for permission to present such a consolidated return.

JUSTICE IN TAXATION

It is only when we have decided what the income of the taxable corporation is that the problem of 'how to tax' arises. Normally the objective of any tax is to bring in a certain volume of revenue to the treasury. But the necessary precondition is that the tax authorities should utilise this instrument of taxation to extract the needed revenue without unduly harming or harassing the taxpayers. In other words, the tax should conform to the canons of justice. Now the application of the canons of justice to corporate taxation cannot be accomplished easily because, as we have seen earlier, this involves considerable subjective interpretations and judgments. However useful statistical techniques may be in other branches of science, they don't help, or help fully, the tax-analyst. They are occasionally suggestive, of course, but actually not much reliance can be placed on them.

Justice in corporate taxation could mean two things :

1. Justice for the corporation which pays the tax : the tax should not be so repressive in its effects that the corporation is made to suffer irreparable damage ; and,
2. Justice in relation to other corporations : in other words, any criteria for taxation should be applied to all the taxpayers, after giving due regard to the individual circumstances—discrimination being avoided as a rule.

To take the first point first : Justice for the corporation with reference to taxation means really taxation within its ability to bear : that is, taxation that is not in excess of the taxable capacity of the corporation. Here the problem is one of determining the taxable capacity. The two points of view regarding the concept of the taxable capacity are, first, the capacity to pay regardless of the ensuing suffering, and, secondly, the capacity to pay without appreciable difficulty. The first view countenances the taxation of the total net profits to what G. Findlay Shirras has called the "limit of squeezability".[86] The other point of view is more common. This takes into account the amount of profit which the corporation can spare without limiting its own normal activities. Even so, it must be frankly admitted that the concept of taxable capacity is most vague, and cannot therefore serve as a practical guide to taxation. The trend of profits seen in conjunction with the trends in price level could give, perhaps, a far better indicator as to the taxable capacity of a corporation.

As regards the second point, Justice in corporate taxation must obviously mean also uniformity of treatment to all taxpayers. In other words, the 'burdens' borne by different corporations should show evidence, not of discrimination, but of impartiality. To put it in yet another way, the tax system should not treat essentially similar classes of taxpayers unequally, or treat essentially different classes of taxpayers equally. This principle is termed by H. M. Groves 'neutrality in taxation', which really means taxation that does not alter the existing allocation of resources. It does not follow, however, that neutrality should be the sole aim of taxation. As Groves judiciously adds : "The thought is not that taxes should be neutral *rather than* equitable ; they should be both. Or perhaps more accurately : taxes should be equitable and they should deviate from neutrality only for an adequate public purpose".[87]

The manipulation of the tax rate is the one elastic instrument with which the Government can try to mete out justice to the corporations. Even then, as Kaldor says, "the choice of the principle on which the burden of taxation can most fairly be allocated between persons is ultimately a moral and not an economic one".[88] Now the choice is mainly between progressive and proportional taxation. Both progressive and proportional rates could be based on the criterion of the ability to pay, and both have protagonists to claim that it alone, the progressive or the proportional rate, is

---

[86] *The Science of Public Finance*, Vol. I, p. 229.
[87] Article in *National Tax Journal*, March 1948, p. 18.
[88] *An Expenditure Tax*, p. 25.

THE ECONOMICS OF CORPORATE TAXATION

the ideal mode of apportionment. The basis of proportional taxation is the nondisturbance of the existing distribution of wealth, whereas progressive taxation aims at decreasing the present economic inequality (that is, it attempts a more equal distribution of income, property, expenditure or any other measure of the economic status of persons). The cornerstone of progressive taxation is the diminishing marginal utility of money. As such it could be applied only to human taxpayers, and not to institutional taxpayers. "Genuinely progressive taxation", says Vickrey, "is necessarily personal taxation. Progressive taxation may be defined as taxation which tends to promote economic equality."[89] In a progressive tax system it is the individuals that are taxed, and not the income or the profits as such; the aim is to contain the economic power that high incomes or profits give to individuals within reasonable bounds, an attempt at a drastic lowering of the economic ceilings of individuals in the hope that thereby the general economic level of the entire community will rise.

As we saw earlier, the attempt to subject to progressive rates the unusually large profits of a corporation without taking into consideration the conditions of the previous or succeeding years is obvious injustice. Actually, progressive taxation as applied to companies can in practice become regressive. If the shares of the corporation with a large income were owned by relatively poor people and the shares of the corporation with a small income were owned by the relatively rich, then the whole object in having progressive rates of taxation must fail. As Seligman says, "the application of the progressive principle to corporations is therefore of dubious expediency".[90] As far as corporations are concerned, proportional taxation will bring about the desired result of equalising the burden of corporations with different levels of income. It is not to be supposed, of course, that a proportional corporation income-tax does not at all produce the effect which progressive taxation brings about, for, in aggregative terms, the taxation of corporate income, by reducing the dividend income, reduces the total disposable income of the larger income groups more than it reduces the total disposable income of the smaller income groups. This is all that we can legitimately hope to bring about.

[89] *Agenda for Progressive Taxation*, p. 3.
[90] *Progressive Taxation in Theory and Practice*, p. 318.

Effects of Corporate Taxation

Perhaps the most vexatious problem in the field of corporate taxation is the difficulty of determining who exactly bears the tax burden ultimately, and what the consequences of this are. The first half of the problem involves 'shifting and incidence', while the second half involves a study of the effects of the tax on the economic system. The tax gatherer may collect a tax from somebody, but the actual burden may quite possibly be borne by someone else. A consideration of this problem is important for policy makers. As we saw at the very outset, the tax is a very useful but at the same time a somewhat dangerous tool; a double-edged weapon, in fact. Its usefulness could be enjoyed only if it is made to do what it is appropriate for it to do; a razor is meant to shave, not to cut, though it can be made to cut if one wants to put it to such perverse use. The question of who really bears the tax burden is of particular relevance in the field of corporate taxation because, unless the tax remains where it is intended, it fails to serve the purpose of the taxation, unless, of course, one takes the 'cynical' view that, after all, it is the business of a tax to bring in revenue, let it come from where it will. If forward shifting takes place, then the tax falls on the consumers; if backward shifting takes place, the tax falls on the factors of production. If the tax is thus shifted one way or the other, then the cry of the corporations that there is 'double taxation' or 'inequity' cannot be very valid. The corporations cannot shift the tax and at the same time complain about the repressive effects of taxation.

SHIFTING AND INCIDENCE

There are broadly three viewpoints regarding the shifting of direct taxes on income and profits. The view generally favoured by the economists is that the direct taxes on profits cannot, and are not, shifted by the taxpayer in the form of high prices. On the contrary, the businessmen say that they can easily shift the taxes, and they actually claim that they are in fact shifting the taxes. They consider corporate taxes as costs, and as costs must be paid for by the public in prices, and are so paid for by the public, like any other consumption tax. The third viewpoint is a *via media* between the above two extreme views. According to this, the taxes over a period of time inevitably come to be widely diffused in the whole economic system. The taxes not only raise the cost of goods and services, but also keep wages lower and limit the yields on risk-bearing investment.

The first view, the economic argument, is best presented in the words of A. C. Pigou: "Income tax is assessed on the profits resulting from trade and industry, and if, as may be presumed, people are already charging the prices that yield them the best profit, the removal by the State of a portion of the profit will not tempt them to fix prices differently".[91] Further, income-tax being a net tax on income, producers cannot transfer their business from one industry to another in order to evade the tax. The price is determined by the marginal producer who makes no profit. A tax on any commodity based on the units affects, not only the cost of the prosperous profit-making producer, but also the struggling marginal producer, whereas a tax on profit affects only the profit-making producer. "But," argues Seligman, "a tax on income is a tax on net profits; and net profits are not cost, but the surplus over cost.... The tax on profits is paid only by the man who makes profits, that is by the intra-marginal producer, not by the marginal producer. But the tax paid by the intra-marginal producer cannot affect the price which is fixed by the marginal producer who pays no tax."[92] W. H. Coates in his Memorandum to the Colwyn Committee on National Debt and Taxation also comes to the same conclusions after a thorough examination of the available facts relating to eight industries in England, although D. Black points out that, even though Coates' technique in analysing the statistics is admirable, his interpretation of the statistics is defective.[93] The Colwyn Committee itself has come to the conclusion that "the broad economic argument is true over practically the whole field and for practically the whole of the time, any exceptions being local or temporary and insufficient to invalidate it."[94] As for corporations shifting direct taxes, the Committee is emphatic

[91] See *Report of Committee on National Debt and Taxation*, p. 109.
[92] *Studies in Public Finance*, p. 73.
[93] See for detailed criticism: D. Black, *The Incidence of Income Taxes*, Part I, Chap. III.
[94] *Report*, p. 119. See also Robert E. Ford, 'Some Economic Aspects of the Present Corporate Income Tax', *Proceedings of the National Tax Association 1947*, pp. 55-9.

that corporations will shift the tax to their shareholders. In large corporations the directors are not individually much affected, and without wanting to run the risk of reduced sales because of increased prices, generally reduce dividend disbursements. This is made possible because of the practical separation of ownership and management. It is illuminating to see what the Committee says on this point : "The enterprise of company, when once established, depends on a small number of managing heads. In the interests of the business, whether the primary purpose be dividend or reserve, the aim of directors will be to make as large a profit as possible. They will of course balance risks against chances of profit, but the Income-Tax although it may exist in the background as a vaguely depressing element, will not normally enter into their calculations .... They are not concerned with the Income-Tax on dividends, which is borne by the shareholders."[95]

As against such striking unanimity of opinion among the economists,[96] the feeling among persons connected with business is that the direct tax on profit is almost entirely shifted to the consumers in the form of higher prices. As Joseph D. Noonan says, even though smaller corporations may not be able to shift the burden, "the giant corporations—the quasi monopolies that control supply and prices—pay little if any of the tax. They simply treat the tax as an item of cost, and set prices to yield the after-taxes profits which they wish to take".[97] The same opinion was expressed by many witnesses to the Colwyn Committee on National Debt and Taxation. Actually one witness went so far as to say that "the difference between direct and indirect taxation hardly exists in actual fact". This witness was convinced that "the burden becomes

[95] *Report*, p. 150.

[96] Except D. H. Robertson, in 'The Colwyn Committee, the Income Tax and the Price Level' (*The Economic Journal*, December 1927), reprinted in *Readings in the Economics of Taxation*. He is of the view that the Committee was wrong in thinking that profit was a pure surplus and had neglected the fact that the supply of enterprise was linked to the profit level, though the practical importance of this mistake was slight because the supply of enterprise is very inelastic.

[97] *Proceedings of the National Tax Association 1956*, p. 182. But the investigations of the National Industrial Conference Board reveal that business taxes are not shifted in the U.S. See Donald C. Miller, *Taxes, the Public Debt and Transfers of Income*, p. 31, and M. H. Gillim, *The Incidence of Excess Profits Taxation*, p. 41 *et seq*.

automatically distributed by a law of political economy that defies all Acts of Parliament".[98]

It is somewhat difficult to accept the opinions of the businessmen without reservation. Rightly does D. H. Robertson chide the Colwyn Committee witnesses for making extravagant statements which they could never substantiate.[99] For one thing, the tax is levied only *after* the profit is made; how then could the tax be shifted to the consumer? Richard Goode correctly says that "it is hard to conceive of a tax on net profits as a cost in any usual sense. The amount of the tax is not known until after the results of the operations of a fiscal period have been ascertained. Moreover, the tax, if a cost, is indeed a strange kind of cost. It is a 'cost' which rises with success but automatically disappears when operations are unsuccessful."[100] H. M. Groves, however, says that "corporate net income tax applies to items of imputed rent and interest deductible as costs and hence concludes that the tax does really reach certain costs and surplus".[101]

Another obstacle to shifting the tax in the form of increased price is the inability of any one corporation alone to control the price of a commodity that is being produced simultaneously by several independent concerns. There are also a variety of other non-economic factors which the corporation has to face in the event of changing the price. As far as the corporations are concerned, the actual administrators are different from the owners. The administrators will naturally give more importance to stability, and hence they will think twice before shifting the taxes on to the prices owing to the fear of losing the market. Even if they should decide to shift, it might not be the whole burden of the tax but

[98] *Report of Committee on National Debt and Taxation*, p. 109. See also J. R. Petrie, *The Taxation of Corporate Income in Canada*, p. 135, fn. 40.
[99] Article on 'The Colwyn Committee, the Income Tax and the Price Level', included in *Readings in the Economics of Taxation*, p. 304.
[100] *The Corporation Income Tax*, p. 50.
[101] *Post War Taxation and Economic Progress*, p. 28. Carl Shoup also comes to the same conclusion in his 'Incidence of the Corporation Income Tax' in the *National Tax Journal*, March 1948. Shoup suggests that companies might have kept their price lower than what they might have charged because of competitive conditions. But should the additional tax burden be 'substantial', the companies would naturally be compelled to shift through increased prices so that the old level of profits might be maintained (pp. 12-7).

only a part of it. According to a sample survey undertaken in the U.S.A., it has been found that only about 60 per cent of the companies take into account the taxes in framing their price policies.[102]

Because of the reduction of the net returns on account of the taxes, it is likely that the risk-taker will tend to withdraw his capital in the long run. Reduced capital would mean reduced output ; and reduced output should mean eventually a higher price. Such is the sort of shift that takes place over a period of some years, and so the tax burden may be said to be transferred after all to the consumers.[103] If, however, the capital thus withdrawn is spent in purchasing real estate and durable consumer goods, then the prices of these will go up. Thus the tax is shifted to the investors generally. Of course, even such a long period shifting is contingent upon factors like a relatively tax-free area—geographical as well as functional—the mobility of capital already existing, and the overall reduction in investment as a result of a tax-produced decrease in either the ability or willingness to invest.[104]

In conclusion we can say that even though the price level may not immediately rise owing to the imposition of the tax, it certainly *tends* to be shifted to the consumers with the passage of time. Economic theory is not quite helpful in locating the incidence, particularly so far as the direct taxation on profits is concerned. As H. M. Groves remarks, "Suffice it to say that no definite conclusion as to the incidence of the corporate income tax is possible and that not improbably the burden is divided between at least stockholders and consumers".[105]

ECONOMIC CONSEQUENCES

Shifting itself is but one of the economic consequences of the imposition of a corporation tax, for the reactions do not stop there.

[102] Lewis H. Kimmel, *Taxes and Economic Incentives*, p. 27.
[103] See C. Lowell Harriss, *A Survey of Contemporary Economics*, Vol. II, p. 265.
[104] See Robert P. Collier's 'The Empirical Evidence of Tax Incidence' in the *National Tax Journal*, March 1958, pp. 51-2.
[105] *Post-War Taxation and Economic Progress*, p. 28. See also M. A. Adelman's 'The Corporation Income Tax in the Long Run' in *J.P.E.*, April 1957. Adelman, however, concludes that, even in the long run, 'there has been no shifting of the corporate income tax either to consumers, or to employees". (*J.P.E.*, April 1957, p. 157.)

It is quite possible that there may be also a certain reaction on the part of the individual on whom the tax falls after the initial shifting has taken place. If the shifting doesn't take place, even then there may be some economic reaction. Now, what are the consequences of a direct tax on the economic plane? Of course, any discussion of the effects of taxation can have meaning only if the tax is unshifted in the short period. Here, accordingly, the impact of the tax on the economy is seen only through investment trends. If, on the contrary, the tax is of the shiftable nature, like consumption taxes, then the impact of the tax on the economy could be studied only through consumption studies.

Like the study of incidence, any analysis of the effects of a particular tax will inevitably involve conjectures and guesses. It is simply impossible to determine with complete exactitude the effects of a particular tax. The tracing of the cause-effect relationship in the field of taxation is made particularly more difficult by the influence of sociological and psychological factors. Moreover, it is quite possible that the long term reactions of the people to taxes are different from the immediate reactions. As Gunnar Myrdal points out, "The effect of a tax must never be examined in isolation, but must be seen in its setting amongst other measures in the complex system of price formation. A measure has different repercussions according to the nature of other measures applied at the same time.... Realistic investigation of the effects of taxes should therefore embrace the whole tax system."[106] It is without doubt true that the effects of particular taxes cannot be isolated. Nevertheless it is not quite a useless pursuit to try to analyse the course of the effects of particular taxes on particular aspects of the economy. It is probable that we may not get accurate results, but then nothing can be mathematically definite or precise with the social sciences. Certain indications can be perceived, certain movements can be foreseen, and these will without doubt be helpful in formulating future policies.

The Colwyn Committee classified the effects of income taxation into two broad categories, namely, effects on the economic capacity and effects on the economic behaviour of the taxpayer. The first

---

[106] *The Political Element in the Development of Economic Theory*, pp. 188-90. See also Ursula K. Hicks's 'The Terminology of Tax Analysis' in the *Economic Journal*, March 1946, p. 45.

is the physical effect, while the second is psychological in nature.[107] An analysis of the physical effects of taxation itself is beset with innumerable difficulties, but the examination of the psychological behaviour of the taxpayer, consequent on the imposition of a tax, is next to impossible. Some economists feel that not much importance should be attached to physical effects : they say that the adverse effects of progressive taxes on incentives etc. depend, less on the taxes themselves, and more on the prevailing social attitudes. The rigours of a particular piece of taxation are felt mainly because of the feeling about them and not because of the physical capacity of the taxpayer.[108] The subjective limitation again ! But, then, while psychology no doubt has its sphere of influence, to say that that is all there is to it is not quite a correct approach to the problem. Apart from the current social attitudes, it is also a palpable fact that people get understandably apprehensive because their economic power suffers real curtailment on account of the taxes.

As far as a corporation is concerned, psychological factors play only a subordinate part, though by no means an insignificant one. Because of steeply progressive personal income taxes, investors are left with diminished funds for investment in the corporate sector. Even if some funds are available, people will not be very anxious to invest them because of the high rates of corporate taxation. After all, the main motive of investing one's money in business is the prospect of high returns. But if high rates of taxation are found at the personal as well as at the corporate level, then the temptation for parting with capital is very considerably reduced. This must certainly affect the investment behaviour of the people with some capital to invest. Another way in which progressive personal taxation may result in the exploitation and eventual migration of the low income shareholders' capital is given by W. L. Crum. When profits are ploughed back in the business, the actual consequence will be the exploitation of the low income shareholders by the high income shareholders. This is how it happens : with ploughing back taking place, the business prospers, and the shares appreciate in some measure. Because neither the

---

[107] A. C. Pigou calls it 'Announcement effects'. *A Study in Public Finance*, p. 55. George Barrel terms it as 'impact effect'. See *The Stock Exchange : A Symposium*, p. 50.

[108] See H. C. Simons, *Federal Tax Reform*, p. 146.

rich nor the poor shareholders are realising their dividends, they are not paying income taxes either. If they had both—the rich as well as the poor—realised their dividends, the high income shareholders would have paid at a relatively higher tax rate than the low income shareholders. In this sense the low income shareholders contribute more than the high income group to the pool of the retained profits that are ploughed back. But even though the immediate cause of the exploitation is the retention of the profits for being ploughed back, the real villain of the piece is the graduation or the progression in the income-tax. This is not only not fair but may also lead to the low income shareholder withdrawing his capital and channelling it into alternative investment directions.[109]

RETARDATION OF RISK-TAKING

Essentially the cornerstone of the private enterprise system is risk-taking, in other words the ultimate risk of losing the principal itself should the business totally fail. Risks are taken because of an anticipated gain—we mean here the net profit after the deduction of taxes. The corporation tax, however, claims a share in the profits so realised after taking the necessary risks. After all, the State does little for the shareholders except claiming a share of the earned profits. Eminent authorities like Sir Josaiah Stamp,[110] J. E. Meade,[111] Lord Robbins,[112] Duncan Black,[113] Nicholas Kaldor,[114] and Alvin Hansen, [115] have accordingly come to the conclusion that "the preference for less risky stock will increase after taxation".[116]

Basically risk-taking is connected with possible losses, not

[109] See W. L. Crum, 'The Taxation of Shareholders', *Q.J.E.*, February 1950, pp. 41-2.
[110] 'Taxation, Risk-taking and the Price Level', *The Economic Journal*, June 1928, p. 209.
[111] *An Introduction to Economic Analysis and Policy*, p. 239.
[112] 'The Long Term Budget Problem', *Lloyds Bank Monthly Review*, April 1938, p. 162.
[113] *The Incidence of Income Taxes*, p. 223.
[114] *An Expenditure Tax*, pp. 112-8.
[115] 'Stability and Expansion', *Financing American Prosperity : A Symposium*, p. 241.
[116] Otto von Mering, *The Shifting and Incidence of Taxation*, p. 197 ; see also p. 213.

counting the ultimate loss of the principal itself. The State claims a share from the person who makes a clear profit through such risk-taking. When he loses in business or loses the invested capital itself, the State has nothing to do with him ; but when he makes a profit, the State promptly steps in to claim its share on the principle of 'Heads we win, tails you lose'. Thus an obvious injustice is done to the risk-taking investor. The offsetting of losses, however, can mitigate this injustice to a certain extent. E. D. Domar and R. A. Musgrave have shown that the reward for taking risks will not be reduced in relation to the risk actually assumed under a *proportional* income-tax, because the offsetting of losses against taxable income will reduce potential losses and gains equally. But under a *progressive* tax system, the prospective reward for risk-taking is reduced beyond question.[117] Yet it must be admitted that no length of carry-over of losses would fully protect the company that never makes enough profits to recover its lost capital. But, then, as Richard Goode concludes, "No feasible plan would completely neutralize the influence of the tax on the return for assumption of risk".[118]

Since the capital, which is mainly employed in starting and promoting the development of a new enterprise, involves some risk, and since investment decisions are subjective, any accurate prediction regarding the marginal rate which unduly discourages equity investment is impossible. If large portions of possible gains are to be abstracted by the Government, then very few investments will appear attractive. Moreover, in most tax systems, interest charges are permitted to be deducted as costs, whereas dividends are taxed. Thus such tax structures have the effect of making risk investments less attractive as compared with less risky ones. The combined result of a steeply progressive personal income-tax (which discourages people from putting forth extra effort because they are not going to retain a sufficient share of the extra profits they make to warrant this extra effort)[119] and the company's

[117] See E. D. Domar and R. A. Musgrave, 'The Proportional Income Taxation and Risk Taking', *Q.J.E.*, May 1944, pp. 388-422. Included in *Readings in the Economics of Taxation*.

[118] *The Corporation Income Tax*, p. 124.

[119] With the help of indifference curve analysis, Otto von Mering shows that if a proportional income-tax is imposed, it may increase, leave unchanged, or decrease the taxpayer's efforts. But a progressive

method of economic financing (that is, financing capital needs through bond-issues to avoid the double taxation of dividends) is to drive the investors to go in for Government tax-exempt bonds or debentures which are 'safe'.

The taxation of corporate income also affects the enterprise of corporations regarding expansion. Corporate taxes, by reducing the net profits, leave less for either dividend distribution or for retention. Either way they act as a deterrent against fresh capital accumulation. For small expanding concerns, the main source of new capital can only be retained earnings, for such concerns cannot attract sufficient new equity capital as much as the well established corporations. In the first place, the established companies will have often ploughed back retained profits, and thus the 'value' of their stock will be high, apart from their goodwill and their long sustained reputation. New companies are generally at a disadvantage in the matter of attracting capital, for unless they can offer prospects of a better return for the money invested than the older, well established companies, people are unlikely to risk their money in new concerns. As Dan Thorp Smith says, "The stock of a new company must, by definition, be sold at its value, since it has no assets other than those secured from the proceeds of stock sold. But stock in an existing company, purchased at less than asset value, has more dollars of assets working for it, as it were. With the same rate of gross and net returns on assets in both companies, the outstanding stock of the established company will offer the greater earnings per share."[120]

Thus, on the one hand personal income-taxes reduce the flow of capital to the corporate sector, and, on the other, corporate taxes stand in the way of large retained earnings being ploughed back for purposes of modernisation and expansion. The effect of this two-pronged attack is to reduce the reward for enterprise. Moreover, it is not enough to consider the discouraging effects of corporate taxation on the existing corporations; attention must be paid also to the many concerns which are as it were still-born. Many a company dies in the minds of its promoters, for they finally shrink from taking the necessary risk in view of the discouraging climate

income-tax tends only to decrease efforts more than a proportionate income tax. (*The Shifting and Incidence of Taxation*, pp. 113-4.)

[120] *Effects of Taxation : Corporate Financial Policy*, pp. 90-1.

of taxation.[121] For the same reason, many companies fail to achieve the expansion that is necessary; the taxes leave behind too little money, and fresh capital cannot be coaxed into the necessary motion of resolved risk-taking.[122] Thus taxation dulls the edge of incentive and locks the free supply of capital, with the result that the formation and growth of new business is adversely affected. There is, of course, another lure for the growth of new firms, namely the possibility of achieving sumptuous long-term capital gains through investment in new enterprises.[123] But, then, the taxation of capital gains, which is in force in many countries, sees to it that even this incentive is eliminated or effectively blunted.

In the foregoing pages it was seen how corporate taxation and personal income-taxation combine to reduce risk-taking, enterprise, capital formation, and the growth of new corporations. It is realised that all these involve also other subjective and objective considerations like the attitude of the State, prospects of trade, etc. Many of the above restrictive effects of additional direct taxes on the private sector can, to a considerable extent, be compensated for through a system of tax-exemptions and concessions. Hence, additional direct taxation, if it is collected at the proper place in the proper manner, need not excessively hamper private capital investment. This applies primarily to the first phase of development in the underdeveloped countries.[124] It is also felt that, even though the corporate tax structure discourages business enter-

---

[121] Fiscal factor is probably secondary when the promoter is making up his mind to launch the Company or not. Non-economic psychological factors like the enthusiasm for novel projects on the one hand and the extent of market on the other have often more influence in founding new companies than the tax structure.

See Butters and Lintner, *Effects of Federal Taxes on Growing Enterprises*, Chap. II and C. Cosciani, *The Effects of Differential Tax Treatment of Corporate and non-Corporate Enterprises*, p. 45.

However, tax structure *is* a prime consideration when a change in the form of business organisation is contemplated.

[122] See C. Cosciani, *The Effects of Differential Tax Treatment of Corporate and non-Corporate Enterprises*, p. 63. See also W. L. Hearne's contribution to *How Should Corporations be Taxed ?*, p. 189.

[123] Butters, Thompson and Bollinger, *Effects of Taxation : Investment by Individuals*, p. 8.

[124] See Paul A. M. Van Philips, *Public Finance and Less Developed Economy*, p. 117.

prise, it is preferable to a steeply progressive personal income-tax and a personal income-tax on the low income groups. For the latter reduces the purchasing power of the people, and this could be very detrimental to business in general. [125]

Corporate taxation is an important subject for critical inquiry, for only such inquiries can offer guidance for the future. The tax is tolerable, and even defensible, only so long as it does not help to devitalise the private sector. The ultimate end of all state activity is the maximisation of social welfare. The weapon of corporate taxation must be carefully handled to achieve the goals of the State. The crucial test of any tax is its consistency with the major objectives of the community. It may have good or bad effects : but the final criterion is whether, on a total view of the matter, the tax is desirable or not, and whether or not the tax will help to achieve the general economic and social goals of the society.

---

[125] See Stanley H. Ruttenberg's contribution to the Symposium on *How Should Corporation be Taxed* ?, p. 192.

CHAPTER II

THE CORPORATE SECTOR IN INDIA

The Capital is there; and so is Capitalism. The waning factor is the Capitalist. He has somehow vanished.... In his place stand the boards of directors....

Adolf A. Berle, Jr.

Introduction

THE emergence of corporations (that is, joint-stock companies with limited liability) as a feature of the Indian business scene is comparatively a recent phenomenon.[1] Even when the corporation was found acceptable to Indian business, it by no means grew fast. The main reason for this tardiness of the growth of corporations lay in the backward economic condition of the country. The necessity of a distinctive form of organisation arises only if there is considerable new business activity stimulated by a new climate for such enterprise. Thus the slow development of joint-stock companies in India but reflects painfully our low tempo of economic and industrial activity. Even the little growth that has actually managed to take place is the result, not of steady or sustained activity, but rather of isolated spurts reflecting certain boom conditions all over the world.

Broadly speaking, in the years of the first world war and afterwards, there was considerable economic activity, and naturally there was witnessed the emergence of a good many corporations in India also. However, the depression years that presently followed, especially the late twenties and the early thirties, caused a definite set-back in the growth of the joint-stock enterprises. And,

---

[1] There are about 6 companies aged more than one hundred years. The oldest of these was established as early as 1788. These early companies were originally mere proprietorship concerns, but were later converted into public limited companies. (K. V. N. Iyer, *Joint-Stock Companies in India : Distribution by Age*, unpublished MS.)

once again, during the second world war, the war effort policy of the Government stimulated Indian industry to a marked extent, and this gave some scope for fresh growth in the corporate sector. The Korean War also stimulated such enterprise for a brief spell, but the post-Korean War depression had just the opposite effect. Now, however, thanks to the Government's avowed and active interest in the economic development of the country, the corporate sector is being allowed to grow, although other prejudicial factors also are lifting up their heads in the context of professed socialistic planning. In this chapter we will examine the nature of the corporate sector in India, the pace of its growth, and touch upon some vital aspects relating to the management of the corporations in India.

THE MANAGING AGENCY SYSTEM

The two chief pillars of the corporate structure anywhere are its management and its financing. In other words, once the corporation has been founded thanks to the initiative and enterprise of the promoters, and the shares of the company have been purchased by a group of capitalists, the question arises: Who is actually to run the business? The Directors are elected by the shareholders, and the Board of Directors will no doubt normally manage the activities of the corporation. The Board of Directors, however, may choose to leave the actual management of the joint-stock company to another party, viz. the managing agents. In the absence of other dynamic entrepreneurs, this unique organisation of managing agents has performed many of the functions that are necessary to ensure the economic growth of the country in general and that of the corporate sector in particular.

The managing agency system has been described by S. K. Basu as "an institutional development of industrial organisation where the promotion, finance and administration of a vast agglomeration of miscellaneous and unrelated enterprises . . . are controlled by a single firm. The managing agency firm may take the organisational form of a partnership, a private or public limited company, or an individual."[2] During the last few decades, the many agencies in India—Indian as well as foreign—have promoted numerous enterprises. These managing agents, not only carried out the prelimi-

[2] *The Managing Agency System*, pp. 4-5.

nary investigation and prepared workable schemes, but also effectively promoted their realisation. Again, during the infant period of the corporation, the managing agents both enabled the corporation to get the necessary venture capital by associating their own name with that of the concern promoted, but sometimes also provided it with adequate funds of their own. Further, they conducted the day-to-day management—like the purchase of stores, distribution of the manufactured products, etc.—of the companies under their agency. In short, the managing agents fostered the growth of industry in almost every possible way. As the 1949-50 Fiscal Commission observed, "In the early days of industrialisation, when neither enterprise nor capital was plentiful, the managing agents provided both, and India's well-established industries like cotton, jute, steel, etc. owed their present position to the pioneering zeal and fostering care of several well-known managing agency houses".[3]

Regarding the promotion of new companies, in the absence of specialised institutions like the great underwriting houses of the United Kingdom, the Investment Bankers of the United States, and the Industrial Bankers of Germany, the managing agents in India had to take up their functions and effectively fill the void. Many factors such as the proverbial shyness of Indian capital, the lack of a well organised capital market in the country, and their own unengaged financial strength have helped the growth of these managing agents as an institutional class and made them the power they have been and still are. In the early stages, British capitalists found the managing agency system the most convenient form of business organisation through which to canalise their investments in India's primary industries like tea, coffee, jute, and other plantations. The managing agencies were resourceful, both in the matter of providing long term and short term credits and in supplying or lending management personnel to the corporations 'managed' by them. Not only were they able to utilise the established reputation of themselves in the field of business and industry, but they were also able to get funds and other facilities from the various corporations managed by them.

Even though the merits of the managing agency system are obvious and are in fact readily acknowledged, certain serious

[3] *Report*, Vol. I, p. 218.

charges also are levelled against it. The most serious charge, of course, is that it leads to heavy concentration of wealth and power in the hands of the few. In fact, some managing agents like Andrew Yule & Co. controlled at one time more than eighty firms. It is not really very conducive to a growing economy that a few managing agents should exercise complete control over a major segment of our industrial economy. The other important charges against the managing agency system may be stated briefly as follows:

1. The system unnecessarily duplicates managing expenditure, for there are the Board of Directors of the company as well as the managing agents to 'run' the company between themselves ; with two such bodies, the cost of management must go up.
2. The more unscrupulous managing agents are likely to manipulate the funds of the managed concerns in a way injurious to the latter.
3. The system of fixing remuneration to the managing agents is also often open to objection.

It has been felt, besides, by many that the prevalence of the managing agency system really cuts at the root of an independent Board of Directors set up by the shareholders themselves.

While the Indian managing agency system has from time to time revealed in its actual working the above shortcomings and the malpractices flowing from them, it must nevertheless be conceded that it has on the whole performed a useful, even an almost meritorious, function in Indian economy at a most critical period. The Government, too, conscious of the utility of the system as a whole but at the same time not unmindful of its essential drawbacks, has introduced many checks and improvements in the new Companies Act of 1956.

'PUBLIC' AND 'PRIVATE' COMPANIES

In the Indian corporate structure there are two kinds of companies, the 'public' and the 'private'. The private company is regarded as a family concern, and the outside public is not supposed to be interested in it. Accordingly, many concessions are granted to private companies that are denied to the public companies. The private limited company is essentially a business association of individuals known to one another. Normally, a private company is one in which the membership is limited to about fifty, the right to transfer shares is restricted, and any invitation to the public to subscribe is prohibited. The private company is generally formed so as to claim the benefits of limited liability. In other words, the private limited company is an organisation by means of which, on the one hand, absolute privacy about the affairs of the company is assured, and, on the other hand, the benefits of incorporation, with limited liability, either by shares or by guarantee, could also be enjoyed. Although both private and public companies are governed by the 1956 Companies Act, many of its provisions do not really apply to the private companies. The reason for this limitation is that the private companies are not allowed to invite the public to buy shares or debentures in them.

But it has been repeatedly urged (especially in the evidence given before the Companies Act Amendment Committee under the chairmanship of Justice A. V. Visvanatha Sastri) that, since many private companies with large capital, besides doing extensive business themselves, also control a number of public companies, these private companies too should be subjected to the same checks as are applicable to the public companies. Attention has also been drawn to the fact that many private companies have much larger businesses than those of many public corporations. Hence the contention is that the various privileges now extended to the private companies should be withdrawn. However, even though considerable sums of money that are invested in the public companies get into the hands of the private companies, it is felt that to abolish the distinction between private and public companies would be too drastic a step and would cause real hardship to the former.[4] It should be sufficient if some form of effective control is exercised by the Government with regard to the functioning of the private companies.

Corporation Finance

FINANCING CORPORATIONS

Apart from its management, finance is the most important factor

[4] See F. R. Ginwalla, *Company Law and Problems of Corporate Enterprise*, p. 10.

that determines the success of a corporation. In a way it could be said that the management is necessary only to manage the finances of the companies, though it is no less true that the managing agents often help to find the finance first and then start managing the corporation for which the finance has been found. The problem of corporate finance is intricate because of the economic, legal and administrative precepts and policies which greatly influence the management in the matter of the financial administration. The financial responsibilities of corporations include the promotion of new companies, administration of the finances during the formative stages of the companies, the tackling of the accounting problem of capital-income distinction, tapping finances for expansion, and finally rehabilitation of corporations if they face abnormal times. However, in a summary form, the financial problem of corporations is simply that of finding the money to run the business and adjusting the income to the expenditure.

CAPITAL

The organisation of any business requires capital, though capital requirements will no doubt vary from industry to industry and even from concern to concern in the same industry. Once the industry is chosen and the size of the company has been determined, the problem of raising the required capital begins. Another important aspect to be considered is the differentiation between the fixed capital and the circulating or working capital. The fixed capital, known also as block capital, is used for providing fixed assets like land, building, machinery, etc. The working capital is utilised for buying raw materials, stationery, etc., for paying salaries, wages, rent of buildings, etc., and providing for other incidental charges in producing the goods for the market. The proportion of fixed to working capital also will vary from industry to industry, and concern to concern, depending upon the volume and the ramifications of the business.

We have used the term 'capital' here in the general or ordinary sense. But the concept of capital is of primary importance for a proper understanding of corporation finance and company law. However, no perfect definition of capital has yet been evolved. Even in legal, administrative and accounting senses, 'capital' is used so loosely that it signifies different conceptions at different times, even though we scarcely notice the fact always. In the most common usage, however, 'capital' is understood as the monetary value of tangible or intangible property that is put into a business when it is started.

SHARE CAPITAL

Before the company invites the public to subscribe, it must first decide the amount of share capital with which it proposes to be registered. This is technically called the authorised or registered capital, and this is important only for fixing the fees and duties payable on the incorporation of the company. A part or the whole of the nominal capital will have to be subscribed, and this would be the issued share capital. This issued capital, again, is composed of the paid-up capital and the uncalled capital (if any). The paid-up capital represents the sum-total of the payments made while receiving the shares, and the uncalled capital represents the balance between the total face value of the issued shares and the amounts already paid. However, the liability of the shareholders is limited only to the total issued capital. If any uncalled capital remains, the shareholders are liable for it also.

The success or failure of the promoters will be seen chiefly in their ability to raise the necessary capital from the risk-takers. In other words, the public must be persuaded, both by the prospects of the new company and the confidence created by the names of the promoters, to buy shares in the company. Many factors like the current economic and political climate, Government policies, etc., besides the reputation of the promoters, will influence the prospective shareholders in deciding whether they will buy the shares or not. In the main, the shares can be either of the ownership variety or the creditorship variety. In the former, the chief types of shares are 'ordinary' and 'preferred'. Debentures and bonds are important types of creditorship securities.[5]

[5] A more complete picture of the instruments of corporate ownership would be: (a) Ordinary shares or equities; (b) Preference shares: (i) redeemable, and (ii) non-redeemable; and (c) Long-term bonds and debentures: (i) redeemable, and (ii) non-redeemable.

These different instruments combine risk, income and control in corporate ventures in different proportions, which facilitate company promoters cultivating different types of investors' psychology. It may be added that, of preference shares and debentures too, there may be diffe-

The ordinary shares provide the basic venture capital, and the ordinary shareholders control the company and enjoy the benefits and bear the responsibilities that are associated with the ownership of any corporation. The preference shares, on the contrary, pertain to a particular part of the share capital which is given a certain preferential treatment over the other shares. The common form of preference relates to the income of the company : the preference shareholder will be given first priority in the matter of the distribution of dividends. A fixed rate of dividend will be distributed to the preference shareholders, and the remaining profits, after providing for reserves, bonuses to employees, etc., will be distributed between the other shareholders. Again, preference shares may be either cumulative or non-cumulative. If the former, then any failure of payment in one year will have to be made good in the succeeding years before ordinary shareholders are paid anything. If they are non-cumulative preference shares, the preference is for each year separately, and the shareholder cannot spread his claim over two or more years. The preference shareholders, however, do not have the right to vote in the company meetings except when their own interests are affected.

The existence of preferred stock gives great flexibility to a company, firstly because of the absence of a fixed maturity date for the repayment of the capital, and secondly because of the power it gives to postpone payment of dividends without serious repercussions, and thirdly because of the possibility it opens of the reorganisation of the capital structure to meet pronounced internal and external change.

There is another kind of share called the 'deferred' share which gives the holder the right to the profits that remain after the claims of the other shareholders have been met. When such shares are issued, the management fixes a ceiling to the dividend rate on ordinary shares. Compared to the other type of securities, these 'deferred' shares carry the greatest risk.

In the first instance, while floating a company, the promoters will issue a certain number of shares ; for consolidation or expan-

rent series of issues on different terms and conditions. All this provides the necessary elasticity for the company management to exploit the market situation best, and to combine control of the concern with sharing of the income with the investors.

sion more shares may be issued from time to time; but after the company has grown substantially, further shares may not be issued for any fresh needs. Instead, the company may decide to float creditorship securities like debentures or bonds. Sometimes, debentures and bonds may be issued even at the time of starting the company. The reason for increasing the indebtedness of the corporation through the issue of such securities may range from urgent expediency to a pre-determined policy. Essentially, this type of security invites the investors to part with their capital as a loan and not as a regular investment in business. Even though all companies cannot issue debentures successfully, yet the debentures of old and well established concerns render a useful service to the economic development of the country. The issue of debentures enables the cautious class of investors to provide capital and also enjoy a better return than that yielded by the Government's gilt-edged securities. Apart from debentures, short term financing of the companies is done by mortgage capital, bank loans, loans from managing agents, deposits from the public and the employees of the company, accrued liabilities for income and other taxes, and miscellaneous credits extended to the business by the suppliers.

SHARE DISTRIBUTION

In India, the most common type of share is the 'ordinary' one. M. A. Mulky has made a study of the securities pattern of Indian industry with the help of a sample of 577 corporations spread over fifteen industries.[6] The study is presumably for the year 1945, and it is stated that nearly 72 per cent of the total capital of the corporations was in the shape of ordinary shares and 20 per cent in the shape of preference shares, while deferred shares accounted for only about $7\frac{1}{2}$ per cent.[7] The Taxation Enquiry Commission has also come to a similar conclusion after a study of 407 companies selected from 17 industries in 1951. According to this study, 70 per cent of the paid-up capital *plus* debentures are made up of ordinary shares, 17.7 per cent of preference shares, ·6 per cent of deferred shares, and 11.7 per cent of debentures and mortgages.[8] An examination of the consolidated balance sheets of industries

[6] *New Capital Market in India* (Bombay, 1947).   [7] ibid., p. 44.
[8] *Report of the Taxation Enquiry Commission*, Vol. I, pp. 276-7.

in cotton textiles, jute textiles, cement, paper, iron and steel and sugar for the year 1954 reveals a similar distribution. The total number of the companies studied was 512, and they represented nearly 96 per cent of the paid up capital in the industries studied, and they represented besides 45 per cent of the paid-up capital of all the public limited companies. It was seen that here 74.8 per cent of the paid-up capital *plus* debentures was composed of ordinary shares, 18.2 per cent of preference shares, .05 per cent of deferred shares, and 5.8 per cent of debentures.[9]

Again, the Reserve Bank of India has made two studies of the capital issues in India from 1948 to the middle of 1960. These issues account for an aggregate amount of Rs. 308.5 crores. Of this capital, ordinary issues accounted for 65 per cent, preference shares for 16 per cent, and debentures for 19 per cent of the total fresh capital. The debenture issues were generally taxable, and the rate of interest ranged from 4 per cent to 6 per cent. Preference shares were generally tax-free, and the dividend rate ranged from 5 per cent to 6 per cent. TABLE I gives the annual issues of fresh capital from 1948 to June 1960.[10]

The ordinary shares in the aggregate account for only 65 per cent of the total whereas Mulky's figure was 72 per cent for 1945 and the Taxation Enquiry Commission's figure was 70 per cent for 1951 and the figure arrived at with the Association of Indian Trade and Industry's consolidated balance sheets was 74.8 per cent. Although the figures are not exactly comparable, still some broad conclusions seem to emerge. Up to 1953-54 it looked as though the importance of the ordinary shares was falling. But with the confidence of the private sector restored and the prevalent buoyant conditions, once again ordinary shares are coming to their own. A low tempo of corporate activity is itself a sign of caution on the part of the investors and no wonder, up to 1953, preference shares and debentures played a higher part than they came to play after 1954.

[9] Calculated from the consolidated balance sheets given in K. C. Shah, *Pattern of Corporate Savings and Investment in India* and *Financial Trends in the Sugar Industry*, issued by the Association of Indian Trade and Industry.

[10] Source: *Reserve Bank of India Bulletin*, August 1956 and February 1961.

TABLE I

ISSUES OF FRESH CAPITAL

(Figures in Rs. Crores)

Year	Ordy. Shares	Col. (2) as % of Col. (6)	Pref. Shares	Debentures	Total Shares
(1)	(2)	(3)	(4)	(5)	(6)
1948	12.8	58	3.4	5.7	21.9
1949	8.9	55	4.1	3.3	16.3
1950	6.5	45	2.6	5.5	14.6
1951	4.3	54	1.3	2.3	7.9
1952	2.9	62	0.4	1.4	4.7
1953	7.2	58	0.4	4.9	12.5
1954	20.4	61	2.4	10.4	33.2
1955	16.3	62	4.4	5.5	26.2
1956	33.1	73	10.5	1.6	45.1
1957	19.1	77	2.0	3.7	24.9
1958	17.5	68	3.1	5.3	25.9
1959	28.8	67	9.7	4.7	43.2
1960 (Jan-June)	24.3	76	3.8	4.0	32.1
Total	202.1	65	48.1	58.3	308.5

Once capital has been secured, the company begins its career in real earnest. Now the management has to face the problems of internal financial arrangements and organisation. Prices and profits have to be determined ; decisions have to be taken regarding reinvestment and the distribution of profits as dividends. Reserves have to be profitably utilised. Finding finances for maintenance and depreciation are among the other cardinal problems to be faced by the management.

If the firm actually begins to make profits, it will first write off the depreciation of fixed assets and meet the tax liability. After allocating a certain part of the remaining profits for dividend declaration, the management will credit the residue to the profit and loss account in the balance sheet. The surpluses will also be transferred to various reserves like the dividend equalisation fund, contingency reserve, investment depreciation reserve, plant replacement reserve, etc. These reserves are useful to the corporation in more than one way. They could be used to expand the concern or consolidate its foundations. Sometimes dividends could be declared even during the 'loss-years' in order to infuse confidence in the minds of the shareholders who may otherwise feel too depressed.

Company Legislation in India

The above paragraphs are no more than an attempt to sketch in broad outline the various aspects of company management in India. Actually, the Indian companies are now governed by the Indian Companies Act of 1956, and such company legislation is intended to protect the shareholders and the general public from unscrupulous persons who tend to misuse the principle and privilege of incorporation with limited liability for their own selfish purposes. Company legislation in India is over a century old, for the first Joint Stock Companies Act became law in 1850. This Act contained 105 Sections and one Schedule. The next Act was the Act of 1866, with 231 Sections and 3 Schedules. In 1913, a new Companies Act was put on the Statute Book, but this was more or less a line by line reproduction of the English Companies Act of 1908. The 1913 Act had 290 Sections and 4 Schedules, and it was frequently amended, the most important of the revisions being Act XXII of 1936 and Act LII of 1951. Even though numerous amendments were thus effected from time to time, the Government was not satisfied with the existing company legislation because of the many loopholes that were noticed in its actual working. Moreover, many changes had been taking place in the structure and management of the corporations. In England, the Companies Act of 1908 (the parent of the Indian Act of 1913) was itself scrapped, and replaced by the more thorough and comprehensive Act of 1948, framed largely in the light of the recommendations of the Cohen Committee. Accordingly, in October 1950, the Government of India appointed a Committee headed by C. H. Bhabha to examine the question of the revision of the 1913 Act in a comprehensive manner. The idea was to examine the whole vast problem of company organisation and management from the wider perspective of the development of trade and industry in the country. The Company Law Committee felt that company law was primarily concerned with means and also with ends. They wanted therefore to provide a good framework for the corporate form of business organisation in India. They thought rightly that the operation of private enterprise under modern conditions must be subject to the acceptance of broad social objectives and recognised healthy standards of behaviour. Thus the Committee had for their objective the adjustment of the structure and methods of the corporate form of business management with a view to bringing about a neat and just pattern of relationship between the promoters, investors and the management. Such a pattern should obviously ensure that

(a) the efficiency of the corporate form of organisation may be increased ;
(b) managerial efficiency may be reconciled with the rights and privileges of the investors ;
(c) the interests of labour and of creditors and other people who take part in the production (directly or indirectly) may be adequately safeguarded ; and, finally,
(d) the attainment of the ultimate ends of social policy may be helped and not hindered by the manner in which the corporate form of business organisation functions in India.

The Bhabha Committee submitted their Report in 1952, and it was widely discussed by publicists, economists, Chambers of Commerce, businessmen, and shareholders. The Companies Bill was at last introduced in the Lok Sabha in 1953. Next year a Joint Committee of the Lok Sabha and the Rajya Sabha was appointed, and they submitted their Report in 1955, making numerous suggestions. The Bill was finally passed in November 1955, and came into effect as from 1st April 1956. The Bill that was referred to the Select Committee had 649 Sections and 12 Schedules; the Act as it finally emerged from the Parliament has 658 Sections, 12 Schedules, and many Forms, as against the 288 Sections and 4 Schedules of the 1913 Act.

THE ACT OF 1956

The intention behind such a lengthy feat of legislation (in its printed form it occupies more than 400 packed pages) as the Act of 1956 was that "the enactment should be a self-contained, complete and exhaustive exposition of the law governing joint-stock enterprise in India. It is intended to help the development of the companies in India on healthy lines and put down the abuses which were noticed in the working of the retiring Act of 1913."[11] The objective being so laudable and the effort correspondingly all-embracing, the new Act affects most of the classes of people connected with companies one way or another, viz., company promoters, company managements, the shareholders, auditors, accountants, etc. in diverse ways, and the Act has also introduced new provisions regarding prospectuses, shares, debentures, investigations, directors, managing agents, and so many other aspects of the corporations. Even now, the Act is in the main based on the English law, though there are 229 Sections which have no connection either with the retiring Indian Act of 1913 or the prevailing English Act of 1948.

But legislative intentions are seldom completely realised in the actual enactments themselves. Critics were not wanting therefore who castigated the Act of 1956 for its "inordinate length, the complexity of its structure, its involved language, the vagueness and obscurity of many of its provisions, the interposition of Government control even in apparently minor matters, the plethora of returns and forms ... the loopholes it has left".[12] The Government

[11] F. R. Ginwalla, *Company Law and Problems of Corporate Enterprise*, p. xxxiv.
[12] Ibid., p. xlviii.

accordingly realised, almost immediately after the Act had come into force, that the whole thing needed revision, and hence appointed the *ad hoc* committee referred to earlier under the chairmanship of Justice A. V. Visvanatha Sastri to report on the amendments necessary to the existing company law. The Committee's Report, already submitted to the Government, is in its turn being widely discussed.

As our purpose here is not to go into exhaustive detail regarding the legislative aspects of the Company Law (these are a veritable Serbonian bog where, in the Miltonic phrase, armies whole might sink), we shall here content ourselves with examining how far the 1956 Act succeeded in bringing changes in the legislation about companies. The important Sections from our point of view are those that relate to

(a) the financing of the companies,
(b) the interlocking of funds, and
(c) the managing agents.

According to Section 86, "The share capital of a company limited by shares formed after the commencement of this Act, or issued after such commencement, shall be of two kinds only namely:

(a) equity share capital ; and
(b) preference share capital."

Holders of equity share capital will be entitled to vote at meetings of the company on all issues. The voting right on the poll will be in proportion to the voter's share in the paid-up equity capital of the company. The Act also makes it clear in Section 87 (2)(a) that holders of preference shares have a right to vote only on resolutions placed before the company that directly affect the rights attached to the preference portion of the capital. Further, under Section 117 of the Act, no company can issue any debentures carrying voting rights, whether generally or in respect of particular classes of business, at any meeting of the company.

HOLDING AND SUBSIDIARY COMPANIES

The Companies Act of 1956 has besides many Sections that deal with the problem of the interlocking of funds by the management which happens to control many companies. Section 4 declares that, subject to certain provisions, a company shall be deemed to be a subsidiary of another if :

(a) that other controls the composition of its Board of Directors ; or
(b) that other holds more than half in nominal value of its equity share capital ; or
(c) the first-mentioned company is a subsidiary of any company which is that other's subsidiary.

For example, if Company B is a subsidiary of Company A, and Company C is a subsidiary of Company B, then Company C is a subsidiary of Company A, by virtue of clause (c) above. Although there is no fixed legal meaning given to the term 'holding company', its definition directly flows from that of a subsidiary company. Section 212 requires that the following particulars should be given in respect of a subsidiary or each of the subsidiaries as the case may be, along with the balance sheet of the holding company:

(a) a copy of the balance sheet of the subsidiary ;
(b) a copy of its profit and loss account ;
(c) a copy of the report of its Board of Directors ;
(d) a copy of the report of its auditors ;
(e) a statement of the holding company's interest in the subsidiary.

On the whole, the information required to be disclosed under this Section is far more comprehensive than required under the corresponding Section 133 of the Act of 1913. The 1936 Amendment, which exempted the investment companies from the operation of Section 132-A of the 1913 Act, was always criticised because most of the holding companies formed by the managing agents were called investment companies in order to dupe the Government. This gave rise to many malpractices, and the present 1956 Act has plugged these particular loopholes effectively.

The Act has further prohibited loans, except for a current account up to Rs. 20,000, by a company to its managing agents, their associates, or companies whose management is subservient to the managing agents above referred to. Moreover, according to Section 295, Government sanction is necessary for loans by a company to any of its directors, or his partner, or relative, or to any of the directors, or his partner, or relative of its holding company; to firms in which any such director or relative is a partner; to private companies in which any of its directors is a member; and to public companies in which any of its, or any two of its, directors hold 25 per cent of the voting powers. The permission of the shareholders is necessary for loans by one company to another under the same management. Government sanction is also required under Section 372 if the company wants to invest more than 20 per cent of its subscribed capital in shares or debentures of companies in the same group or more than 10 per cent of the subscribed capital of any single company in the group; banking and insurance companies, however, are exempt from the operation of this Section. In an earlier Section, two corporations ('bodies corporate') are declared to be under the same management if certain officers (namely, managing agent, managing director, manager, secretary, treasurer) of one company fill a corresponding post in the other company, or if a majority of the directors of one company constitutes (or at any time within the six months immediately preceding constituted) a majority of the directors of the other company. But companies under the same group include, not only companies under the same management, but also the managing agents of the investing company.

Overloaded though it is with much unavoidable and even some avoidable legal jargon that sometimes seems to darken issues instead of throwing light upon them, inflated certainly to almost inordinate length, the Act of 1956 nevertheless must be said to have taken the first decisive step—though only the first step—towards the abolition of the managing agency system. It is true that, as the immediate aim of the legislation was to eliminate the malpractices in company administration in general, the Act now gives special importance to the malpractices in the managing agency system, since these agencies happen as a matter of fact to control a large area of our entire corporate sector. The Act, however, has in effect given a fresh—though somewhat attenuated—lease of life to the managing agents; they are permitted to continue, though with rather circumscribed powers.

Sections 324-327 of the Act lay down the tests of eligibility with regard to the appointment of managing agents. According to Section 325, no managing agency company can, after the commencement of this Act, appoint a managing agent to manage its own affairs, on the excellent principle that a physician should at least be able to heal himself. Section 326 states that the appointment or reappointment of a managing agent can be made by a company only at its general body meeting, and this too will be subject to the approval of the Union Government who should be satisfied that the appointment of the managing agent is not against the public interest, that the managing agent proposed is a fit and proper person to be appointed and the conditions of the agreement proposed are fair and general, and, finally, that the proposed managing agent has fulfilled any conditions which the Union Government requires him to fulfil. Another salutary provision is made under Section 332, which disqualifies a person from holding office as managing agent in more than 10 companies after 15 August 1960. The Act has also various other clauses that aim at limiting and controlling the remuneration and allowances of managing agents, the transfer of the office of the managing agents, loans to managing agents, restriction on investment, etc.

More than one opinion has been expressed regarding the managing agents.[13] Eminent industrialists like Babubhai Chinai, Homi Mody, Tulsidas Kilachand and G. D. Somani have ventilated the view that the 1956 Act has armed the Government with powers of control over the private sector of industry—powers that are much too sweeping in character—thereby placing the private sector practically at the mercy of the executive. The critics feel that the malpractices of a few unscrupulous men cannot afford warrant for the many fetters now imposed by the Act on the large mass of honest captains of commerce and industry. Even though the Companies Act has not actually abolished the managing agency system, Government's ultimate intention is clear enough; and the view is therefore advanced that the Government should not be too hasty in deciding once for all about the future of the managing agency system which has, after all, contributed greatly

[13] See Chapter I entitled "Views and Attitudes, 1935-1955", in NCAER, *The Managing Agency System : A Review of its Working and Prospects of its Future.*

in the past to the growth of commerce and industry in India.

It is certain that this recent spate of company legislation will definitely influence the nature of the growth of corporations in India. The growth of the corporate sector in our country has followed a rather haphazard course of development all these decades, and it is yet to be seen whether these various pieces of Government legislation will be really conducive to the rapid growth of the corporate sector in India and will thereby help the nation to register rapid economic progress, or whether they will merely create difficulties, legal, financial and organisational, that may actually retard such progress. To say the least the position needs careful watching.

History of the Corporate Sector in India

THE BEGINNINGS : THE NINETEENTH CENTURY

The present corporate sector in our economy is the result of a long process of growth from very humble beginnings. In fact, the very early joint-stock companies were founded by European businessmen, and these companies were mostly situated in the three presidencies of Bengal, Bombay and Madras. For example, in 1899-1900, 86 per cent of the total capital invested in India was concentrated in Bombay and Bengal. TABLE II[14] also proves the fact that joint-stock companies, while they no doubt increased in number during the last two decades of the century, did not grow with equal rapidity in the matter of the capital invested in them.

It may be seen that the growth was by no means a very rapid one, rather less striking during 1892-1900 than during the preceding ten years. Though the companies had increased in number in 1892 by 90 per cent over the 1882 figure, the total paid-up capital had increased only by about 70 per cent. During the next eight years, the number of companies rose by about 40 per cent, but the paid-up capital only by just 30 per cent. These eight years saw significant increases in the number of companies in banking, mills and presses, and in the trading group. After the Companies Act of 1862 was passed in England, making the principle of limited

[14] Source : Company Law Administration, *Progress of Joint-Stock Companies in India.*

TABLE II

NUMBER AND PAID-UP CAPITAL OF JOINT-STOCK COMPANIES

(Figures relating to paid-up capital in crores of rupees)

Industrial Group	1882 Number of Companies	1882 Paid-up Capital	1892 Number of Companies	1892 Paid-up Capital	1900 Number of Companies	1900 Paid-up Capital
Banking	146	2.18	273	3.94	407	3.79
Mills & Presses	100	6.75	245	12.06	364	17.93
Mining & Quarrying	19	0.74	57	1.62	54	1.66
Planting	122	2.8	158	3.75	148	3.46
Trading	95	1.95	168	3.79	279	5.85
Others	23	1.26	49	1.43	88	2.01
Total	505	15.68	950	26.59	1340	34.90

liability the cornerstone of company law, this new form of business organisation became very popular in England during the last decades of the nineteenth century. But the opportunities afforded by this way of doing business evidently did not catch the imagination of the Indian business community. Actually, during the eighteen years from 1882 to 1900, the companies in India had increased only by 835 and the paid-up capital by Rs. 19.22 crores. The new form of business organisation was utilised only by a few pioneering individuals, their friends and relatives, who pooled together their financial resources for starting new enterprises in the corporate form. Even in the matter of choosing the types of business to invest their money in, the Indian businessmen were content with the enterprises which had already been successfully run by the Europeans.

THE TWENTIETH CENTURY

In the early decades of the twentieth century, however, joint-stock companies began to grow more rapidly than in the previous century. This was principally because of the increasing pace of industrialisation then in evidence in the country. In 1909-10, the number of joint-stock companies in the country was 2,216 with a paid-up capital of Rs. 61.00 crores. This meant an increase of 65 per cent in the number of companies and nearly 75 per cent in the paid-up capital over the 1900 figure. The noteworthy feature here is that the paid-up capital was not only increasing at a fast rate, but increasing at a rate faster than the rate of increase in the number of companies. It is clear capital was flowing in rather more freely than before into the corporate sector, and this was a good augury indeed.

On the eve of the first world war, the total number of companies in India was 2,744, with a paid-up capital of Rs. 77.00 crores. During the first fifteen (rather less than fifteen) years of the century, then, the number of companies as well as the amount of the capital invested in them had risen by more than 100 per cent : the number from 1,340 to 2,744 and the paid-up capital for Rs. 34.90 crores to Rs. 77.00 crores. Besides, the growth during the 1900-15 period was 70 per cent more than what had taken place during the last quarter of the nineteenth century ; and the paid-up capital of the Indian joint-stock companies in 1914 was nearly 120 per cent more than the paid-up capital in 1900. Whereas during 1882-1900 the number of companies increased faster than the amount of the paid-up capital, during 1900-14 the very reverse was the case, the paid-up capital increasing rather faster than the number of companies.

This sudden rise in the number of companies and the amount of paid-up capital is generally attributed to the fast spreading Swadeshi movement that gave a fillip to Indian-made goods in preference to goods imported from abroad. The growing national sentiment generated during the 'Bandemataram' and 'Partition of Bengal' agitation was turned against the imported foreign goods, especially cotton textiles, and consequently a great demand arose among the people for goods manufactured in India. It was also during this period that pioneers of Indian industry like J. N. Tata and his son Dorabji Tata established the first iron and steel factory at Jamshedpur. Besides, the Government had by this time changed its policy and decided to purchase the necessary stores, etc. for State purposes within the country, at least whenever possible.[15] This also gave the needed incentive for the formation of new corporations in India backed by reasonably adequate capital.

THE FIRST WORLD WAR AND AFTER

But it was during the war of 1914-18 and during the immediate post-war years that the growth of the joint-stock companies registered major advances. Even though the total number of companies decreased due to liquidations, the total paid-up capital shot up from Rs. 77 crores in 1914 to Rs. 99 crores in 1918. This was mainly due to the demand for goods created by the war. However, difficulties in the importation of machinery caused a certain slackening in the pace of progress during the later stages of the war.

After the war, for one thing the supply of machinery from foreign countries became easier, and, for another, an enormous quantity of pent-up demand was released, with the result that industrialisation began to take place rapidly. During the period between 1918 and 1922, the number of joint-stock companies rose to 5,189 and the paid-up capital to Rs. 231 crores. While the number of companies had hardly doubled, the paid-up capital had almost exactly trebled in the course of only eight years. Yet, comparatively speaking, the progress during the next ten years—the 1922-32 period—was far from satisfactory. And, strangely enough, such was the situation in spite of the policy of discriminating protection in favour of Indian goods followed after 1923. As against the three-fold increase in the paid-up capital during 1914-22 (that is, from Rs. 77 crores to Rs. 231 crores), the rise during the following decade ending in March 1932 was only to the extent of Rs. 55 crores, the paid-up capital in the joint-stock companies in 1932 being Rs. 286 crores, though the number of companies had increased from 5,189 in 1922 to 7,997 in 1932. But it must be remembered that, out of the ten years 1922-32, the last four were sorely afflicted by the world depression, and consequently many liquidations of companies took place.

Once again, from 1932 onwards, the number of companies as

[15] See article entitled "Government Purchase of Stores for India: 1858-1914" in *Bengal : Past and Present*, January-June 1961.

well as the amount of paid-up capital began registering a steady if slow progress up to 1937. The number went up from 7,997 in 1932 to 11,229 in 1937, and the paid-up capital from Rs. 286 crores to Rs. 312 crores. During the 15 years from 1922 to 1937—by and large lean years in our economy—while the number of companies had increased from 5,189 to 11,229, that is to say, the number had doubled in fact, the paid-up capital increased only from 231 to 312 crores of rupees, in other words it had increased only by one-third. To put it in another way, the companies had increased in number six times as fast as the total paid-up capital of the companies increased. Lean years, though they may throw up entrepreneurs, can seldom find funds to anything like an equal extent.

In 1937 an event of some magnitude happened : Burma was separated from India, with the result that the number of companies and their paid-up capital were reduced by 278 and Rs. 25.7 crores respectively. These figures represented 2.6 per cent of the total of the companies but as much as 8.2 per cent of the total paid-up capital. Evidently some of the richer companies had been in Burma, and the separation gave rather a jolt to Indian economy. After the separation and on the eve of the second world war two years later, India had 11,114 companies with a total paid-up capital of Rs. 290.4 crores. The dent caused by the separation of Burma had not been closed yet.

The growth in the number of companies and their paid-up capital during the inter-war period had by no means been spectacular. On the contrary, it had been almost disappointing. Of course, during the inter-war period, especially the thirties, the world economic situation had itself not been very conducive to rapid economic growth in India. Being a primary-goods producer, India suffered considerably during the depression years. Another factor which contributed to such a slow growth in our corporate sector was the political climate in India. Indians then were more interested in the political emancipation of the country rather than with organised economic development. Two of the crests of the Gandhian *satyagraha* and civil disobedience movements fell during this period—namely in 1920-22 and 1930-32. Actually, during the pre-1939 period, a large portion of Indian capital was diverted to trading as distinct from manufacturing enterprise. Many of our capitalists did not give their thought to the rapid industrialisation of the country but were content to make quick profits by engaging in money-lending, the export and import business, and agency work. This was roughly the situation till the second world war broke out in 1939.

THE SECOND WORLD WAR PERIOD

The second world war, however, stimulated economic activity in India to a considerable extent. During the war period the companies in India increased in number and increased their paid-up capital as TABLE III for the 1939-45 period clearly shows.

TABLE III

NUMBER AND PAID-UP CAPITAL OF JOINT-STOCK COMPANIES[16]

Year	Number of Companies Incorporated	Total Paid-up Capital (in crores of rupees)
1939	11,114	290.4
1940	11,372	303.7
1941	11,638	309.6
1942	12,049	325.2
1943	12,770	336.1
1944	13,689	353.7
1945	14,859	389.0

Again, as during the first world war, the reasons for such stimulus to economic growth are easily seen. In the first place, thanks to the war, imports fell markedly. For example, while cotton imports totalled Rs. 1,415 lakhs in 1938-39, they accounted for a paltry Rs. 137 lakhs in 1942-43, showing a decline of more than 90 per

[16] Source: Company Law Administration, *Progress of Joint-Stock Companies in India.*

cent. Such was the fate of many other articles as well, for their imports too fell drastically. The sudden gap thus created by this non-availability of necessary consumer goods had to be filled somehow by indigenous production. The fall in imports specially helped industries like paper, matches, glass, leather-goods, and soap to take root in the country. There was another factor, too, which helped the advance of industrialisation and consequently led to the formation of more and more joint-stock companies. When Russia and Japan entered the war, India became an important source of supplies to China, Russia and the Near East, not to mention the other theatres of the global conflict. It became necessary accordingly to utilise India's industrial capacity to the uttermost. By the end of December 1942, the aggregate value of the contracts given by the State Department was of the order of Rs. 455 crores. Many industries like iron and steel, woollens, and chemicals had to work to their maximum capacity for making their contribution to the war effort. The only difficulty—and a major one it certainly was —which Indian industry experienced during these years of hectic expansion was the near-impossibility almost of importing machinery from abroad, often from the embattled countries themselves. They could neither spare the machinery nor could it, even when available, be safely transported across the seas to India.

THE POST-WAR PERIOD

When the war ended in 1945, as after the first world war, in the immediate post-war years there was witnessed again an unprecedented growth in the formation of joint-stock companies, thanks to a new spurt of industrialisation. There was an enormous growth in the civilian demand for consumer goods which, for the duration of the war, had been in terrible short-supply. India had now also the opportunity of capturing the markets of China, Iran, Arabia, Egypt, Indonesia, and other Asian underdeveloped countries, because the advanced Western countries, which were the original suppliers to these Eastern countries, were now war-ravaged and needed time to set their own industries in order, and also to meet first the local demand for goods which had been in short-supply during the war-period. The result was that the number of companies in India and the amount of their total paid-up capital grew rapidly after the war as indicated in TABLE IV.

TABLE IV

NUMBER AND PAID-UP CAPITAL OF COMPANIES INCORPORATED[17]

Year	Number of Companies	Total Paid-up Capital (in crores of rupees)
1945	14,859	389.0
1946	17,343	424.2
1947	21,853	478.7
1948	22,675	569.6
1949	25,340	628.3
1950	27,558	723.9
1951	28,532	775.4

The number of companies has nearly doubled within six years, and so has the paid-up capital: an impressive record of expansion indeed, and particularly so during 1947-48 and 1949-50, when Rs. 90 and Rs. 95 crores respectively of fresh capital came to be invested in the corporate sector.

It has been estimated by the Company Law Administration Wing of the Government of India that, after the creation of Pakistan in August 1947, nearly 2,000 companies, with a total paid-up capital of Rs. 18 crores, had gone over to Pakistan. Twenty years earlier, in 1937, it had been Burma's separation; now it was a more radical operation, the carving out of Pakistan. But the Company Law Administration remarks with regard to the companies that had gone to Pakistan's share: "These companies had their registered offices in Pakistan and it is, however, not known how many of them migrated to India, and how much of their capital was already in

[17] Ibid. The FICCI however thought that in 1947-52 progress in private investment would have been higher but for the higher prices of plant and machinery and uncertain delivery dates. See *The Economic Weekly*, January 26, 1954, p. 114.

India or crossed the frontiers later on".[18] Anyhow, the partition of the country and the consequent diminution in our corporate sector were not very markedly reflected in the number of companies still in India, for, while the year 1947 shows the number as 21,853, for the very next year, 1948, the first year after the partition, the number was 22,675, actually an increase of over 800—and this in spite of the 2,000 companies that went to Pakistan's share. With the attainment of independence in August 1947, joint-stock companies in India grew in number and strength more rapidly than ever. As mentioned earlier, in the immediate post-Partition period, the Korean War acted for a brief spell as a spur to increased corporate activity and quickened the pace of economic growth.

TABLE V

NUMBER AND PAID-UP CAPITAL OF COMPANIES INCORPORATED[19]

Year	Number of Joint-stock Companies (in thousands : as on the 31st March)	Total paid-up Capital (in crores of rupees)
1951	28.5	775
1952	29.2	856
1953	29.3	898
1954	29.5	945
1955	29.6	970
1956	29.9	1024
1957	29.4	1078
1958	28.3	1306
1959	27.5	1510
1960	26.9	1593
1961	26.1	1725

[18] *Progress of Joint-Stock Companies in India* (Brochure issued by the Company Law Administration, 1955), p. iii.
[19] Source: Ibid. and relevant issues of the *Monthly Blue Book of Joint-Stock Companies in India*. Figures for 1959, 1960 and 1961 are provisional.

Anyhow, up to 1951, economic activity in India was more or less guided by fortunate circumstances; but in 1951, the Government took the momentous decision to promote India's progress through economic planning, and thereby introduced a new factor with incalculable possibilities. The First Plan period (1951-56) saw a net increase of 1,520 in the total number of companies doing business, with a net increase of Rs. 235 crores in paid-up capital. TABLE V indicates the growth of the corporate sector during the First Plan period. In six years the number of companies increased by hardly 5 per cent, while the paid-up capital increased by nearly 40 per cent.

THE PRIVATE AND THE PUBLIC CORPORATIONS:
THEIR RELATIVE GROWTH

Comparing the performance during the post-independence era of the two divisions of the corporate sector, namely the public and the private companies, the latter seem to be showing a more pronounced tendency to grow than the former, especially in number. At the same time, while the number of public companies seems to be actually decreasing, the amount of the paid-up capital in the public companies shows an upward trend. The comparative TABLE VI is most suggestive.[20]

There were but 207 private companies in 1917 with a paid-up capital of Rs. 5.8 crores; the number was 20,299, with a paid-up capital of Rs. 334 crores, in 1956, almost a hundred-fold increase in number and nearly a sixty-fold increase in paid-up capital in the course of forty years. Further, the table shows that in 1955-56, more than twice as many private companies as there were public companies, had between them less than half as much paid-up capital as the public companies had. It is also interesting to observe that, between 1951 and 1959, while the public companies decreased in number by nearly 46 per cent and increased their capital by about 54 per cent, the private companies increased in number by about 21 per cent and also increased their paid-up capital by almost 400 per cent.

It would not be difficult to account for the spectacular rate of growth of the private companies and the tardiness in the growth of the public companies. In the first place, it was the tightening

[20] Ibid. Figures for 1958-59, 1959-60 and 1960-61 are provisional.

TABLE VI

NUMBER AND PAID-UP CAPITAL OF PUBLIC AND PRIVATE COMPANIES

Year Ending 31st March	Public Companies Number	Public Companies Paid-up Capital (in crores of rupees)	Private Companies Number	Private Companies Paid-up Capital (in crores of rupees)
1916-17	2,306	85.0	207	5.8
1918-19	2,350	95.6	439	11.0
1927-28	4,108	205.9	1,722	71.5
1938-39	6,859	213.0	5,255	77.0
1945-46	10,129	323.0	7,214	101.0
(Indian Union only)				
1950-51	12,568	566.5	15,964	208.9
1951-52	12,413	606.8	16,810	248.9
1952-53	12,055	628.8	17,257	268.8
1953-54	10,248	631.3	19,280	313.6
1954-55	10,056	661.3	19,569	308.3
1955-56	9,575	690.4	20,299	333.8
1956-57	8,810	714.6	20,547	363.0
1957-58	8,296	773.6	19,984	532.7
1958-59	7,760	784.10	19,719	725.7
1959-60	7,306	811.6	19,615	781.5
1960-61	6,745	876.1	19,363	848.5

up by the Company Law Administration that led to the closure or weeding out of a number of so-called public companies that were hardly functioning or were companies only in name. Secondly, capital being proverbially shy in the Indian climate, it has on the whole been easier for the promoters of private companies to secure the necessary capital from their relations and friends than for the promoters of public companies to collect funds through public issues. The business spirit is still confined to a narrow section of the population (a legacy, perhaps, of the old 'caste system'—still dying hard!—that made business the preserve of one particular caste), and it is this section that is ready and eager to exploit the advantages of limited liability over simple partnership, especially when (as it is happening now) the circle of ownership widens gradually. The so-called 'democratisation' of business enterprise is yet to take deep root in India, and the threatened 'organisational revolution' has not occurred here so far, at least not visibly. The average investor in India has still to develop 'investment-mindedness' of sufficient momentum and sense of direction to stake his investment more on the intrinsic merit of the venture concerned than on the men at the moment promoting it.

THE NEW COMPANIES AND THE OLD

It will be seen from the foregoing rapid historical sketch that one striking feature of the growth of the corporate sector in India is that, even though companies have been numerically growing in India since the last century, the real momentum came only after the second world war, and this has been sustained ever since at a more or less steady pace. But while the expansion of the corporate sector is impressive and unmistakable, in one particular the character of the growth cannot be said to be very satisfactory, for the expansion in the paid-up capital has been mainly borne by the companies already in existence. It may be that this is to some extent at least only to be expected, for it is but natural that companies that are well established and are making steady profits will be inclined to plough back their profits, whereas people are likely, even in an encouraging climate for investment, to be rather hesitant to risk their capital in new enterprises. But unless the hesitancy or shyness is decisively overcome, a real tempo of industrial expansion cannot develop. The growth of paid-up capital, due entirely to new registration, is indicated year by year in TABLE VII for the 17-year period from 1941 to 1958.

TABLE VII

JOINT-STOCK COMPANY REGISTERED NEWLY YEAR BY YEAR[21]

Year	Number of Companies Newly Registered	Authorised Capital (in crores of rupees)	Paid-up Capital (in crores of rupees)
1941-42	1165	71.8	1.14
1942-43	1306	96.9	1.46
1943-44	1443	107.5	3.36
1944-45	1476	119.4	0.91
1945-46	2877	284.8	2.18
1946-47	4807	557.3	7.99
1947-48	3267	283.9	6.95
1948-49	3235	200.6	5.59
1949-50	2440	145.4	3.31
1950-51	2104	120.7	2.50
1951-52	1866	152.3	5.42
1952-53	1333	96.4	3.92
1953-54	1937	153.9	0.39
1954-55	1203	226.8	5.06
1955-56	1448	156.9	0.69
1956-57	848	210.65	10.67
1957-58	961	102.71	2.77

[21] Ibid.

Not only is the disparity between the authorised and the paid-up capital very marked (the proportion being very marked particularly for 1955-56 and 1953-54, nearly 225 : 1 and 400 : 1 respectively), the growth in the companies as a rule seems to bear but a poor relation to the fresh capital invested in them. Actually, in the eight years following independence, it has been noticed that, as compared with the paid-up capital brought in through new registration rather a little more capital has been lost through liquidations. If the corporate sector has nevertheless grown and is growing still in spite of everything, it is only thanks to the enormous rise in the paid-up capital of the older companies functioning with increasing success in the present climate of industrial expansion. Taking the figures for the first Five Year Plan period alone, it is seen that, while the paid-up capital of the new companies averages about Rs. 25,000, the paid-up capital of the entire corporate sector averages about Rs. 3 lakhs per company. The disparity would be even greater if the averages of the new and the old companies alone are contrasted.

PROFITS

Paid-up capital is only one of the many features that reflect the growth of the corporate sector. There are also other reasonably sure indicators like the value of the output manufactured, the amount of productive capital employed, and the net profits of the joint-stock companies. It is not possible here to measure with any accuracy the significant role played by the corporate sector in the light of the value of the output and the amount of productive capital employed owing largely to the non-availability of the relevant data. But at least an attempt could be made to study the growth of corporate activity in India by a scrutiny of the net profits.

In the process of growth of corporate economic activity, profits occupy a very prominent place, for it is they that supply the main motive force in a free enterprise society. Ample profits enable corporations to get much of the capital they require without approaching the capital market, and profits also induce the prospective investors to part with their funds readily. In the realm of corporate finance, profits, savings, and investment are the three key factors that mobilise a self-generating tempo of advance.

Actually, savings and investment really depend upon profits to a very large extent ; in very simple terms, profits lead to savings, and savings to investment. Hence a study of profits, not only helps us to mark the main trend in corporate growth, but also enables us to understand the mechanism of corporate finance and investment.

From the economist's point of view, no accurate definition of 'profits' has yet been formulated. For our practical purposes, however, we can take 'profits' to mean on the one hand 'normal' profits which constitute the remuneration of the entrepreneurs (like the Directors of a company and its managing agents), and, on the other hand, 'pure' profits, which are actually the reward of the investors for taking the necessary risk. Thus the corporate net profit does not exactly correspond to the economists' concept of profit as a reward for uncertainty bearing. We should, perhaps, conclude that the corporate profit is nothing but normal profit *plus* profit for risk taking. But the difficulty here is in the actual application of the principle, for profits are, as M. H. Gopal rightly confesses, "one of the hardest kinds of income to measure",[22] and it is not possible to distinguish with any degree of precision between various types of income in the shape of profits.

The crucial problem is one of collecting the relevant data about the profits of corporations. There are three sources from which such data might be collected, namely, the corporation's account books, its income-tax returns, and its annual report including the balance sheet and the profit and loss account. The company's own account books are the most reliable source for the evaluation of the profits of the company, but they are not readily or easily made available by the management. The income-tax returns are also not possible to get at, and even if they are somehow made available, they cannot be relied upon, because income-tax returns are often a trial of strength and ingenuity between the accountants and auditors of the firms on the one part and the income-tax legislation and the tax officers on the other part. As for the third source, it is also not very satisfactory because the Annual Report, balance sheet and the profit and loss account are seldom very precise. "In a very large number of concerns", A. D. Gorwala writes, "there is a considerable gap between the profit shown and

[22] *The Theory of Excess Profits Taxation*, p. 69.

THE CORPORATE SECTOR IN INDIA 91

the actual profit . . . . . the amount of this gap appears nowhere in the accounts, but passes directly to the individuals managing".[23] But for want of any more reliable or more easily accessible source, we have to depend on the balance sheets and the profit and loss accounts for the measurement of the profits of companies, since their own account books are not readily available for scrutiny.[24]

As we are concerned here with the profits of the entire corporate sector, it is not feasible to analyse, even if they were made available, the balance sheets and profit and loss accounts of all companies functioning in India, for these run into tens of thousands. Hence we are obliged to seek the help of the tax-statistics compiled by the Central Board of Revenue.

TABLE VIII gives the net profits of all joint-stock companies in India from 1937-38 to 1959-60.[25]

While examining the figures given in the table, it must be remembered that the amount shown for any year is actually the profit for the previous year. From the figures, however, we may have an idea of the profits made by the companies year by year. These amounts include also the amounts paid as taxes. We see that, according to the table, the profits of companies and other associations assessable at company rates have risen by nearly eight times in the course of twenty years, that is, from Rs. 27.72 crores in 1937-38 to Rs. 212.97 crores in 1959-60. It is also clear that the corporate sector has done better than the unregistered firms and associations of persons, whose profits have risen by only six times during the same period, that is, from Rs. 6.02 crores to Rs. 34.93 crores.

However, the figures provided by the Central Board of Revenue cannot be entirely relied upon. There are obvious defects, dictated

---

[23] *The Illustrated Weekly of India*, 27 January, 1957.

[24] See M. C. Munshi, *Industrial Profits in India*, p. 18. Discussing the analysis of balance sheets, the Ministry of Commerce rightly points out that the considerable time-lag between the publication of the balance sheet and the close of the year to which it relates accentuates the difficulty of linking up the profits to the economic conditions just preceding; "generally speaking, however, it is safe to assume that the profits declared during any particular year reflect in the main the conditions during the preceding year". (*Review of the Trade of India* : 1938-39, p. 22.)

[25] Source : Relevant issues of the *All India Income Tax Reports and Returns* issued by the Central Board of Revenue.

TABLE VIII

PROFITS OF INDIAN JOINT-STOCK COMPANIES AND UNREGISTERED FIRMS AND ASSOCIATIONS OF PERSONS

Year	Companies (Public & Private) Amount (rupees in crores)	Index (1939-40 =100)	Unregistered Firms & Associations of Persons Amount (rupees in crores)	Index (1939-40 =100)
1937-38	27.72	75	6.02	62
1938-39	37.76	102	7.03	72
1939-40	37.03	100	9.77	100
1940-41	47.39	128	10.95	112
1941-42	56.48	153	10.66	109
1942-43	97.68	264	10.20	104
1943-44	134.50	363	15.03	154
1944-45	168.76	456	13.50	138
1945-46	169.44	458	13.68	140
1946-47	148.38	401	13.78	141
1947-48	157.92	426	12.86	132
1948-49	169.47	458	17.89	183
1949-50	185.60	501	17.43	178
1950-51	145.92	394	21.99	225
1951-52	199.99	540	27.16	278
1952-53	201.40	543	22.33	229
1953-54	219.96	594	26.73	274
1954-55	197.54	533	29.44	301
1955-56	188.14	508	33.97	344
1956-57	235.94	637	32.69	331
1957-58	219.70	593	34.47	349
1958-59	265.93	718	37.94	388
1959-60	212.97	575	34.93	358

by the exigencies of the tax assessment, and at best the figures are useful in so far as they give us an indication of the trend or course of company profits. The data given relate to the total number of assessments completed in a year ; and they also include a number of assessments of earlier years, and often some of the assessments of a year are carried over to the next year. The coverage too is not quite comprehensive. There are many companies which are not required to pay any tax on account of their income being absorbed by the development rebate, depreciation, etc., and hence are excluded from the cumulative data provided by the Central Board of Revenue. Again, the new companies that have actually begun production are not included here on account of the sanctioned tax-holiday. Further, income through capital gains does not come within the purview of the table of statistics, because the income-tax law excludes capital gains. Thus the above table can be taken only as a general and not very accurate indicator of the corporate growth, subject of course to the limitations already referred to. Apart from the statistical shortcomings, there are also other factors like companies resorting sometimes to deliberate evasion or to the avoidance of revealing the real position about their financial affairs, which also detract somewhat from the reliability of the figures arrived at by the Central Board of Revenue largely on the basis of the data supplied by the companies themselves.

Apart from the statistics of the Central Board of Revenue, the Company Law Administration Section of the Ministry of Commerce maintains an index of industrial profits in India. This does not suffer from some of the defects of the C.B.R. statistics as explained above, but, in its turn, it is useful only to the extent of the usefulness of balance sheet studies. This index[26] (TABLE IX) is prepared with the figures for profit given in the *Investor's Year Book*, published annually by Place, Siddons and Gough of Calcutta.

The profits taken into account are profits of manufactures less provisions made for taxes, interest, commission and other miscellaneous items. The contributions made towards depreciation and other reserves are not deducted from the figures for profits, but allowance is made for the transfer of money towards the profit account from contingencies and capital or reserve funds from the

[26] Source : *Progress of Joint-Stock Companies in India* (up to 1953) ; and *Monthly Abstract of Statistics*, July 1959 (1954-56).

TABLE IX: INDEX OF PROFITS (Base 1939 = 100)

Year	All Industries	Jute	Cotton	Tea	Sugar	Paper	Iron & Steel	Coal	Cement
1940	138.0	359.1	142.5	99.1	100.3	236.3	103.8	100.8	102.8
1941	187.0	344.4	316.6	146.8	137.8	284.7	133.7	82.6	128.8
1942	221.8	351.1	491.3	228.1	126.7	321.7	110.1	80.5	169.1
1943	245.0	276.3	640.0	142.3	157.8	352.8	111.8	95.6	147.9
1944	238.9	310.6	492.1	110.5	133.5	271.5	117.8	237.0	214.4
1945	233.6	327.6	423.3	150.7	108.9	279.5	120.2	258.3	211.6
1946	229.2	415.4	408.9	198.8	122.4	266.4	101.3	198.5	194.1
1947	191.6	313.2	317.7	216.3	171.5	167.6	86.1	171.8	142.5
1948	259.9	361.2	548.1	127.9	381.3	257.0	96.3	201.0	252.6
1949	181.5	—89.3	292.0	138.4	216.4	316.7	116.0	287.2	295.0
1950	246.6	456.9	356.6	271.2	262.4	479.0	134.2	209.2	333.4
1951	310.5	679.1	551.1	103.9	420.8	604.1	157.7	178.4	419.7
1952	190.6	183.4	262.8	—88.8	409.1	566.8	162.6	220.4	293.4
1953	261.2	326.2	379.4	391.4	419.8	512.7	179.4	145.5	279.0
1954	320.8	354.7	398.9	743.8	336.1	666.1	226.3	361.0	341.4
1955	334.3	277.5	535.0	183.1	413.5	747.8	307.3	200.4	409.7
1956	326.5	—27.2	568.4	346.6	454.0	749.2	293.3	148.6	430.2

sale of Government loans or from charges incurred by managing agents, directors, debenture holders, etc. The coverage of companies in the principal industrial groups—Jute, Cotton, Tea, Sugar, Paper, Iron & Steel, Coal and Cement—whose profits have been taken into account in compiling the index series, in terms of paid-up capital in the respective group totals, is between 35 per cent and 98 per cent, and the overall coverage of all eight groups works out to be slightly above 60 per cent. Judged, on the other hand, by the total paid-up capital of all the companies in the entire field of trade and industry, the coverage of the sample might not exceed 25 per cent. Besides, this is a chain index, because both the base and the base year vary from year to year; and this is also an index of the trend of profitability (unlike the index given along with the C.B.R. statistics), which is meant to indicate how profits of companies in the same group in two consecutive years vary from year to year. Here we are able to make a direct comparison between the level of profits in one year and that in the immediately preceding year or succeeding year, without rigidly referring it only to the base year (here 1939), which may be remote from the year we are actually considering. There is also considerable elasticity here, because items may be added or omitted each year so that the percentage coverage may be maintained. Each figure now indicates how, relatively to the previous year, the trend of profits is to increase or decrease, and in what proportion. The increase or decrease in the trend of profitability might be the result of various factors: more production, boom conditions, price control, etc. Without being too specific or quite comprehensive, the chain index does indicate the trend of profitability at the different points of time, both in the eight groups of industry separately analysed, and also in all the industries taken together.

Company Law Administration have discontinued preparing this index after 1956. There is however another index of profits of Indian industries compiled by the Reserve Bank of India that commences from 1950. Two sets of figures are available—one is the index for the profits after tax while the other represents Gross profits *plus* tax (TABLE X).

This index [27] is also prepared with the figures provided by the companies in their balance sheets and profit and loss accounts.

[27] Source: *Monthly Abstract of Statistics*, September, 1960.

TABLE X: INDEX OF PROFITS (Profits after taxes: Base 1950=100)

(Figures in brackets are the indices of Gross profits *plus* depreciation)

Year	Jute	Cotton	Tea	Sugar	Paper	I & S	Coal	Cement
1951	150.2 (145.5)	156.5 (145.4)	53.2 (64.1)	169.0 (151.5)	149.0 (148.9)	157.1 (132.8)	96.1 (108.2)	119.9 (128.0)
1952	28.5 (78.0)	35.1 (72.4)	(19.3)	122.5 (129.6)	138.6 (146.5)	168.7 (142.7)	128.3 (122.9)	129.5 (128.9)
1953	62.1 (72.5)	63.3 (90.8)	142.6 (140.8)	154.7 (142.1)	132.7 (154.9)	166.2 (141.8)	76.4 (94.9)	114.3 (124.5)
1954	58.6 (71.9)	62.9 (93.1)	238.6 (251.0)	150.2 (139.8)	112.8 (129.5)	232.0 (181.6)	91.5 (101.9)	136.4 (150.1)
1955	43.2 (62.7)	150.3 (145.2)	69.3 (82.5)	172.4 (173.3)	174.2 (181.5)	326.5 (234.3)	135.4 (132.4)	151.8 (168.9)
1956	(22.2)	139.8 (143.3)	146.6 (126.3)	207.2 (209.7)	109.4 (188.2)	282.2 (226.1)	63.2 (104.5)	150.6 (154.9)
1957	196.6 (84.4)	(71.7)	50.7 (71.6)	225.0 (228.6)	137.8 (216.2)	279.7 (214.8)	119.4 (141.1)	124.8 (160.5)
1958	508.5 (131.0)	5.5 (81.5)	82.7 (89.4)	201.2 (218.2)	222.1 (271.9)	318.9 (242.7)	148.5 (151.4)	102.2 (177.6)

Strictly speaking, these two indices cannot be compared because they are based on different samples, but they are both useful if we wish to infer only the broad trends. A careful scrutiny of the indices, taking into account the qualifications already mentioned, shows how factors like business cycles, the nature of demand, the imposition of controls, and the prevalence of competitive conditions have influenced the trends in profitability in the corporate sector.

BUSINESS CYCLES

Business cycles are more or less rhythmic fluctuations in the economy. The major characteristics of such cycles are fluctuations in employment, output, and money income. In the words of G. von Haberlar, the primary features of any business cycle are two : "The one is the fact that the cyclical ups and downs of production and employment are accompanied by a parallel movement of the money value of production and transactions, the second is the fact that the cyclical fluctuations are more marked in connection with the production of producers' goods than in connection with the production of consumers' goods."[28] Business cycles either increase or decrease the demand for goods and services, and thus influence the level of profits through their effect on the scale of operation of the corporations. Another way in which the business cycles affect profits is by their effect on the price of goods. If the prices fall, in the short period the cost structure cannot be changed to reduce the prices, and naturally the profits must come down. Thus the depression of the thirties affected the profits portion of the corporate sector considerably. The second world war period was one of boom conditions, but in the post-war period the boom conditions began to thin down slowly, till the Korean War brought about boom conditions once again. A mild depression or recession followed the Korean War boom, and now we see another revival. All these are broadly reflected in the profit index.

NATURE AND EXTENT OF DEMAND

The profits of the corporate sector are also greatly influenced by the nature and extent of the demand for the goods it produces. In the depression period the demand naturally sinks to a low level, and that is mainly the reason for the reduced price level and

[28] *Prosperity and Depression*, pp. 277-8.

the consequent dwindling profits. This applies both to the countries and industries depending on the internal market, and those that depend on the outside market. During the pre-war period, Government's protection policy saved industries like sugar, paper, and iron and steel from the effects of the depression abroad, and that is the reason why the indices of these industries showed an upward trend. Profits rose sharply from 1939 to 1943 owing mainly to a spurt in the war effort and the mounting orders placed by the Government. From 138.0 in 1940, the all-India index rose to 245.0 in 1943, but from then onwards profits began to decrease slowly, almost imperceptibly for the next three years, owing to the gradual thinning of war orders and the end of the war in 1945. The bottom was reached in 1947, the partition year ; but in 1950, however, the Korean War boom increased overseas demand, particularly of jute, cotton and tea, and thus profits also mounted up, and took the general index from 191.6 to 310.5. Once the Korean War boom ceased, however, the indices of these commodities fell sharply, with the result that the general index also declined from 310.5 in 1951 to 190.6 in 1952.

Apart from the external demand, the internal demand for goods and services are also on the increase of late, especially due to the new developmental activity. Goods like cement, iron and steel, and coal are required in increasing quantities, because of the enormous constructional activities of recent years. Accordingly the indices have shown a tendency to fall : this could very well be due to the non-availability of foreign exchange which has considerably slowed down the construction work of many an important project.

CONTROLS

Normally, in a competitive economy, prices are fixed by the operation of the forces of supply and demand. But in abnormal times like war, famine, etc., it will be a grave hardship if such unrestricted freedom were allowed, and hence Governments are obliged to resort to price controls. If a ceiling is fixed for prices, then it keeps the level of profits at an artificially low level. Occasionally a minimum selling price also is enforced with the result that it artificially raises the prices. During the war and the post-war periods, the coal industry had to be given such artificial price support, and besides, during the war years, the prices of several other products too were controlled. When Government needs certain goods in large quantities in times of emergency, price fixing is generally undertaken ; and by this process the profits are frozen. This is actually what happened to many industries in which profits were frozen at a fairly high level during the war. When, in 1947, most of the price controls were removed, profits began to show an upward trend. All the indices except those of tea thus increased between 1947 and 1948 ; Jute, from 313.2 to 361.2, an increase of about 15 per cent ; Cotton from 317.7 to 548.1, an increase of over 70 per cent and so on.

COMPETITIVE CONDITIONS

The level of profits is also dependent on competitive conditions in the industry. Whatever competition there might have been, it existed only in the pre-war period. In that period, there was considerable competition among the members of the coal and cement industries. But now the increasing desire to unify the various units and the Government policy of licensing to prevent overcrowding have tended to give almost monopoly power to many industries in the corporate sector. Again, there is a marked trend of late, namely increase in the 'groups of enterprises.' These tendencies towards monopolistic conditions have also played a part in influencing the level of profitability. In fact, it is not possible to say with any certainty that this cause or that cause alone was responsible for a particular effect, because always opposing forces are at work in the economy. For example, in a depression period, the profits will tend to fall, but the buttressing power of protection will prevent the profits from falling catastrophically. In like manner, in war time, profits tend to rise sharply, but price controls will try to keep the profits within reasonable limits. Thus profits are largely affected by the arbitrary fixation of prices and the effectiveness of the governmental machinery to enforce the levels so fixed.

CORPORATE SAVING

Profits no doubt play an important part in a free enterprise economy, but the importance flows mainly from the fact that the corporate sector can, and does, retain a considerable portion of its profits for further expansion. In this connection it is interesting to hear H. T. Parekh : "Industrialisation is a function of capital investment. Modern techniques of production require not only large initial capital but necessitates continuing investment for modernisation and expansion as a price for remaining in the business."[29] Every year it is not feasible for the company to go to the capital market for additional funds, and hence, when savings from profits are available, it is best to utilise the savings for ensuing such continuous growth. Corporate saving is thus the *sine qua non* for the development of the corporate sector. Now, what are the factors that induce the management to save and plough back a certain part of the disposable profits?

THE DIVIDEND POLICY

Foremost comes the dividend policy of the corporation, for increased corporate saving and liberal dividend declaration inevitably pull in opposite directions. Actually, a company's reputation is largely determined by its dividend policy. The company's share values on the market are also influenced by the dividends it declares, because the value of the shares fluctuates in response to the yield as dividends. Hence many companies follow a stable dividend policy; in other words, the rise or fall of net profits is not allowed to be unduly reflected in the dividend declared by the company year by year. Sometimes, again, the dividend policy is influenced by the tax liability of the shareholders. The companies may not choose to declare high dividends even when the level of profits warrants such declaration, because that must necessitate, after all, the payment of taxes at a higher rate by the shareholders.

The size of the companies also influences the decision of the management regarding the quantum of the profits to be retained. From a theoretical angle, the need for saving varies inversely with the size of the corporation. This is because the smaller the corporation, the more restricted is its ability to procure new capital, and hence the greater the need for drawing upon profits to supply the deficiency.[30] However, this is not universally the case, for a company may be small, and yet have a good name and standing in the capital market. On the other hand, the above argument regarding the size of companies will hold good if the company is

[29] *The Future of Joint-Stock Enterprise in India*, p. 10.
[30] See J. Ellwood Amos, *The Economics of Corporate Saving*, p. 57.

not only small but also new ; ploughing back of profits is necessary for consolidation as well as expansion.

The company's programme of expansion will thus also be taken into account in determining the proportion of the profits to be kept back. If the management suspects that they are unlikely to get sufficient response in the capital market, they will naturally be obliged to keep back a portion, large or small, of the profits. Sometimes it is possible that a company may not have a volume of profits large enough to enable them to set apart a sufficient amount for retention and ploughing back. In such cases, the company may actually declare a higher dividend than is warranted by the profits to attract prospective investors.

For some companies, again, the nature of the business is such that they must have sufficient liquid cash on hand even if they don't have any plans for expansion. This factor also influences the decision of the companies regarding the amounts of the profits to be retained.

The Government too may interfere and regulate the dividend policy of the corporate sector. In an economically developed country, such interference is mainly occasioned by the Government's concern with the state of the economy. In other words, during inflationary periods, the Government may direct that the corporate sector should not distribute dividends ; while, during the deflationary periods, the corporate sector will be encouraged by the Government to distribute large dividends. However, in an underdeveloped economy like India, the main concern of the Government will be only to ensure economic development by all means in its power. As retention of profits will help the corporate sector to save and invest, the Government will enact and enforce measures that will encourage the corporations to distribute less by way of dividends and retain more for ploughing back. The Government can either employ taxation for this purpose or issue direct orders to the corporate sector. The undistributed profits tax and provision for rebates on the amount of profits not distributed are among the types of taxation measures that discourage or encourage profit retention. Sometimes the Government may statutorily prohibit the companies from declaring a high dividend, as was attempted by the Public Companies (Limitation of Dividends) Act of 1949— though this particular Act was not much of a success, and not a single tear was shed when it lapsed in March 1950. Even though the Government can in theory, and sometimes does actually, try to regulate the level of profits retained, such Government interference is open to criticism, and has been criticised, on many grounds. Limitation of dividends upsets the capital market and promotes the growth of many undesirable trends in corporate financing. It is not necessary that all corporations should utilise the saved funds for really productive purposes, for it is quite possible that wasteful expenditure may be undertaken by the corporations. The cardinal criticism against dividend limitation is that such Government interference must necessarily mean reduction of the freedom of the companies to utilise the profits in the best possible manner.

If the management holds a relatively large proportion of the shares of the company, it may not like to give up its managerial control. The need for capital may compel the management to go to the capital market; yet, even though it may be easy to secure capital in the market, the company may nevertheless decide to resort to retained profits just to prevent outsiders from getting control of the company by taking large blocks of shares. In closely held companies, retention of profits may also be used to avoid personal liability. Thus, various considerations—psychological, prudential, financial, adventurous, even selfish—may operate, singly or in collusion, in determining the proportion of the profits to be retained.

ROLE OF RETAINED PROFITS IN THE CORPORATE SECTOR

TABLE XI gives a comparative picture of how corporate income was disposed of.

These figures show what part retained profits play in the various developed countries. We find very few countries retaining less than 50 per cent of the net corporate profits. "If British or American experience is any guide", writes Kaldor, "successful companies plough back, during the critical period of their expansion, not 40, but 90 to 95 per cent of their disposable profits, or even more".[31] The difference between developed and underdeveloped countries is that, even if the percentage of corporate savings is low in advanced countries, still the net accretion to the total saving will be

[31] *Indian Tax Reform*, p. 87.

TABLE XI
USES OF NET CORPORATE INCOME
(Average 1950-59)[32]

Country	Percentage of Corporate Income before Taxes			Percentage of Corporate Disposable Income	
	Net Saving	Direct Taxes	Dividends	Net Saving	Dividends
Norway	47.7	46.0	6.3	88.3	11.7
Japan	47.0	40.9	12.1	79.3	20.7
Australia	34.4	31.2	34.4	49.1	50.9
UK	33.4	39.2	27.4	54.6	45.4
France	31.4	34.4	34.2	47.9	52.1
West Germany	31.0	54.3	14.6	68.1	31.9
Finland	30.0	59.2	10.8	73.9	26.1
Canada	27.8	46.4	25.8	51.1	48.9
New Zealand	26.8	48.7	24.5	52.2	47.8
USA	20.8	49.5	29.7	41.2	58.8

considerable, whereas in undeveloped or underdeveloped countries, whatever may be the percentage of retained profits, it will still yield but a poor accretion to the pool of saving because the corporate sector is but at the early tentative stages of development. Actually, in advanced countries the capital market is approached by corporations only when a very rapid expansion of investment is visualised, the normal expansion schemes being generally financed from internal sources.[33] During the fifties many countries were recovering and progressing economically after the war, and hence we see them depending on external finance to a considerable extent. For instance, the share of external finance to total finance of capital formation works out to be 60.5 per cent (1951-59 average)

[32] UNO, World Economic Survey 1960 (New York: 1961), p. 31.
[33] This, at any rate, was the position of the American manufacturing companies between 1915 and 1943. (Cf. S. P. Dobrovolsky, *Corporate Income Retention*, p. 6.)

for Japan, 51.3 per cent (1950-54 average) for Canada, 55.5 per cent (1952-58 average) for Australia, 38.5 per cent (1950-55 average) for France, 48.4 per cent (1950-59 average) for West Germany, 37.2 per cent (1950-59 average) for USA and 37.1 per cent (1950-58 average) for UK. One cannot be dogmatic about the relative dependence of external finance being solely due to higher levels of investment. They might also be due to other factors like tax policy, growth of corporate income, dividend policy and the liquidity position of corporations.[34]

In India, while it is clear that the corporate sector saves a considerable part of its profits to plough back, still we do not have any comprehensive data regarding the proportion to the total profits that the corporate sector saves as a whole. For a broad analysis of the trends, however, the data supplied by the Central Board of Revenue could be used. For a rough approximation, we can deduct from the net income assessed by the corporations (Private and Public) the sum-total of taxes *plus* the dividend income assessed. There are, no doubt, certain anomalies here. For one thing, the dividends might be the dividends of previous years. Again, certain companies may declare dividends even if they have sustained a loss for reasons already stated earlier. Moreover, the figures in TABLE XII (prepared with the help of the Central Board of Revenue's statistics) reflect savings made by profit-making companies only, and the net savings in the corporate sector will naturally be smaller to the extent of the dis-saving by companies sustaining losses.

Not only do the figures reflect the savings only of profit making companies, but intercorporate dividends introduce another complication as well. The difference between the companies' accounting year and the assessing year has also to be borne in mind. As far as the statistics are concerned, because of huge arrears of pending assessments for several years, the incomes published for these years tend to be understated. Larger amounts were actually earned, but they have not gone into the statements, because they have not been charged to tax yet. Exaggeration—both in the number of assessees and in the quantum of income—is possible because of the method of preparation of the statistics which tabulate the incomes assessed in a particular year, irrespective of the year or years during which the incomes were earned.

[34] UNO, *World Economic Survey* 1960, pp. 52-53.

TABLE XII
CORPORATE PROFITS AND SAVINGS[35]
(in crores of rupees)

Year	Net Profits plus Taxes (1)	Profits minus Taxes (2)	Taxes (3)	Dividend (4)	Corporate Saving (5)	(5) as % of (2) (6)
1940-41	47.39	37.13	10.26	11.62	25.51	70
1941-42	56.41	37.33	19.08	13.83	23.50	65
1942-43	97.68	52.47	45.21	17.85	34.62	69
1943-44	134.50	44.68	89.82	23.44	21.24	47
1944-45	168.76	58.93	109.83	29.81	29.12	49
1945-46	169.44	55.95	113.49	30.89	25.06	45
1946-47	148.38	40.27	108.11	29.90	10.37	25
1947-48	157.92	70.63	87.29	28.70	41.93	60
1948-49	169.47	74.22	95.25	41.43	32.79	45
1949-50	185.60	96.80	88.80	40.94	55.86	58
1950-51	145.92	70.80	75.12	38.22	32.58	46
1951-52	199.99	104.44	95.55	52.29	52.15	50
1952-53	200.35	96.88	103.47	45.42	51.46	53
1953-54	219.96	122.40	97.56	54.88	67.52	56
1954-55	197.54	110.75	86.79	58.01	52.74	48
1955-56	188.14	105.68	82.46	45.97	59.71	57
1956-57	235.94	127.44	118.50	55.21	62.23	49
1957-58	219.70	109.19	110.51	55.01	54.18	50
1958-59	265.93	128.53	137.40	69.54	58.99	46
1959-60	212.97	103.45	109.52	60.58	42.87	41

The table indicates that in India retained profits are a major factor in the corporate sector, rising steadily, though with minor fluctuations, from Rs. 25.51 crores in 1940-41 to Rs. 58.99 crores in 1958-59. The fall in 1959-60 to Rs. 42.87 crores should be mainly attributed to the increased dividends made necessary by the abolition of grossing and also to a lessened quantum of total profits.

[35] Only income-tax and supertax are included for the years 1954 to 1960. The assessment year for income-tax falls next to the accounting year of the companies. The assessment year, say 1949-50, should thus normally be related to the accounting year, 1948-49.

The part played by retained profits in the corporate development has shown a slight increase. For example, the average percentage of retained profits to net profits during the 1946-52 period was 47.3 per cent. This rose to 51.3 per cent in the period between 1953-58.

It is worth while to compare these figures with the figures arrived at after a study of a sizeable number of companies by the Taxation Enquiry Commission and the Reserve Bank of India. TABLE XIII is compiled by the Taxation Enquiry Commission after a study of 492 joint-stock public companies.

TABLE XIII

NET PROFITS AND RETAINED PROFITS[36]

(in crores of rupees)

Year	Profits after Tax (1)	Distributed Profits (2)	Net Transfers to Reserves (3)	Retained Profits (4)	(4) as % of (1) (5)
1946	27.80	15.51	9.67	10.78	38.8
1947	24.39	15.12	8.32	8.57	35.0
1948	31.30	15.28	16.35	15.71	50.0
1949	19.62	15.10	6.62	4.24	21.6
1950	30.36	17.86	11.96	12.11	39.9
1951	39.02	20.61	16.71	17.93	46.6
Total	172.48	99.49	69.54	69.29	40.1 (average)

According to this table, the corporate sector tends to save about 40 per cent of its net profits on the average. According to a study by the Reserve Bank of India also, based on a bigger sample of 750 companies, nearly 40 per cent of the net profits are ploughed back.

For the years 1941, 1942 and 1943, M. H. Gopal has constructed an index based on a sample survey of 445 joint-stock companies comprising 20 per cent Jute, 11 per cent Cotton, 19 per cent Tea,

[36] Source: Taxation Enquiry Commission, *Report*, Vol. I.

3 per cent Sugar, 15 per cent Coal, 3 per cent Engineering, 1.5 per cent Banking and 27.5 per cent others. The Jute firms chosen represented 84 per cent, Cotton 44 per cent, Coal 70 per cent and Banking 60 per cent of the paid-up capital in the respective business groups.

Year	Index of Average Net Profits	Percentage of Net Profits Distributed	Percentage of Saving
1939	100	62.9	37.1
1941	282	33.6	66.4
1942	259	27.0	73.0
1943	327	24.6	75.4[37]

Although the results derived with the C. B. R. statistics and M. H. Gopal's indices are not strictly comparable, still it is interesting that the percentages given in the former (70, 65, 69) should roughly correspond to the percentages for the same years given by M. H. Gopal (66.4, 73.0, 75.4).

Comparing the results respectively of the C. B. R. statistics and of the Taxation Enquiry Commission—Reserve Bank of India samplings, we find that the C. B. R. figures tend to overstate the percentage of retained profits by about 6.5 to 12 per cent. Apart from the fact (a point that could not be stressed too often) that these two sets of calculations are not exactly comparable due to technical reasons, such differences may also be due to two factors. Firstly, in the C. B. R. statistics, we have not separated the actual retained profits and the net transfers to reserves. As both these were clubbed together in the statistics, they necessarily inflated to a certain extent the percentage of profits retained. Secondly, the T. E. C.—R. B. I. samplings include only the nation's largest public limited companies, whereas the C. B. R. estimates include even the smallest concerns, as also private companies which are closely managed. In India as elsewhere, the small concerns find it

[37] Source: 'Industrial Profits Since 1939' in *The Eastern Economist*, 12 May 1944.

difficult to obtain sufficient external capital, and they naturally are more dependent on retained profits for expansion than are larger and longer or better established firms. The bigger companies can hence always go to the capital market with a better chance than the smaller companies of successfully floating new issues, and consequently they can, without undue risk, distribute more by way of dividends. As the C. B. R. statistics comprise *all* concerns, big and small, they show a bigger percentage of the net profits as having been retained and ploughed back.

In spite of its major role, the profit that is ploughed back is not sufficient by itself to meet all the contingencies that may face corporations from time to time. In India many factors are responsible for the companies saving considerable amounts for ploughing back. Thanks to the steeply progressive personal taxation, individuals are being left with a diminishing net income for new investment. When the funds available for investment are thus reduced, the psychology of the investor also undergoes a change. He will not be prepared to risk the security of his money for a smaller rate of dividend, rendered inevitable due to personal taxation at steeply progressive rates. Thus, on the one hand, the amount available for investment is reduced, and, on the other, there is also a steady diminution of the willingness to invest. The result is that less capital flows to the corporate sector from prospective investors.

In India, again, the various financial institutions are not quite helpful in matters relating to the financing of joint-stock companies. The Indian banking system is based essentially on the British system, and provides working capital (short-term loans) only, and that too but to a few reliable corporations. As George Rosen points out, the larger managing agents who control these reliable firms also control banks and insurance companies, so that capital is easily procured.[38] Even so, banks and insurance companies have not, after all, contributed much to corporate financing. For example, on 31 December 1959, only 2.7 per cent of the total investment of 93 Indian Scheduled Banks and 248 non-scheduled Banks (which form almost the entire Indian Banking Sector) was in the shape of shares and debentures of joint-stock companies: Rs. 24.33 crores out of Rs. 885.22 crores. Actually this represents a decline from 3.7

[38] *Industrial Change in India*, p. 125.

per cent in 1951 to 2.7 per cent in 1959.[39] Again investment by the Life Insurance Corporation on ordinary and preference shares and debentures formed but 14.4 per cent of the total assets on 31-12-1958 and 14.3 per cent on 31-12-1959.[40] After analysing insurance investments in many countries, an R.B.I. study concludes that "the ratio of shares and debentures to total assets in India at 15 per cent at the end of 1960 was much lower than in other countries, excluding Sweden where the Law prohibits investments of life funds in common stocks."[41] Since thus banks and insurance companies will not liberally invest in the corporate sector engaged in industry and business, the money has to be found either from the private investor or through corporate saving for ploughing back. If the private investor too is shy for reasons already stated, ploughing back may almost be about the only reliable means of embarking on expansion of the corporate sector.

In India, especially during the war period, the Government followed a policy of restricting dividend distribution, mainly as an anti-inflationary measure, and retention of profits was encouraged by measures like discriminatory taxation and stationary dividend limitation. This actually proved a blessing in disguise to the corporate sector.

Ploughing back of profits has become by now a very common feature [42] of the corporate sector, and there is no doubt about the useful role it has played in forging the developmental process in the corporations. If dividends are distributed, they might be—at least a portion might be—used for consumption. Hence retained profits raise the level of savings from a national point of view. Moreover, the funds are left in the hands of the corporations which have, generally speaking, the capacity to put these funds to profitable use. Retained profits cost relatively much less than other forms of external capital. Apart from using the funds made available through corporate saving for expansion purposes, sizeable amounts are also retained to constitute a profit reserve which might act as a

[39] See relevant issues of R.B.I., *Trends and Progress of Banking in India*.
[40] Calculated from data given in the *Insurance Year Book* 1960.
[41] *RBI Bulletin*, November 1961, p. 1816.
[42] According to Joan Robinson, "The habit of ploughing profits into the firm is partly due to the pressure of competition, for any business which is not constantly struggling to expand is liable to shrink and collapse". *The Accumulation of Capital*, p. 40.

cushion to absorb sudden shocks and vicissitudes in the business. Actually, in recent times, thanks to high taxation, individual savings are more and more replaced by institutional and corporate saving. No wonder that, in expanding economies, corporations save a large chunk of their income, which is fruitfully ploughed back in business and industry.

DANGERS OF EXCESSIVE PLOUGHING-BACK OF RETAINED PROFITS

However good retention of profits may be, it is not entirely a blessing without drawbacks. J. Ellwood Amos, for example, points out that corporate saving tends to eliminate competition.[43] This arises from the fact that the policy of indiscriminate ploughing back may lead to monopolies. After all, monopolies come to be created because the existing firms go on expanding continuously, extending their tentacles in direction after direction, assuming an increasingly menacing octopus look, with the result that new companies find it more and more difficult to obtain capital in the open market. This, again, is more due to the fact that, with increased corporate savings, which means diminished dividends, less capital flows into the market, and thus less capital is available there. Thus excessive corporate savings are apt to reduce the economic function of the capital market itself by as it were attenuating its resources. The capital market in consequence will not be allowed to regulate where the capital shall flow and where it shall not. As a leading article in *Indian Finance* pointed out, "the trouble is that 'ploughing back' cannot be guaranteed to give us the re-equipment precisely where it is needed. Industry is composed of different cells with different needs and different prospects. The only way to secure a proper distribution of available and limited capital resources is to put them upto tender, as it is in the new issue market."[44] If a new product or invention is rejected by the monolithic corporations, it becomes very difficult indeed for the new entrepreneurs who would like to give it a chance to get the necessary capital from the investors, because the hands of the latter are largely tied up by dividend limitation. Thus excessive ploughing back leads to social waste, however veiled it may all be, because the capital is not made available to those who can use it to the best advantage of the

[43] *The Economics of Corporate Saving*, p. 84.
[44] Issue dated 6 November 1954, p. 869.

society.[45] The retained profits might, on the contrary, be utilised to foster the pet schemes of the management, in luxury buildings with luxury fittings, or be invested in companies in which most of the shareholders may not really be interested.

There are other dangers also in excessive retention of profits. Internal financing hides the cost and profitability of the new investments. Evasion of tax liability, greater scope for manipulating the value of shares, and over-capitalisation are the other dangers which owe their existence mainly to excessive accumulation of reserves. This does not, however, mean that corporate saving is bad at all times and places. The usefulness or futility of corporation saving can be known only by looking into each individual case.

CORPORATE INVESTMENT

What we mean by corporate investment is the amount of capital spent on increasing the total assets of the corporation, and corporate saving is only one of the three sources from which flow funds for corporate investment. The other two sources are borrowings and fresh capital subscribed out of individual savings. New investments in a company consist of additions in assets which enable it to produce more. Whereas individual savings are channelised into all types of investment, corporate savings mainly enter the concerns which saved them, being a kind of financial inbreeding. While considering the investments made, due attention must be paid, not only to the new capital subscribed and the capitalised reserves, but also the borrowed capital and the depreciation and other reserves which are motivated to increase the assets of the corporation. TABLE XIV represents the increase in the paid-up capital added year by year and also the paid-up capital of newly registered companies for the corresponding years.

Of course, these figures represent only the increase in investment in so far as it is the result of fresh issued capital subscribed by the savings of individuals and companies, and capitalised reserves.

[45] This is more so in under-developed countries like India. Considerable mal-investment can occur when a small number of large corporations plough back undistributed profits into expanding their own concerns and "where a more diffused investment through the economy would bring larger returns to the economy as a whole". See The U.N. (Dept. of Economic Affairs) publication, *Measures for the Economic Development of Underdeveloped Countries*, p. 37.

TABLE XIV

RISE IN PAID-UP CAPITAL[46]

(in crores of rupees)

Year	Paid-up Capital (of Existing Companies) Increase During the Year	Paid-up Capital of Newly Registered Firms
1939-40	13.3	—
1940-41	5.9	—
1941-42	15.6	1.14
1942-43	10.9	1.46
1943-44	17.6	3.36
1944-45	35.3	0.91
1945-46	35.3	2.18
1946-47	55.2	7.99
1947-48	90.1	6.95
1948-49	58.7	5.59
1949-50	94.1	3.31
1950-51	53.0	2.50
1951-52	80.4	5.42
1952-53	41.8	3.92
1953-54	47.3	0.39
1954-55	38.2	5.06
1955-56	54.0	0.69
1956-57	53.4	10.27
1957-58	228.7 (includes Rs. 155.7 crores of Hindustan Steel)	2.77

They do not therefore include investments carried out by either loan capital or depreciation or other reserves.

[46] Relevant issues of the *Monthly Blue Book of Joint-Stock Companies* and *Monthly Abstract of Statistics*.

CAPITAL FORMATION

The Taxation Enquiry Commission and the Reserve Bank of India have estimated the gross capital formation in the corporate sector from 1946 to 1957. The T.E.C. have calculated the gross capital formation for 448 companies between 1946 and 1951. In this period, the gross capital formation for these 448 companies was Rs. 359 crores, and the sources were as follows :[47]

(Rupees in crores)

Paid-up capital	86
Borrowings	95
Depreciation	74
Savings	46
Excess Profits Tax Refunds	30
Others	28
Total	359

On the basis of this sample, the T. E. C. have estimated the total gross capital formation in the corporate industrial sector, making their calculation with respect to the paid-up capital of their sample. The gross capital formation during the five years, 1946-51, in the manufacturing sector for all public limited companies, is thus estimated at Rs. 671 crores, out of which the addition of Rs. 317 crores of gross fixed assets in the period works out to an annual rate of Rs. 63 crores.

The Reserve Bank of India's estimate of 751 companies between 1951 and 1955 was Rs. 442.73 crores. However, for the years 1956-1959, the sample was increased to 1001 companies ; and the capital formation in the years 1956, 1957, 1958 and 1959 was Rs. 254.72, Rs. 235.16, Rs. 152.82 crores and Rs. 122.54 crores respectively. The rough estimate of gross capital formation during the period, 1951-1959, for all public limited companies in the industrial sector, made on the basis of the ratio of the paid-up capital of the companies included in the Reserve Bank of India study to the total paid-up capital of all public limited companies

[47] Source : T.E.C., *Report*, Vol. I.

in the sectors covered, is given in TABLE XV. According to this estimate of total gross capital formation, the average annual gross investment comes to about Rs. 186 crores in the manufacturing sector.

TABLE XV

ESTIMATE OF CAPITAL FORMATION IN THE CORPORATE SECTOR IN INDIA[48]

(in crores of rupees)

Year	Capital Formation in the Sample	Estimated Capital Formation in the Entire Corporate Sector
1951	123.83	186
1952	31.85	48
1953	48.96	74
1954	102.00	153
1955	136.09	204
1956	254.72	340
1957	235.16	319
1958	152.82	191
1959	122.54	159

TABLE XVI is the result of an attempt made to estimate the gross capital formation of public limited companies in the manufacturing sector from 1939 to 1954. The basis of these estimates is the consolidated balance sheets and profit and loss accounts of corporations which control 96.5 per cent of the paid-up capital in the six major industries in India, namely, Cotton Textiles, Jute Textiles, Sugar, Paper, Cement, and Iron and Steel. The number of companies in the various industries range from 410 to 524. To estimate the

[48] Source: *RBI Bulletin*, January 1957, October 1958, August 1959, September 1960 and September 1961.

TABLE XVI

ESTIMATE OF THE CAPITAL FORMATION IN THE INDIAN CORPORATE SECTOR BASED ON THE GROSS CAPITAL FORMATION IN SIX MAJOR INDUSTRIES[49]

(in crores of rupees)

Year	Gross Capital Formation in the Six Major Industries	Estimate of Gross Capital Formation in the Corporate Sector as a Whole
1939	25.97	60
1940	13.03	30
1941	45.13	105
1942	65.59	153
1943	100.57	234
1944	14.75	34
1945	9.03	21
1946	34.95	81
1947	41.52	97
1948	107.39	250
1949	—7.55	..
1950	57.63	134
1951	89.56	208
1952	8.70	20
1953	15.32	35
1954	40.76	94

capital formation in the corporate sector with samples from only some of the industries (in this case, more or less the whole area is taken up for examination) is ordinarily fraught with many difficulties. For example, the industries selected may have some

[49] Sources: K. C. Shah, *Pattern of Corporate Saving and Investment in India* and *Financial Trends in Sugar Industry* (Assn. of Indian Trade and Industry) for column (2); column (3) calculated by the author.

characteristics which are peculiar to them alone, and may not be therefore representative of the corporate sector as a whole. Again, some industries grow or decline in some periods, and the choice of them as the representative industries is likely to yield biassed or wrong conclusions. During war time, for instance, the munitions industry will not only grow very rapidly, but will also grow faster than the consumer goods industries. If such industries are selected as the sample, the results will be unduly exaggerated. Hence the results of such sample studies must always be viewed with due reservations.

In the present instance, however, the results seem to be rather nearer the correct figures. The T.E.C. estimate, as we saw earlier, the gross capital formation of public limited companies in the period, 1946-51, after examining 448 companies representing all industries in the manufacturing sector, to be Rs. 671 crores. According to the present estimate also, the gross capital formation of the public limited companies between 1946 and 1951 is Rs. 671 crores. This remarkable correspondence indicates that the present estimate cannot be very far wrong. During the war period, however, there is the possibility of this estimate being a little exaggerated. Because of the non-availability of machinery from foreign countries, especially those involved in the war, and the difficulties of war time transport to India, only certain industries like Iron and Steel were able to develop. Even so, the exaggeration cannot be anything more than slight (if not negligible) because some industries like Aluminium, Heavy Engineering, and Chemicals, which are not included in the above study, also registered considerable growth during the period.

SIZE OF CORPORATE INVESTMENT

We have seen earlier how corporate profits and savings are determined. More or less similar factors determine the size of corporate investments also. As a matter of fact, corporate investment depends upon certain social and psychological factors. Investment is undertaken mainly because of an anticipated gain. A gain can be expected only if there is the possibility of the economy being run smoothly. There must be plenty of investment opportunities, and these opportunities must be such that the corporate form could be exploited with success. The reason for the present phenomenal development of joint-stock enterprises flows from the circumstances of modern factory production. On the one hand, savings were available in small quantities, and, on the other, heavy investment was required for undertaking huge projects : the many had to come together to mount the necessary financial backing for such projects. The result was the emergence of the corporation as a form of business organisation.

The demand for goods and services, and the supply of raw materials and machinery, are the other factors which determine the level of investment in the economy. During periods like wartime, investment rises sharply owing to the enormous demand for all types of goods. During the recent war, Indian industry could have developed much more than what actually materialised but for the difficulties in importing new machinery from abroad. As investment is dependent upon the entrepreneur's anticipation of gains, business cycles play a large part in determining it. As far as India is concerned, the period after 1939 has been one of continuous boom except for a small interval, the post-Korean-War recession. This prevalence of boom conditions could be easily seen in the growth of the paid-up capital in the corporate sector.

Governmental policies are another major factor in determining the level of corporate investment, especially so when the Government undertakes the gigantic task of developing the country through national economic planning. Protection is an important tool in the hands of the Government to improve the indigenous industries, and after 1940, Indian industries are being given increasing tariff protection. Industrial policy, company legislation, labour legislation, tax policy, loan programmes and export-import policies, all affect the growth of corporate investment—sometimes favourably, sometimes prejudicially. Actually all these Governmental policies interact on one another, and the cumulative effect could be seen only if the investment process is viewed as a whole. All these factors (business cycles, the nature and extent of demand, government policies, etc. etc.) combine to determine the economic climate which, if it is favourable, will stimulate corporate investment.

RELATION OF CORPORATE PROFITS TO THE NATIONAL INCOME

The percentage of net company profits to the net national income in 1958-59 works out to be roughly 2.1 per cent. In a highly industrialised country like the U.S.A., the average percentage net corporate income before taxes to national income for the years 1950-59 works out to be 10.7 per cent. In U.K. it was 1.29 per cent and Japan 8.6 per cent.[50] Even though the U.S.A. is richer (in terms of per capita income) than the U.K., the lower percentage is due to the fact that agriculture still forms a very prominent part of the American economy, and the corporate form is not suited to agricultural operations. However, this percentage is not all, for the indirect contribution of the corporate sector to the national income through wages, salaries, and value added to the product, is much larger. Even though the actual percentage, viz. 2.1 per cent (for 1958-59), is low, it is nevertheless the most organised sector in the economy even in India, and hence the importance of the corporate sector to India's economy.

CONCLUSION

In the preceding pages we have seen how the corporate sector and some of its constituents have grown, and how corporations occupy a vitally significant place in Indian economy. It should be the task of the policy maker to remove the obstacles to the further growth of the corporate sector, and create conditions that will allow it to develop properly and at a steady pace. This is most essential, especially at this crucial stage in India's economic development.

[50] UNO, *World Economic Survey* 1960, p. 30.

CHAPTER III

THE EVOLUTION AND STRUCTURE OF THE TAXATION OF CORPORATE INCOME

The tax rates bark more than they bite.

A Modern Saying

Introduction

CORPORATE TAXATION IN INDIA

IT was seen in the first chapter that the taxation of companies involves a great deal of controversy, starting with the question whether they should be taxed at all or not. Controversies and theories apart, there are very real difficulties involved in the taxation of corporate income. In spite of the absence of a definite theoretical sanction favouring such taxation and the various practical difficulties arising therefrom, many countries rely on this form of taxation as one of the chief methods of increasing their revenues. India too is among the countries that thus resort to corporate taxation to augment their revenue. Even though corporate taxation did not originally play an important part in our fiscal system, at present it is playing no small role in our national economy.

JURISDICTION OF THE CENTRAL GOVERNMENT

Under the Indian financial system, throughout the history of company taxation, it is the central government that has been exercising the right to tax the companies. According to the Government of India Act of 1935—which gave India a federal form of Government—the Central Government retained the right to the taxation of all kinds of income except only agricultural income. The Constitution of the Republic of India, which has adopted many features of the 1935 Act, has retained this feature also.

According to the Indian Constitution (I List, Article 43 of the Seventh Schedule), the incorporation, regulation, and the winding up of trading corporations (including banking, insurance, and financial corporations) are matters which come within the jurisdiction of the Union Government. Article 85 of the same Schedule makes clear that the Union Parliament has exclusive power to make laws relating to the corporation tax. The Constitution also defines the corporation tax as any tax that is payable by companies, a tax in the case of which the following conditions are fulfilled :

(a) it is not chargeable in respect of agricultural income ;

(b) no deduction in respect of the tax paid by companies is, by any enactments which may apply to the tax, authorised to be made from dividends payable by the companies to individuals ;

(c) no provision exists for taking the tax so paid into account in computing, for the purpose of Indian income-tax, the total income of individuals receiving such dividends, or in computing the Indian income-tax, payable by or refundable to, such individuals.

In this manner, the Indian Constitution has laid down that it is the duty of the Union Government to govern the corporations generally and that they have the exclusive right to levy corporation taxes.

Income-Tax Legislation in India

THE BEGINNINGS

The taxation of corporate income in India is as old as income-tax legislation in India.[1] The British rulers introduced the first Income-tax Act in 1860. Incomes below Rs. 500 and above Rs. 200 were taxed at the rate of 2 per cent, and all incomes above Rs. 500 at the rate of 4 per cent. An amendment in 1863 reduced the higher tax rate to 3 per cent. During this period agricultural income also was taxed. However, due to many reasons, like the scope for false returns and the weak assessing machinery, the tax proved to be a complete wash-out. Again, by taxing the industrial and commercial incomes in 1864 on the basis of their earlier assessment, the tax was turned almost into a mockery. Not a tear was shed, therefore, when the tax expired in 1865.

As the Government's financial position deteriorated, direct taxation had to be resorted to once again in 1867, when income-tax

---

[1] See for a history of early Income tax legislation : J. P. Niyogi, *The Evolution of the Indian Income-Tax*, pp. 15 *et seq.* and S. M. Pagar *The Indian Income Tax : Its History, Theory and Practice*, Chapter II.

was reimposed with certain modifications under a new name, the license tax. It was a tax on trade and the professions on the basis of the annual income. This tax was levied on all industrial and commercial incomes which exceeded Rs. 200 per year, and the rate of assessment was 2 per cent. Assessees were divided into five classes, and the lowest class paid Rs. 4 and the highest class paid Rs. 200. Joint-stock companies were placed in a separate class, the maximum tax payable by such a company being Rs. 2,000. However, this tax too was abolished in 1868, and was now replaced by a 'certificate tax'. This new tax was a more comprehensive one, with a higher exemption limit and sharper graduation rates.

The very next year, 1869, the Income-tax Act II was passed, converting the certificate tax into a general income-tax. Actually the reason behind the move was largely financial; even though the Act did not adversely affect the persons who were paying the former tax, it extended the liability to those sections of assessees who were till then exempted from the payment of tax. Under this dispensation, the companies were charged at the rate of $1\frac{1}{2}$ per cent, Government Securities at $2\frac{1}{2}$ per cent, while the rate of tax on income from all other sources was nearly doubled. The tax rates were again increased in 1870, and the exemption limit was also raised. Finally, the tax was withdrawn in 1873, as the authorities thought that there was not much use in continuing it. The cardinal reasons for the failure of the tax were uncertainty and inefficiency. On the one hand, people were never quite certain as to how much they owed, and, on the other hand, the petty tax officials indulged freely in fraud and extortion for personal gain, thereby rendering the yield from the tax largely nugatory.

However, direct taxation could not long be dispensed with. The see-saw moved again, and four years later, in 1877, a 'license tax' was imposed on the trader. Many of the defects of the earlier taxes were rectified. Various provinces, like Bombay, Bengal and Madras, introduced local Acts to suit local conditions. Even so, frequent changes were a feature of taxation during the next few years. This haphazard tax structure (it was no firm 'structure' really) continued up to 1886, when once again an income-tax found a place in the Indian fiscal system.

The period between 1860 and 1886 is very important, for during this period were made the pioneering efforts at widening the tax base. The authorities were quite aware of the haphazard structure of the new taxes, the inequity of the license tax, popular dislike of direct taxation, etc. But more often than not, they were compelled to continue the taxes due to the Government's weak financial position caused, no doubt, by the fall in the price of silver, famines, and successful political pressure to abolish import duties on cotton. The authorities, however, realised the worth of these pioneering attempts, as A. Colvin the finance member said in a confidential memo dated 14 May 1884 : " . . . experience has been acquired ; positions previously unoccupied, have been gained and retained ; . . . a striking unanimity has been arrived at as to what is inadmissible, unworkable and unadaptable to India ; while, finally, the practice of direct taxation has been received into and assimilated by the body of the people . . . "[2]

THE ACT OF 1886

The Income-tax Act of 1886 remained practically unaltered for as long a period as 30 years. This tax retained many desirable features of the earlier license taxes. Income was now divided into four classes :

1. Salaries ;
2. Interest on securities ;
3. Profits of joint-stock companies ; and
4. Other incomes, which included income from house property.

No tax was levied on a shareholder in respect of profits of companies which had already paid the tax ; nor was the tax levied on the share received by a Hindu undivided family. Incomes below Rs. 500 per year were not taxed. Apart from agricultural incomes, profits of shipping companies and interest on stock notes[3] were also exempt from the tax. The aggregates of income from the different sources were used only in so far as they helped the autho-

[2] From the *Ripon Mss.*, at the British Museum, Add. Mss., 43586.

[3] Stock notes were an interesting experiment of the Government of India for encouraging small investors. They were really Government Securities of the denominations of Rs. 10, 25, 50 and 100, bearing interest at 4 per cent and issued at par. (See C. N. Vakil, *Financial Developments in Modern India*, pp. 298-9.)

rities to determine the minimum taxable limits. The sources of income and the rate of taxation under each head were given in the Act itself.

PERIOD OF INTEGRATION : 1886-1916

The Act of 1886 continued up to 1916, when the first world war necessitated increased taxation, and naturally income-tax had to make up its share. Even though neither the principle underlying the tax nor its actual administration was unexceptionable, yet the experience in the income-tax field gained by the Government during the three decades preceding was well worth the trials and tribulations involved. V. K. R. V. Rao rightly calls it a period of integration, and goes on to say : "Its unbroken existence for 30 years was doubly useful. To the Government, it laid bare the defects that underlay the Indian System and showed the way to reform. In the people, it bred an intelligent, though gradual, acquiescence in the continuance of the tax."[4] The tax became, in fact, an integral part of the Indian fiscal system, and laid the foundations of the present income-tax structure in India. TABLE I [5] gives the total tax collected and the tax on income from business for selected years, the tax on income from business being the tax paid by the joint-stock companies.

Although the income-tax revenue was unspectacular, the part played by business taxes was relatively impressive, covering between 55-60 per cent of the total. On the whole, the yield of the business taxes showed a steady upward trend, indicating unlimited future potentialities.

THE ACT OF 1916

In 1916 a graduated scale of income-tax was introduced for the first time. Separate rates were charged for various types of income. The company tax rate was one anna in the rupee. The increase in the rates and the steeper graduation necessitated a change also in the system of assessment. The first change made was the provision for the refund of income-tax to the shareholders of companies by way of small income relief. Presently, the 1916 Act was

[4] *Taxation of Income in India*, p. 47.
[5] Source : *Financial Statements* of the Government of India for the relevant years.

TABLE I

Year	Total Tax Collected (in lakhs of rupees)	Tax Collected from Business (in lakhs of rupees)	Percentage of Total
1886-7	136.9	78.1	55.8
1887-8	139.7	79.1	56.4
1890-1	157.8	88.4	55.2
1894-5	178.6	99.5	55.3
1897-8	187.5	106.1	55.8
1899-1900	193.3	109.2	59.1
1902-3	208.2	118.4	56.9
1904-5	188.0	104.9	55.8
1906-7	211.7	120.4	56.9
1910-11	229.6	126.1	55.4
1913-4	284.0	163.8	58.3

superseded in 1918 by another Act which brought about many changes. Under this Act, total income and taxable income were differentiated for the first time. The tax levy was imposed in respect of the taxable income of the year of assessment, whereas in the earlier Acts, the income of the previous year had been taken into account for the purpose of assessment. Moreover, the joint-stock companies were now compelled to furnish returns of their profits. This new Act, however, was far from satisfactory in the matter of its practical administration. Besides, a novel judicial interpretation of the word 'income' compelled the Government to take action with a view to amending the Act. In the *Board of Revenue* vs. *Arunachalam Chetty* case, a Full Bench of the Madras High Court, with Justice Sadasiva Iyer dissenting, decided against the Crown that 'income' meant only what actually came in, and that nothing could be regarded as income unless it was actually received. This rather upset the long-standing practice of the mercantile community. Actual working of the Act showed up various other defects as well that called for rectification. Accordingly, the Government of India appointed Committees consisting of officials and non-officials in the various provinces to report on the working of the income-tax legislation then in force. The Income-tax Act of 1922 was largely based on the recommendations of the above Committee.

SUPERTAX

Before the 1922 Act, supertax was levied in accordance with the provisions of a separate Act. In the 1922 Act, on the contrary, Supertax provisions also were included. Supertax is an additional tax on income above a certain arbitrary high level fixed by the Act. Originally, supertax was a war-time measure introduced in India in 1917. Incomes below Rs. 50,000 were exempted, and the tax was levied at progressive rates; and the same rates applied to companies also. In the case of companies, only the undistributed profits were taxed, the distributed profits being taxed in the hands of the stock-holders, if they were liable to supertax, as part of their income. In other words, while the individuals were taxed on their total income, supertax was levied on the undistributed profits of the companies. The net effect of this method of assessment was the disinclination on the part of companies to build a reserve of accumulated profits for further development, and many complaints were made by the business community about this sort of disincentive caused by the tax. Accordingly, in 1920 this Act was amended, and joint-stock companies whose incomes exceeded Rs. 50,000 were charged at a flat rate of one anna in the rupee, instead of at a progressive rate schedule. The shareholder was not credited with the tax paid by the company, and the supertax became more or less a corporation profits tax. However, unlike the practice of other countries, supertax was not allowed to be deducted from taxable income for income-tax purposes. From 1917 to 1922, the Supertax Acts were 'Principal Acts', but in 1922 the Income-tax Act and the Supertax Act were merged into a single Act known as the Income-tax Act of 1922 which, in spite of many major and minor amendments of later years, has held the field almost to this day. But henceforth the new comprehensive Act of 1961 will take the place of the 1922 Act and its numerous amendments.

THE ACT OF 1922

The 1922 Act introduced many important and far-reaching changes in the Indian tax structure. In the first place, the Act established a change in the year of assessment. The tax was now to be assessed on the income of the previous year, instead of the previous year's income merely serving as the measure of the income of the year of assessment. Prior to the enforcement of the 1922 Act, the rate of tax also was determined by the Act itself and used to be appended as a schedule to the Act. The 1922 Act, on the contrary, deals merely with the basis, methods, machinery and administration of assessment, but not with the tax rate itself. The rates at which income-tax and supertax are to be charged are now separately determined by the Annual Finance Acts. This innovation in income-tax legislation was introduced largely with a view to securing elasticity in the fiscal system, because under the new dispensation the rates could be adjusted conveniently with reference to the annual budgetary requirements.

AMENDING ACTS

Between 1922 and 1939, there were twenty-three amending Acts. Excepting in the years 1932, 1935, 1936 and 1938, there was at least one amending Act every year. In the tax years up to 1938, a 'step system' was used for the assessment of income-tax. Companies and **registered firms**, however, had to pay income-tax at the maximum rate prescribed for income-tax on their total income, whatever it might be. Thus, in so far as corporations are concerned, there has never been under the Act any exemption limit for income-tax. Till 1938, however, there was an exemption limit for supertax payable by the companies. In the 1920 Act the exemption was, as we saw above, Rs. 50,000 ; but, in 1931-32, the limit was lowered to Rs. 30,000.

It is only in the period after 1938 that the Indian tax structure, with special reference to the joint-stock companies, has undergone considerable growth. Beginning with the 1939 amendment to the Indian Income-tax Act, there has been a spate of amendments to the Act, especially during 1948-59, resulting in major and far-reaching changes. Apart from income-tax and supertax, new taxes like the Excess Profits Tax, Business Profits Tax, Capital Gains Tax, the tax on excess dividends, the tax on bonus shares, and the Wealth Tax were (or are) being levied on companies. It is also during this same period that we have been witnessing both the tightening up of the income-tax administration and the introduction of liberal provisions encouraging saving, investment and economic development.

STATUS OF COMPANIES

In India the judicial decisions have always held that taxes paid by the company are paid by it as a separate entity; the companies are not paying taxes on behalf of their shareholders but only on behalf of themselves as assessees of income-tax. In the *Mrs. Guzdar* vs. *C.I.T.* case, Justice Chagla held that, "Not only are a company and a shareholder separate and independent entities under the general law, but even under the Indian Income-tax Act, a company is a separate entity for the purpose of assessment from a shareholder. A company pays income-tax on its income ... (not) on behalf of the shareholders.... In fact and in law, income-tax is paid by the company as a company on its own income, and the shareholder also in fact and in law has to pay tax on his own income."[6] In the *Lalitha Bai* vs. *Tata Iron and Steel Company Ltd.*, Chief Justice Beaumont also held that "in the case of a company the tax has to be paid by the company direct, and not on behalf of the shareholders."[7] The same opinion has been expressed in the judgment on the *Raja Bahadur Vishveshvara Singh* vs. *C.I.T.* case. Whatever the controversies on the subject as indicated in the first chapter, it is clear from the above decisions that Indian judicial opinion accepts the theory that companies have a status and a personality distinct from those of the shareholders; the company is an entity in itself, and not merely the sum of the shareholders.

The advantage in securing the status of a 'company' in so far as income-tax assessment is concerned mainly rests on the fact that company income is chargeable at flat rates, which are lower than the highly graduated rates applicable to individuals and partnerships with large incomes. For the purpose of Indian income-tax, companies now constitute a separate class of assessees. According to Section 2 of the Income-tax Act, a company means either a company which has been registered under the Indian Companies Act or any Association, Indian or non-Indian, whether incorporated

---

[6] Cited in the *Taxation Enquiry Commission Report*, Vol. II, p. 151.
[7] This and the following case are cited by M. S. Srinivasan in his *Lectures on Income-tax*, pp. 66, 72.

or not, which is declared by the Central Board of Revenue to be a company for the purposes of the Act. Any foreign company has also to be first declared a company for the purpose of this Act, and generally such declaration is a formal affair if the said foreign company exhibits the formal characteristics of a company limited by shares and is a legal 'individual' according to the laws of the home country. The distinction between an Indian and a non-Indian company was first introduced only in the Finance Act of 1948. The object of this pointed differentiation was to confine to the Indian companies alone the then newly introduced concessions to small companies and concessions regarding undistributed profits.[8]

DIVISION BY DICHOTOMY

In the Indian Income-tax law, the definition and classification of companies derives largely from the principle of 'Division by Dichotomy'. In the previous chapter the definition of companies as given in the Companies Act was cited. Company legislation is interested mainly in the sound management of the companies and in ensuring that no exploitation of gullible investors takes place. But income-tax legislation has to take into account many aspects touching adequacy, equity, administrative convenience, etc., regarding Government's relationship with the companies, and consequently it is not at all surprising that the treatment of companies by the tax law is extremely complicated.

It is not necessary that all joint-stock companies should be alike in structure and intention, even though superficially they might have several common characteristics. Apart from the advantage already referred to regarding flat taxation rates which companies enjoy, the corporate form of organisation could also be utilised in such a way as to avoid certain types of tax liability which attract themselves to individuals and partnerships. In certain private and public companies which are controlled only by a few persons, the owners have the power so to regulate the distribution of dividends that their personal tax liability is reduced to a considerable extent. This method of tax avoidance not only reduces the revenues of the state but also leads to "inequities as between shareholders of different companies, and also to the utili-

[8] Section 8, Annual Finance Act (1948).

sation of accumulated profits for the purposes of consumption".[9] The company law does not require the Directors of a Company to distribute its income as dividends among the shareholders. Directors could, if they like, leave the profits undistributed to avoid tax liability as individuals. Such and other similar cases of possible or real tax avoidance and inequity led the tax authorities to differentiate between the various types of companies and treat them appropriately. The Indian Income-tax Act does not explicitly define *private* or *public* or *holding* or *subsidiary* companies, and, consequently, what the Companies Act says in the matter is to be treated as generally acceptable. But as regards classification of companies for the purpose of income-tax assessment, there are four groups of companies, each group with two types of characteristics, either type of one group matching with either of the types in the other groups.

CLASSIFICATION OF COMPANIES

The following are the four groups, with the dual variations in each of them :

First Group :   (a) Companies in which the public is interested considerably ;
(b) Companies in which the public is not interested considerably.

Second Group : (a) Companies which are Indian ;
(b) Companies which are not Indian.

Third Group :   (a) Companies which have made the prescribed arrangements for the declaration and payment in India of the dividends, and for the deduction of supertax therefrom, payable to non-resident shareholders ;
(b) Companies which have made no such arrangements.

Fourth Group : (a) Companies with an income of Rs. 25,000 or less ;
(b) Companies whose total income is above Rs. 25,000.

[9] *Report of the Taxation Enquiry Commission* (1953-4), Vol. II, p. 171.

SECTION 23A OF THE ACT

It must be noted that, as far as the income-tax is concerned, no distinction is made between private and public companies as such. Actually, there is no difference in any basic principle employed in the assessment of private or public companies, and they are both of them treated alike. But in order to arrest the possibilities mentioned earlier regarding the evasion of supertax, our income-tax legislation has an important Section, namely 23A, which applies to certain classes of companies—not necessarily private companies alone. The crucial feature of Section 23A is the specification of provisions regarding the distribution of dividends. Under this Section, companies could be compelled to distribute more of the profits as dividends than the companies would ordinarily care to. In some cases, this Section is applied equally to companies which are 'public' from the angle of Company Law. However, *all* 'private' companies come within the purview of this Section.

Section 23A of the Income-tax Act was originally enacted in 1930 following the practice in this regard in the United Kingdom. This Section aims at compelling the private limited companies (and even some of the public companies) not to retain profits beyond a certain 'reasonable' level, but to distribute a 'reasonable' part of the profits to the shareholders within a 'reasonable' time, failing which the shareholders would be liable to a special tax. An officer of the Income-tax Department could pass an order under this Section only if he was satisfied that a "company's profits and gains are allowed to accumulate beyond its reasonable needs, existent and contingent, having regard to the maintenance and development of its business". We thus see that this action under this Section called for judgment of motives and also estimation of future ('contingent') possibilities, and it is no wonder that the Section proved "virtually a dead letter, only one (order) having been passed under that sub-section from its insertion in 1930 upto the end of the year 1935-36".[10] The Income-tax Enquiry Committee (1936), therefore, suggested the removal of qualitative judgments (e.g. 'reasonable') and recommended the prescription of quantitative tests. Accordingly, the provision was suitably altered by the Amendment Act of 1939, and in the result this Section

[10] *Income-tax Enquiry Report* (1936), p. 66.

gained a distinct, and an operatively useful, shape. The Section was further amended in 1955 and 1956.

COMPANIES IN WHICH THE PUBLIC IS SUBSTANTIALLY INTERESTED

Income-tax legislation in India has made a very vital distinction between companies in which the public is substantially interested and companies in which the public is not so interested. This peculiar distinction enables the authorities to differentiate between the assessment of one class and that of the other class in many ways, especially in the matter of privileges and reliefs. It should be remembered that the main justification for the enactment of Section 23A was the social and economic policy flowing from broad considerations of equity and justice. According to this Section, a company in which the public is substantially interested must satisfy the following conditions :

A. If the company is owned by the Government, or if not less than 40 per cent of the shares of the company are held by the Government, it may be deemed a company in which the public is substantially interested.

B. Otherwise, for being deemed a company in which the public is substantially interested, the company should *not* be a private company as defined in the Company Law, and it should besides satisfy some more conditions, namely,

(1) At least 50 per cent of the company's shares (not being shares entitled to a fixed rate of dividend, whether with or without a further right to profits), carrying not less than 50 per cent of the voting power, should have been purchased and held unconditionally by the public throughout the previous year. However, if 50 per cent or more of the shares of a company are owned by another company in which the public is *not* interested, then the first company also is deemed to be one in which the public is *not* substantially interested. Again, it is enough for "an Indian company whose business consists wholly in the manufacture or processing of goods or in mining or in the generation or distribution of electricity or any other form of power" to be one in which the public is substantially interested, if 40 per cent of its shares (unlike the other companies' 50 per cent) are held by the public ;

(2) The shares should also be dealt in recognised stock exchanges in India ; or, in the words of the Act, it should be assured that "the said shares (40 per cent or 50 per cent, as the case may be) were at any time during the previous year the subject of dealing in any recognised stock exchange in India or were freely transferable by the holder to other members of the public" ;

(3) At any time in the previous year, less than six persons should not have controlled more than 50 per cent of the company's shares. Further, in the case of industrial companies engaged in the manufacture or processing of goods or in mining or in generation or distribution of electricity or any other form of power, less than six persons should not control more than 60 per cent of the company's shares. Owners who are closely related are to be treated as only one person. For example, if two brothers own each 30 per cent of the shares, it will be considered that 60 per cent of the shares are owned by only one individual. The Act further explains the term 'relative' explicitly as "husband, wife, lineal ascendant or descendant brother or sister".

The purpose behind these 'conditions' is obvious. Since public companies enjoy special privileges under the Income-tax Act, small groups of self-seeking individuals should be effectively prevented from exploiting these privileges under the guise of running public companies. In short, public companies should be really 'public' companies and not merely notionally such.

NON-INDIAN COMPANIES

As we saw earlier, the Indian Income-tax law made a clear distinction between Indian and non-Indian companies only in the Finance Act of 1948. Before that, a company meant just "a company as defined in the Indian Companies Act of 1913, or formed in pursuance of an Act of Parliament or of Royal Charter or Letters Patent or of an Act of the Legislature of a British Possession, and included any foreign association carrying on business in British India, whether incorporated or not, and whether its principal place of business was situated in British India or not, which the Central Board of Revenue may by a general or a special order declare to be a company for the purpose of this Act". Truly an omnibus definition! As we pointed out earlier, the main reason for bringing in the new distinction was to restrict the fiscal benefits of the Income-tax Act only to the Indian companies, although this kind of preferential treatment necessarily brought about other complications as well. Non-Indian companies have to be formally recognised by the Central Board of Revenue, and if they are not so recognised and accorded the status of companies, their tax liability will be greater than if they are so recognised.

COMPANIES WITH NON-RESIDENT SHAREHOLDERS

The differentiation in the Third Group is a safety valve against non-resident shareholders escaping supertax liability. The companies will have to bear the supertax also if they have not made any arrangements to distribute the dividends. The effective arrangements to be made by a company for the declaration and payment of dividends in India (Jammu and Kashmir excepted) and for the deduction of supertax therefrom will be as follows :

1. The Share Register of the Company for all shareholders shall be regularly maintained at its principal place of business within Indian territory (Jammu and Kashmir excepted), (*i*) from a date not later than the 1st day of November 1948 in respect of the assessment for the year ending 31 March 1949, and (*ii*) in respect of any assessment for a subsequent year, from a date not later than the 1st day of April of such a year ;

2. The general meeting for passing the accounts of the previous year relevant to the year of assessment and for declaring any dividends in respect thereof shall be held only at a place within the territory of India (excluding Jammu and Kashmir) ; and

3. The dividends declared, if any, shall be payable only within the territory of India to all shareholders.[11]

Thus, while computing the total taxable income, it is necessary that the residential status of the corporation should be settled. This is because the incidence of the tax differs according to the residential status of the assessee. The Indian income-tax law no-

[11] Appendix 1 of *Income-tax for the Layman*, issued by the Central Board of Revenue.

where exactly defines 'residence'. However, no company can have more than one residence, because, according to Clause C of Section 4-A of the Act, residence relates to a particular year and is settled by criteria which do not permit of residence at more than one place in the course of the same year.

COMPANIES WITH A LOW INCOME

In the Fourth Group, the differentiation is on the basis of income and it is made with a view to giving relief to the low income corporations. A lower rate of taxation is applicable to companies with incomes below Rs. 25,000, as against companies with higher incomes.

One important point that should be remembered is the prevalence of various rebates which help to reduce the effective tax as distinguished from the formal tax which often appears crushing. After taking into account the permissible rebates, companies are finally required to pay taxes at various effective rates, depending upon the situation in which they are classed under one or more of the four Groups described earlier.

REFUNDS TO SHAREHOLDERS

In India, the major taxes paid by the companies or corporations are income-tax and supertax, otherwise known as the corporation tax. According to the Indian Income-tax Act, companies are liable to pay income-tax and also supertax on the total income of every previous year at rates which are prescribed by the Annual Finance Acts. While income-tax as applied to individuals and Hindu undivided families is based on the progressive principle, companies are required to pay income-tax at the maximum rate fixed for individuals by the Annual Finance Act ; and the maximum rate is applied irrespective of the income of the company. There is thus no income limit for tax exemption so far as corporations are concerned. But as company income was considered to be doubly taxed, certain provisions were enacted to give some relief at least to the shareholders. According to Section 49B of the Income-tax Act, the income-tax paid by the company is supposed to have been paid by the shareholders. The assumption is that the company just acts as a sort of tax collector in respect of the income-tax payable by the shareholders on their dividend incomes. Every shareholder (if he is not liable to pay tax at the maximum rate on his personal income, including the dividends) will be entitled to get a refund calculated on his dividends received from any company whose profits are liable to income-tax at the difference between the rate applicable to his total income and the rate applicable to the companies. For this purpose the dividends received are grossed up in the following manner :

If (r) is the full rate of company income-tax in pies per rupee and (x) the percentage of the company's profits liable to tax, the gross dividend for every unit of dividend will be

$$\frac{1}{1 - \left(\dfrac{x}{100} \times \dfrac{r}{192} \right)}$$

The grossed up dividend is added to the shareholders' total income and the refund is given on this basis. However, income-tax on the profits retained by the company is neither creditable to the shareholders or refundable to the company. This system of refund, based on the British system of taxation, enables the shareholders to get back a considerable portion of the income-tax paid by the corporation. But India has now given up this practice of refunds since the passing of the Finance Act of 1959-60, and has switched over to the American system of taxation, according to which company profits are taxed once and for all by a single tax at a uniform rate, and no credit is given to the shareholder in his assessment. More or less, this is also the system that is followed in North America, many countries in South America, and Europe, Australia and South Africa.

SUPERTAX OR CORPORATION TAX

Apart from the income-tax which is levied on the entire income of the companies, the Union Government also levies a corporation tax on the same income, and neither is allowed as a rebate in assessing the other. This tax is often called supertax on companies, but this is not altogether proper because the Constitution itself has labelled this tax a corporation tax. Before 1939, supertax was levied on the companies with an exemption limited to Rs. 50,000. The shareholders, however, were not given any credit for the supertax paid by the company. The nice discrimination here is that the supertax is paid by the company as company on behalf of the company, whereas the income-tax is supposed, by a legal fiction, to be paid by the shareholders themselves with the company for their tax-collector. Viewed from this angle, the term supertax is rather a misnomer, for it is inconceivable that the 'super' can be altogether independent of the 'base'; it would therefore be most appropriate to call it by the right name of corporation tax. The Taxation Enquiry Commission (1924) has observed that "its justification lies partly in the fact that companies derive certain advantages and enjoy certain privileges as the result of incorporation; and partly in the fact that the portion of the profits of companies which is not distributed as dividends, but is placed to reserves, escapes assessment to supertax".[12] But there are not wanting Indian authorities who declare that the corporation tax is not any return for any special privileges; for example, R. N. Bhargava says: "if the corporation tax is a tax on privilege, it should be levied when the privilege is granted, that is, when the joint-stock company is incorporated. It should also be related to the privilege granted. But the corporation tax bears no such relationship. The tax is not levied so long as a corporation incurs losses. If it earns an income the tax liability varies in proportion to income."[13] However, even these authorities are united in saying that a corporation tax is justifiable on the ground of 'ability to pay'.

THE EXEMPTION LIMIT

The Taxation Enquiry Commission of 1924 expressed the opinion that, "if the tax is recognised as a corporation profits tax, it becomes clear that the exemption limit of Rs. 50,000 is illogical. Small companies derive relatively as much advantage as large ones from the privileges of incorporation, and the amount of profit made by a company bears no necessary relation to the wealth or poverty of its shareholders"; the Commission therefore recommended "that the present exemption limit which seems to have been made on a false analogy should be abolished".[14] The Income-tax Enquiry

---

[12] *Report*, pp. 213-4.
[13] *The Theory and Working of Union Finance in India*, p. 191.
See also V. K. R. V. Rao, *Taxation of Income in India*, p. 182.
[14] *Report*, p. 214.

Committee also endorsed this view of the Taxation Enquiry Commission.[15]

Accordingly, in the Indian Income-tax (Amendment) Act, 1939, the exemption limit in case of supertax on companies was removed, and all companies, irrespective of their income, were made to pay this tax and at the same tax rate. But, in practice, the tax (in the words of Nicholas Kaldor) is "levied at different rates according to varying criteria, such as the nature of the company, the source from which the income is drawn (whether it represents profits of the assessee company, or dividends paid by another ; if the latter, according to the kind of activity pursued by it) and according to whether the profits are distributed or retained".[16] There is one basic rate undoubtedly, but hardly any company is made to pay at that rate, for the rebates invariably qualify the basic rate considerably. Different classes of companies are allowed to claim various rebates depending on individual conditions, and in the result the effective rate at which the companies pay the corporation tax is lower than the basic rate.

SUMMARY

The substance of what was sought to be explained in the previous paragraphs could now be stated briefly. The tax for any assessment year is levied on the total income of the corporations for the corresponding previous year at the rates fixed by the Annual Finance Acts. The final determination of the tax would depend upon : (1) the status of the corporation (whether it is resident or non-resident) ; (2) the place or places where the income of the company is earned ; (3) the Group to which the company belongs (whether it is Indian or non-Indian, whether it has made the necessary arrangements for declaring dividends or not, whether it comes under the Section 23A category or not, etc.) ; (4) the company's total computed income ; and (5) the bonus shares issued and the dividends distributed by the company. The variable factors are so many and human ingenuity (at the tax-gatherer's no less than the tax-payer's end) is so great that the taxation of corporate income presents one of the most complicated problems thrown by advancing civilisation. An annually altering or alterable basic tax rate, a whole complex of provisions relating to rebates, ambi-

[15] *Report* (1936), p. 18.   [16] *Indian Tax Reform*, p. 85.

guity in interpretation, the rising mass of judicial decisions on the subject, the conflicting pulls of present need and long-term equity, all contribute to the baffling intricacy of the whole problem of corporate taxation in India.

Rate Structure of Company Taxes

RATE STRUCTURE OF COMPANY INCOME-TAX

As we saw earlier, the rates of taxation of income in India are determined by the Annual Finance Acts. If the growth of the rate-structure of the taxes affecting corporations is examined, it will become abundantly clear that the evolution has proceeded from a comparatively simple to an increasingly complex scheme of taxation with more and more proliferating qualifications and exceptions. It is evidently the price that we have to pay for industrial and technological advance.

Taking into consideration the history of the income-tax rates falling on companies, we can divide the period into five distinct sectors: (*i*) Pre-1939, (*ii*) War-time (1939-45), (*iii*) Pre-Independence (1945-47), (*iv*) Pre-Plan (1947-51), (*v*) After 1951 (Plans I and II). Before 1939 we find that the income-tax rates were stable at a comparatively low level. From 1922 to 1930, income-tax was levied on the total income of the companies at the rate of 18 pies in the rupee. This rate was presently raised to 19 pies, and in 1931 it was again raised to 29.25 pies. From 1932 to 1935, the rate was 32.50 pies in the rupee. The next year saw a slight reduction to 30.33 pies, and in the next Budget a further reduction was announced. This rate—28.17 pies in the rupee—continued up to 1939.

Just when the corporate sector was beginning to shake off the economic sluggishness of the thirties and show marked signs of new vitality and growth, the taxes on corporations also began to expand with alacrity. In 1939-40, income-tax was charged on the entire income at 30 pies in the rupee, and there was no surcharge. This basic income-tax rate of 30 pies in the rupee was adhered to till 1946.

SURCHARGE ON INCOME-TAX

The Central Government had been given the right to levy surcharges on the taxes on income by the Government of India Act of 1935 (Section 138). The whole surcharge revenue was to accrue only to the Centre, whereas the income-tax revenue was to be shared by the Centre and the States in a certain proportion. Government took advantage of this position and resorted to the levy of surcharges on income-taxes during the Second World War, instead of raising the basic income-tax rate itself. Actually, surcharges had been levied earlier in 1936-37, but had been promptly discontinued soon afterwards; it was the financial pressure exerted by the exigencies of the war that now necessitated the imposition of surcharges on all taxes paid on income.

There was, however, no surcharge for the year 1939-40, the first year of the war. Introducing the Second Finance Bill for the year 1940-41, Sir Jeremy Raisman, the Finance Member, said in the Legislative Assembly on 5 November 1940 while proposing a 25 per cent surcharge for Central purposes on all taxes on income: "In relation to the needs of the present situation, the sacrifices which I have to ask of the community at this stage are not excessive". He proposed a levy of 25 per cent surcharge only for the remaining four months of the current year. But as the rates of income-tax had to be fixed for the whole year at one time, the intention of a 25 per cent surcharge on 4 months' income was carried out by actually levying a surcharge of one-twelfth (i.e. $1/4 \times 1/3 = 1/12$) on the income-tax rates for the year. In the next year, i.e. 1941-42, the surcharge was increased from 25 per cent to $33\frac{1}{3}$ per cent. This meant another 10 pies in the rupee to be paid in addition to the usual 30 pies in the rupee as income-tax. In 1942-43, the surcharge was again raised to 15 pies in the rupee; in 1943-44, it was 20 pies; in 1944-45, it was 24 pies; and, finally, in 1945-46, it was 27 pies in the rupee, while income-tax *plus* surcharge was 57 pies in the rupee.

POST-WAR AMALGAMATION AND AFTER

In the first post-war Budget for the year 1946-47, Sir Archibald Rowlands, the Finance Member, amalgamated the basic income-tax rates and the surcharge rates. In the name of greater simplicity and rationalisation, the surcharges were removed and the loss in revenue was made good by upgrading the rates of income-tax. For one thing, during the post-war period the bulk of the developmental expenditure was to have been undertaken by the Provincial Governments, and because of the upgrading of the basic rates themselves, the Provinces could now hope to get more revenues, since income-tax was shareable while surcharge was not. For another reason, of course, there was the plea for simplification of the company income-tax structure. Anyhow, in 1946-47, the basic income-tax rate shot up from 30 pies to 60 pies in the rupee, and this rate was maintained till 1949-50. In 1950-51, the rate was reduced to 48 pies in the rupee. From 1951-52 onwards, once again surcharges were levied, the tax-payer now having, as it were, "the worst of both worlds". The rate is now maintained at 48 pies in the rupee, with a surcharge of 5 per cent of the total tax paid.

RATE STRUCTURE OF CORPORATION TAX

The rate structure of the corporation tax has also undergone changes similar to the rate structure of the company income-tax. During the pre-war period, corporation tax was charged at the rate of one anna in the rupee on the income with an exemption limit of Rs. 50,000. Actually, ever since supertax (company supertax being really corporation tax) was incorporated into the Income-tax Act, income-tax rates were subject to changes though supertax rates hardly ever changed. In 1940-41, a surcharge at the rate of 1/3 of the supertax rate was levied. In 1941-42 this was continued. In 1942-43, the supertax rate itself rose to 18 pies in the rupee, and the next year to 24 pies, and it rose again by 12 pies in 1944-45; but there were no surcharges. The rate was reduced to just one anna in 1946-47, only to be sharply raised to two annas in the now notorious Liaquat Ali Khan Budget of 1947-48. The rate was 3 annas in the rupee in 1948-49, and this was further raised to 48 pies (4 annas) in the rupee in 1949-50. The 1950-51 Budget increased the rate still further by half-anna, and another quarter-anna was added to the rate in the 1951-52 Budget. This rate was not changed till 1956-57, when the rate became six annas and nine pies in the rupee.

TOTAL TAX BURDEN

From all this we can see that the history of the rate structure is one of continual rise, at times very steep indeed. Even though the basic rates were as indicated above, there have also been many qualifications hedging the rates so that the effective rates have been much lower than the basic rates. Before detailing the various exemptions and qualifications, it will be instructive to examine the total tax burden (that is, income-tax and supertax, with their respective surcharges) as it has fluctuated over a period of several years. It is, of course, not very proper to club together income-tax and corporation tax, because a portion of the income-tax paid by the company is, after all, refunded to the shareholders. However, from the company's own point of view, there is hardly any difference between income-tax and supertax, for both represent, in the account books of the company, only debit items.

TABLE II gives in a summary form the shares claimed by the taxes on every rupee earned by the corporations from 1939-40 to 1957-58.

This table reflects picturesquely the steady increase in the tax burden borne by the companies. The upward movement was arrested and slightly even lowered in the immediate post-war budgets; but soon afterwards the burden started growing heavier than ever before, the post-freedom crest of 143.4 pies in the rupee for 1956-57 being much higher than the war-time crest of 90 pies for 1944-45. Of course, as we have said earlier, these rates are more apparent than real; rates and rebates have to be studied together to arrive at the real position, and we shall address ourselves to this problem now.

FORMAL RATES AND REAL RATES

The present combined rate of income-tax and corporation tax is visibly much higher than it was in 1939-40: the combined rate is, in fact, $3\frac{1}{2}$ times the rate prevailing immediately before the war. Many causes like the financing of the War and the recent developmental expenditure have contributed to this position. On the other hand, as already pointed out, while the formal rates look truly formidable, the actual rates are much less so. The reason is that it is customary of late for the Indian tax legislation to lay down certain rates which are the maximum rates at which various classes of assessees will have to pay taxes, and at the same time to make it possible for most of the assessees to take advantage of several concessions and rebates that will effectively reduce the tax liability. Thus tax-rate law and the rebate-bye-laws have to be taken to-

TABLE II
RATES OF COMPANY TAXATION[17]
(in pies[a] per rupee)

Year	Income-tax	Surcharge on Income-tax	Corporation Tax	Surcharge on Corporation Tax	Income-tax + Corporation Tax
1939-40	30	nil	12	nil	42
1940-41	30	2.5	12	4	48.5
1941-42	30	10	12	4	56
1942-43	30	15	18	nil	63
1943-44	30	20	24	nil	74
1944-45	30	24	36	nil	90
1945-46	30	27	36	nil	93
1946-47	60	nil	12	nil	72
1947-48	60	nil	24	nil	84
1948-49	60	nil	36	nil	96
1949-50	60	nil	48	nil	108
1950-51	48	nil	54	nil	102
1951-52	48	2.4	57	nil	107.4
1952-53	48	2.4	57	nil	107.4
1953-54	48	2.4	57	nil	107.4
1954-55	48	2.4	57	nil	107.4
1955-56	48	2.4	57	nil	107.4
1956-57	48	2.4	93	nil	143.4
1957-58	30	5	50	nil	85

[a] 192 pies made one rupee.

gether to get a clear picture of the actual tax liability of the assessees. Till 1948 there were no rebates in respect of income-tax, and even afterwards, there has not been as much complication with regard to the income-tax as with the levy of the corporation tax. As regards the corporation tax, the system of rebates was introduced only in 1944.

REBATES ON INCOME-TAX

Compared to the corporation tax, income-tax on companies has

[17] Source : Annual Finance Acts.

remained on the whole a simple affair. As we noted earlier, shareholders in India were until recently entitled to a refund from the Government in respect of income-tax paid by the company. According to the Finance Act of 1948, a rebate is given in respect of undistributed profits. An additional tax is levied on dividends paid in excess of the available net profits after taxation. Small companies with incomes less than Rs. 25,000 per year are charged at a lower rate. The Finance Act of 1948 introduced, besides, the distinction between Indian and non-Indian companies. According to this Finance Act, Indian companies with incomes over Rs. 25,000 per year and *all* non-Indian companies had to pay income-tax at the rate of 5 annas and supertax at the rate of 3 annas in the rupee. However, all companies, including Indian companies with incomes less than Rs. 25,000, were entitled to a rebate of one anna in the rupee on supertax, if the prescribed arrangements were made for deduction of supertax at the source. An Indian company is effectively prevented from not making such prescribed arrangements for deducting supertax because, under Section 18(3-E) of the Indian Income-tax Act, the company has to collect supertax at the source from the shareholders, and, under Section 18(7), the company will be responsible to the Government for such collection. There is also another rebate of equal value for Indian companies with incomes over Rs. 25,000 per year for ploughing back profits. In other words, a rebate of one anna in the rupee is given on the amount by which the total income, after reduction by seven annas of the tax in the rupee, exceeds the dividends declared. This rate of seven annas is composed of five annas of income-tax, three annas of supertax, *minus* the rebate of one anna. In the company's income, only nine annas will thus remain for distribution. Sometimes the companies may distribute from accumulated savings also. To discourage this, an additional charge is levied on Indian companies on the excess dividends declared, that is to say, the dividend-amount that exceeds total profits *minus* the seven annas in the rupee of the tax. The rate of this extra charge on excess dividends is calculated in the following manner. It is assumed correctly that any distribution over the current net income of the company must come from past undistributed profits. Accordingly, the levy is at a rate equal to the difference of 5 annas and the amount of tax (if any) actually borne by such excess in the previous years. The tell-tale reason for levying this extra charge is to make available the tax concessions only to those who actually retain the profits in the business.

An Indian Company with an income less than Rs. 25,000 per year had to pay under the Finance Act of 1948 only $2\frac{1}{2}$ annas in the rupee as income-tax; supertax, however, was at the rate of 3 annas in the rupee. A rebate of half an anna in the rupee was given for ploughing back profits remaining out of the total income after the payment of tax at $4\frac{1}{2}$ annas in the rupee on the total income; here, again, this rate of $4\frac{1}{2}$ annas is composed of $2\frac{1}{2}$ annas of income-tax, three annas of supertax, *minus* the rebate of one anna. Unlike companies with an income over Rs. 25,000 per year, these smaller companies were not subject to an additional charge if the reduced total income fell short of the dividend declared. In the 1949 Finance Act, however, this concession to the small Indian company was also withdrawn. In the next Finance Act (1950), the distinction between Indian and non-Indian companies in the matter of granting rebates was abolished. The rebate was now given to those companies which had made the prescribed arrangements for deducting dividends in India and deducting super-tax whether the companies were Indian or non-Indian. No significant change has been introduced in the Finance Acts of the subsequent years up to 1959 regarding the income-tax on companies.

REBATES ON CORPORATE TAX

Companies pay a flat rate of corporation tax on their profits. The rates, like the income-tax rates, are regulated by the Annual Finance Acts. Here also the effective rates are much lower than the prescribed basic rates, though, for the years 1946 and 1947, while the minimum rates were prescribed, the effective rates actually increased.

Before 1944, companies paid a uniform rate of tax as could be seen in the table already given. After the 1944 Finance Act, however, the tax burden of the companies began to depend to a great extent on the dividend distributions. A glance at the history of the corporate tax structure is sufficient to indicate the Government's desire to regulate and control the profits made by the joint-stock companies. All along, Government have been trying, with the aid of taxation measures, to see that companies distribute only a reasonable portion to the shareholders and maintain healthy reserves for expansion.

The Finance Act of 1944 introduced for the first time a rebate to companies from the supertax on the declared dividends. The rebate was one anna in the rupee on so much of the company's total profits as was *not* distributed in the shape of dividends other than dividends payable at a fixed rate on preference shares. The same scheme continued in the assessment year of 1945-46 also. However, in the Finance Act of 1946, the same scheme was followed in a different way. Instead of specifying a particular basic rate first and then giving rebates for the undistributed income, there was now first a low basic rate, and an additional supertax was levied on that part of the total income which did not exceed the amount of dividends on ordinary shares. The tax was, naturally enough, on a progressive scale. Unlike the procedure followed in 1944 and 1945, the Finance Act of 1946 specified that no additional supertax was payable if the dividends declared by the company were less than or equal to 5 per cent of the capital of the company. Here 'capital' means "the paid-up share capital at the beginning of the previous year for the assessment for the year ending on the 31st day of March, 1947 (other than capital entitled to a dividend at a fixed rate) *plus* any reserves other than depreciation reserves for bad or doubtful debts at the same date as diminished by the amount on deposit on the same date with the Central Government under Section 10 of the Indian Finance Act, 1942". Not exactly or sparklingly lucid, and perhaps inviting no end of legal wrangling with regard to its precise interpretation, but some attempt at comprehensive definition was called for, and this was the best the Act could provide. There was no perceptible change in the next Finance Act regarding the taxation of companies.

POST-INDEPENDENCE RATE AND REBATE STRUCTURES

It was only after India achieved freedom that considerable changes took place in the company tax structure. In the first Finance Act after independence (1948-49), the rate of corporation tax was 3 annas in the rupee, with a rebate of one anna for making the prescribed arrangements. As far as the corporation tax was concerned, the distinction between Indian and non-Indian companies was not now operative, for the tax was levied at the uniform rate of 4 annas in the rupee. The following, however, is a summary of the permissible rebates under the Act :

1. A public company, with a total income not exceeding Rs. 25,000 per year, which has made the prescribed arrangements for declaration and payment in India of dividends, will get arebate of 3 annas in the rupee ;
2. A public company like the above, but with an income exceeding Rs. 25,000 per year, will receive a rebate of 2 annas in the rupee;
3. This is to apply to private companies also, if they make the prescribed arrangements ;
4. Finally, any public company whose shares are sold in the stock exchange but has not made the prescribed arrangements will get a rebate of only one anna.

As we have seen earlier, the last mentioned class of companies refers only to foreign firms, as Indian companies are effectively prevented from not making the prescribed arrangements for the distribution of dividends.

In the 1950 Finance Act, the rebate structure was the same, but the basic rate was raised from 4 annas to $4\frac{1}{2}$ annas in the rupee. Another quarter anna was added in the next year and the rate and rebate structure continued without further changes till 1953, when fresh changes were brought about.

The change introduced in 1953 related to the treatment to be meted out to the dividend income from a subsidiary company. In the previous years only a rebate of one anna was given to public companies which had not made the prescribed arrangements but whose shares were sold in the stock exchange. But in 1953, a rebate at the rate of one anna and a half in the rupee was given on the dividends received from a subsidiary Indian company, and a rebate of half an anna on any other income. This was to encourage foreign companies to invest in—or form subsidiary—Indian companies. In the 1954 and 1955 Finance Acts, again, no change was made in the rate structure. The Finance Act of 1956 enhanced the basic supertax rate to $6\frac{3}{4}$ annas in the rupee with the following rebates :

1. A public company with a total income not exceeding Rs. 25,000 per year, which had made the prescribed arrangements, will get a rebate of 5 annas in the rupee ;

2. Companies with incomes exceeding Rs. 25,000 per year, which have made the prescribed arrangements, will be entitled to a rebate of 4 annas in the rupee;
3. A rebate of $3\frac{1}{2}$ annas in the rupee will be given on income from subsidiary Indian companies to foreign companies who have not made the prescribed arrangements, while the rebate will be only one anna in the rupee for other income to these companies.

From the 1949-50 Finance Act onwards, it has been specifically stated that supertax will not touch the 50 per cent level of the taxable income. The supertax should not exceed, according to the Finance Acts, the combined total of (i) the supertax payable on Rs. 25,000, *and* (ii) 50 per cent of the total income *minus* Rs. 25,000.

EXCESS DIVIDENDS AND BONUS SHARES

A tax on excess dividends and a tax on bonus shares also find a place in the Finance Act of 1956. If any company declares dividends higher than 6 per cent of its paid-up capital—the dividends not being payable at a fixed rate—then the rebates allowed to that company on the supertax will be reduced in the following way:

		Rate
1.	On that part of the dividends exceeding 6 per cent but below 10 per cent of the paid-up capital:	2 annas in the rupee;
2.	On that part of the dividends exceeding 10 per cent of the paid-up capital:	3 annas in the rupee;
3.	On the amount representing the face value of any bonus shares or the amount of any bonus issued to its shareholders during the previous year with a view to increasing the paid-up capital:	2 annas in the rupee, i.e. $\frac{1}{8}$ or 12.5 per cent of the face value of the shares.

Under the Finance Act of 1957, the basic rate has been increased to $8\frac{3}{4}$ annas in the rupee, but the assessees are entitled to the rebates that were available in 1956-57 ; there is, however, a change in the tax on excess dividends :

		Rate
1.	On net dividends that exceed 6 per cent but less than 10 per cent of the paid-up capital:	10%;
2.	On net dividends that exceed 10 per cent but less than 18 per cent of the paid-up capital :	20%;
3.	On net dividends that exceed 18 per cent of the paid-up capital :	30%.

The tax rates for Section 23A companies, on the other hand, have been fixed only in two slabs, 10 per cent on the slab of dividends over 6 per cent of the paid-up capital, and 20 per cent on the slab of dividends over 10 per cent of the paid-up capital. This change in favour of Section 23A companies is brought in because of the statutory condition which requires these companies to distribute a large chunk of their profits to the shareholders to avoid a penal supertax.[18]

The tax on bonus shares also has been increased from 12.5 per cent to 30 per cent on the face value of the shares.

SECTION 23A COMPANIES

We have seen all along that the amount of tax paid by the companies depends to no small extent upon the dividend declarations. The basic idea behind these tax measures is evidently the desire to encourage the ploughing back of profits in the business for its further expansion. But in the matter of the special taxation measures pertaining to the companies falling within the scope of Section 23A, we find quite the opposite motive operating, in other words, a desire to discourage, not encourage, the excessive ploughing back of profits. What is the reason for this apparently ambivalent attitude ? On the one hand, the conviction regarding the necessity for the ploughing back of profits has gained wide approval, and hence undistributed profits receive a measure of favourable treatment ; on the other hand, there is also the necessity to check evasion of personal supertax through the formation of closely controlled limited companies, and hence there would appear

[18] Taxation of excess dividends has been abolished by the 1959-60 Budget.

to be a need for penal provisions to prevent such evasion. Dividend declaration becomes, in effect, a kind of Bed of Procrustes; companies should beware of declaring too high or too low a dividend, for in either case they are likely to be visited with penalties.

According to Section 23A of the Indian Income-tax Act (after 1939 but before 1955), if certain companies did not declare as dividends 60 per cent of their profits,[19] then the income-tax authorities could pass an order declaring that the entire distributable profits had been declared. Accordingly, the shareholders will be assessed on the dividend income from these companies, whether they actually received any money or not. Thus the shareholders of such closely held corporations, instead of avoiding supertax, suffered actually extra burdens if the company failed to distribute at least 60 per cent of its profits. Further, if the past accumulations of the company equal 100 per cent of its paid-up capital *plus* its loan capital or the actual cost of its fixed assets, whichever is greater, the entire distributable profits should be distributed. Thus a virtual limit is placed on the accumulation of reserves by these companies. One way of putting this would be to say that the shareholders are penalised for the 'sins' of the company. Almost always the main motive behind the formation of private companies is to evade personal supertax, and Indian private companies are no exception to this rule. According to a sample survey conducted by the Taxation Enquiry Commission (1953-4), 86 per cent of these Section 23A companies were controlled by one to four persons, and 31.4 per cent of the companies were controlled by one person only. And there is hardly a Section 23A company in which the majority of the shares is controlled by more than six persons.[20] All this means excessive concentration of wealth and economic power in a few hands under conditions that make for

---

[19] Here 'profit' means the total assessible income *minus* the following:— (1) the amount of income-tax and supertax payable by the company in respect of its total income but excluding the amount of supertax (if any) under this Section; (2) the amount of any other tax under any law for the time being in force on the corporation by the Government or by the local authority in excess of the amount (if any) which has been allowed in computing the total income; and, (3) in case of a banking company, the amount actually transferred to a reserve fund under Section 17 of the Banking Companies Act of 1949.

[20] *Report*, Vol. II, p. 177.

further such concentration through avoidance of personal supertax liability : hence the attempts of the tax-gatherers to arm themselves with sufficient powers, not only to collect the legitimate taxes that are due, but also to exert a check on more and more concentration of wealth and economic power in fewer and fewer hands.[21] This apart, there was also experienced very real difficulty in assessing the shareholders on their dividend income. "Very often," writes Girish Chandra Sharma, "assessments of many shareholders were completed long before the assessment of the company, and if Section 23A was applied to its assessment later, it meant reopening of the assessments of the shareholders."[22] There was in consequence much unnecessary work and unpardonable delay in the assessment and collection of supertax, and this too cried for reform.

REFORMS UNDER THE FINANCE ACT OF 1955

With a view to avoiding the delay and the confusion in assessing the (deemed) dividend income in the hands of the shareholders, certain new reforms were introduced in the Finance Act of 1955, and this was slightly amended in 1956. Under the 1955 Act, it is the company which has to bear the tax if it fails to distribute a sufficient portion of the profits as dividends. Section 23A has prescribed different minimum percentages for distribution of dividends to different classes of companies. If the minimum prescribed is not distributed, the penal supertax rates will be applied. We can now classify the minimum percentages that are applied to various classes of companies and the penal supertax rates applicable to them if they fail to distribute the prescribed minima :

Class of Company	Minimum to be Distributed	Penal Supertax
1. Ordinary non-public company i.e. a company in which the public is not interested :	60% of distributable profits :	6 annas in the rupee ;

[21] Only a small number of cases have needed the application of these penal provisions. *Report of the Direct Taxes Enquiry Committee*, p. 47.
[22] *Taxation of Companies*, p. 80.

2. An investment company in which the public is not interested :	100% of distributable profits :	8 annas in the rupee ;
3. Any non-public company in which the public is not interested, whose accumulated profits and reserves are more than either (i) the cost of fixed assets, or (ii) paid-up capital *plus* loan capital whichever is greater :	do.	do.
4. A non-public industrial Indian company (i.e. one engaged in the manufacture or processing of goods or in mining or in the generation or distribution of electricity or any other form of power) :	60% of distributable profits in 1955-6 and 1956-7 ; 50% in 1957-8 ; 45% being the current rate :	4 annas in 1955-6 ; and 6 annas in the rupee afterwards :
5. In the case of an Indian company a part of whose business only consists in activities referred to in the previous clause,		
(a) in relation to the said part of the company's business :	Originally 60% but now reduced to 45%, provided the company is not a mere investment company :	6 annas in the rupee ;
(b) for the remaining part :	Originally 100%, now reduced to 90% of distributable profits :	do.

The reduced limits to industrial companies are fixed after considering the need for them to retain sufficient funds for purposes of expansion. However, under the present system, the tax burden would be (ultimately) higher on the ordinary not-very-rich shareholders, while the burden is correspondingly lighter on those who are in the highest supertax brackets, because the tax paid by the company will after all be less than what they would have to pay.

One particular problem in the taxation of Section 23A companies has evoked considerable comment. On the one hand, these companies are penalised by a supertax if they fail to distribute a prescribed percentage of the distributable profits, and, on the other hand, such a company is also penalised if it distributes dividends equal to 6 per cent or more of the paid-up capital. It is quite possible, under the circumstances, that in particular instances, the private companies may attract penal rates of taxation simultaneously both on account of the distribution and the non-distribution of their profits.[23] Of course, authorities like Girish Chandra Sharma point out that such a kind of overlapping will occur only in stray exceptional cases. But he also immediately warns that, "in any event, it may be sometimes necessary for the Board of Directors to calculate at what point they should stop distribution so that the supertax liability of the company under Section 23A and the Finance Acts is kept at the minimum".[24]

This Section is not applicable to foreign companies operating in India through branches and subsidiaries owned fully by these foreign companies. Again, all subsidiaries of foreign companies which are not closely controlled are free from the application of the penal provisions of Section 23A, which are mainly intended for Indian companies alone.

DEFINITION OF 'DIVIDEND'

It is necessary to point out that more items are included under 'dividend' for the Section 23A companies than for the ordinary companies. Like 'income', 'dividend' also is left undefined in the Income-tax Act. Dividend is ordinarily a distribution, in the form of money or shares, by a joint-stock company of the profits earned by it to its shareholders. Before 1939 also there was no definition of the term 'dividend'; it was interpreted according to the ordinary

[23] See N. Kaldor, *Indian Tax Reform*, p. 86.
[24] *Taxation of Companies*, p. 114.

meaning attached to it in the light of the various judicial pronouncements. It was felt, however, especially by the Income-tax Enquiry Committee,[25] that such practice led to a frantic search for loopholes and consequent evasion of taxation. In accordance with the suggestion of the Income-tax Enquiry Committee, there was now included, though not a definition, at least a description of 'dividend'. Section 2(6A), which deals with 'dividend', gives a list of what constitutes dividend income and what does not. The Indian Income-tax system thus categorises five instances of what 'dividend' is and three instances of what 'dividend' is not :[26]

'Dividend' includes
(a) any distribution by a company of accumulated profits whether capitalised or not, if such distribution entails the release by the company to its shareholders of all or any part of the assets of the company ;
(b) any distribution by a company of debentures (debenture-stock or deposit certificates in any form, whether with or without interest) to the extent to which the company possesses accumulated profits, whether capitalised or not ;
(c) any distribution made to the shareholders of a company on its liquidation, to the extent to which the distribution is attributable to the accumulated profits of the company immediately before its liquidation, whether capitalised or not ;
(d) any distribution by a company on the reduction of its capital to the extent to which the company possesses accumulated profits which arose after the end of the previous year ending next before the 1st day of April 1933, whether such accumulated profits have been capitalised or not ; and,
(e) any payment by a company, not being a company in which the public is substantially interested (within the meaning of Section 23A), of any sum (whether as representing a part of the assets of the company or otherwise) by way of advance or loan to a shareholder, to the extent to which the company in either case possesses accumulated profits ;

but 'dividend' does *not* include
(a) a distribution made in accordance with sub-clause (c) or

[25] *Report* (1936), pp. 66-8.
[26] *Income-tax Manual,* Part I, 14th Edition (1957), pp. 4-5.

sub-clause (d) in respect of any share issued for full cash consideration where the holder of the share is not entitled in the event of liquidation to participate in the surplus of assets;

(b) any advance or loan made to a shareholder by a company in the ordinary course of its business where the lending of money is a substantial part of the business of the company; and,

(c) any dividend paid by a company which is set off by the company against the whole or any part of any sum previously paid by it and treated as a dividend within the meaning of clause (e) to the extent to which it is so set off.

The whole agonisingly complicated and laboriously comprehensive construction of the above Section of the Act reflects the understandable anxiety of the Government as tax-gatherer to see that the shareholder does not evade his tax liability. The net is spread as wide as possible, the ways of escape are carefully closed, the pulling strings are sharp and strong. The sole criterion is whether or not the shareholder has received a benefit, of one or another kind, as a return for his investment; if he has received such a benefit, it is 'dividend' for all practical purposes, and he should pay the prescribed tax to the Government. Of course, no categorisation can ever be absolutely fool-proof or unexceptionably comprehensive. Hence, from time to time, clauses have to be added or modified as and when fresh loopholes are discovered. For example, in sub-section (b) of Section 2(6A), the term 'deposit-certificates' was added by the 1955 Finance Act, as a result of a judgment by the Madras High Court in the *C.I.T. of Madras* vs. *M. P. Viswanatha Rao* case.[27] The High Court held that a deposit-certificate is only a post-dated cheque, and it is neither a debenture nor does it entail a release of assets; it was consequently held *not* taxable.

Part (e) of the Section is peculiarly important, as this part discriminates only against the Section 23A companies.[28] According to (e), any payment made by a company (in which the public is not substantially interested), carrying on any business other than money-lending, to its shareholders by way of a loan or advance is considered as a dividend. But this is operative only if the company

[27] Cited by V. S. Sundaram, *The Law of Income-tax in India*, p. 106.
[28] Suggested by the *Report of the Taxation Enquiry Commission* (1953-4), Vol. II, p. 164.

possesses accumulated profits. This clause is mainly intended to check the evasion of taxation on dividends received in the name of loans or advances, but in point of fact not intended to be repaid.

ARE BONUS SHARES 'DIVIDENDS'?

Another very ticklish problem in the study of dividends is the ambiguous position of bonus shares: Are they to be included under dividends or not? The Indian income-tax system definitely keeps out bonus shares from the purview of dividends, for obviously bonus shares cannot be taxed on the same footing as regular dividends. As the Select Committee said in its Report on the Income-tax Amendment Bill of 1938: "We have recast and expanded the definition of 'dividend', primarily in order to ensure that no distribution falling under this head shall be taxed unless there is a release of assets. Under the amended definition a debenture will be, when issued, treated as a dividend, but an ordinary bonus share will not be liable to taxation until it is actually paid off". We have already seen the main problem relating to bonus shares in the first chapter. In India, the Finance Act of 1956 introduced a tax on the face value of the bonus shares issued. This was done rather in spite of the Taxation Enquiry Commission's view that they had "come to the conclusion that bonus shares are not income in any sense of the word as understood in income-tax".[29] This was no casual conclusion, but had been arrived at after considerable discussion and weighing of expert judicial opinion both from the United States and Great Britain, for example the decisions in the famous *Eisner* vs. *Macomber* and *Inland Revenue* vs. *Blott* cases wherein it had been held that bonus shares were *not* taxable.[30] Apart from these two cases, there are other cases too like *Towne* vs. *Eisner*, in which it was decided as follows: "A stock dividend really takes nothing from the property of the corporation, and adds nothing to the interests of the shareholders. Its property is not diminished and their interests are not increased.... The proportional interest of each shareholder remains the same. The only change is in the evidence which represents that interest, the new shares and the original shares together representing the same proportional interest that the original shares represented before the

[29] *Report* (1953-4), Vol. II, p. 162.
[30] Ibid., Vol. II, pp. 162-3.

issue of the new ones."[31] Here the essential and controlling factor is that the shareholder gets nothing out of the corporation's assets for his exclusive and private use. Of course, there are dissenters to this view also; for example, in the *Inland Revenue* vs. *Blott* case, although the majority of the judges concluded that "the shares credited to the respondent in respect of the bonus, being distributed by the company as capital, were not income in the hands of the assessee", two judges expressed a contrary view. Lord Sumner, one of the dissenting judges, said in his note that "It takes two to make a paid-up share. A share issued... is a share to be paid for; paid for by the allottee in meal or in malt; in money, unless by contract between himself and the company he is enabled to satisfy his obligation to pay by some other consideration moving from himself to the company. Under the contract in question, what consideration so moves from the shareholders? None that I can see, except the discharge of the company's debt for a dividend, which has become due to him by being declared. When debt from dividend is set off against debt for calls and the account is squared, the equivalent of payment of a dividend takes place."[32]

KALDOR'S VIEWS

On the other hand, Kaldor subscribes to the more commonly held view that there is no case in equity for taxing bonus shares: "A tax on bonus issues has been urged from time to time... on the ground that a bonus issue is the method by which shareholders obtain profits on their holdings without paying tax on it. On closer examination, however, this claim is shown to be unfounded." Yet the ghost of a lurking suspicion remains to induce the uncomfortable feeling that the shareholders do gain something somehow, and so Kaldor immediately adds: "It is true the shareholders may, and to some extent normally do, enjoy an appreciation in the value of their holdings resulting from bonus issues".[33] But, then, it is impossible to isolate this consequential appreciation in practice from other factors affecting the market valuation of shares so as to fix rates of taxation on the benefit derived. It would

---

[31] Cited from an extract in Rosewell Magill, *Taxable Income*, p. 32.
[32] Cited from V. S. Sundaram, *The Law of Income-tax in India*, p. 111.
[33] *Indian Tax Reform*, p. 91.

therefore be better on the whole to give the benefit of the doubt and treat bonus shares as other than dividends in disguise.

VIEWS OF THE ROYAL COMMISSION (1955)

The same position is also taken by the Royal Commission on the Taxation of Profits and Income (1955). They too feel that bonus shares do not represent taxable income.[34] But while expressing this view, the Commission also point out that "while the operation of capitalising profits and issuing 'bonus' shares in respect of them presents in a dramatic form what is involved in the process of corporate saving, we do not take the view that the issuing of 'bonus' shares, which leaves the shareholder's position substantially unaltered, is itself an important aspect of the matter. What matters for the present purpose is the improvement of the shareholder's position through corporate saving, without his share of the saving passing through his hands as taxable income".[35] Bonus shares undoubtedly mean an *appreciation* or *improvement* in the value of the shareholder's position, but this is no measurable quantity and hence not properly taxable.

TAX ON BONUS SHARES

From the foregoing discussion it must be clear that doubt of one or another kind has assailed even the authorities who have felt on the balance that bonus shares are *not* 'income' and hence not taxable.[36] The Indian Taxation Enquiry Commission had also its own doubts on this matter and hence came to the guarded and hesitant conclusion that "the privilege of issuing bonus shares free of income-tax in the hands of the shareholders does confer some

---

[34] *Final Report* (Cmd. 9474) : "We find it impossible in this any benefit accruing to the shareholder in the nature of income" (p. 242).

[35] Ibid., p. 32.

[36] Business interests have throughout opposed a tax on bonus shares: for example, see *The Role of Joint-Stock Companies in India's Economic Progress*, issued by the Forum of Free Enterprise, p. 83, and 'Taxation of Bonus Shares' in *Economic Trends*, April-September 1955, issued by the Association of Indian Trade and Industry, pp. 71 ff. See also above, pp. 67-68. Bonus shares were not actually a regular source of finance in the Indian Corporate Sector and it is only after the Second War that Bonus issues have become important. See S. S. Srivastava, "Extent of Auto-Financing in Major Indian Industries", *Indian Journal of Economics*, October 1960, p. 186.

advantage both on the shareholder and the company, and there *may be* a case for *a small duty* payable by the company on the issue of bonus shares".[37] The qualifications are masterly: 'may be' ... 'a small duty'; and the Government seized them readily and found in them a justification for a tax on bonus shares. Moving the Bill in Parliament, the Finance Minister said: "There has been a certain amount of criticism against making bonus shares a subject matter of tax on the ground that this is contrary to the recommendation of the Taxation Enquiry Commission. This criticism is apparently due to the misunderstanding of the scope of the proposal. It is not proposed to tax the shareholder himself on the value of the bonus shares as if it were a dividend in his hands. What is proposed is that the issue of bonus shares should be taken into consideration while calculating the corporation tax payable on its total income. The burden thus falls on the company and not directly on the shareholder."[38] This was all right as far as it went, and was perhaps in consonance with the spirit of the Taxation Enquiry Commission's recommendation for a 'small duty' so long as the rate was 12.5 per cent, as it was at first. What is inequitable is not the imposition of such a tax (or duty) *per se*, but rather the arbitrary increase in the rate in the very second year after its introduction, for, as a matter of fact, Government increased the rate suddenly from 12.5 per cent to 30 per cent, obviously because it was thought necessary to prevent by any means whatsoever the avoidance of the excess dividends tax. 'May be' has acquired the force of an imperative, and 'a small duty' has become 30 per cent. It is needless to point out that this is but another flagrant instance in our fiscal policy of 'giving an inch and taking an ell', of the merely financial motive getting the better of the larger equity motive.[39]

BONUS SHARES AND 23A COMPANIES

It would have been much wiser, however, if the bonus shares

[37] My italics. *Report*, Vol. II, p. 164.   [38] April 1956.

[39] It is fair to add that more than the financial motive, the motive in introducing this tax appears to be to prevent the use of bonus issues to disperse the percentage which dividend payments bear to paid up capital and thus avoid the newly introduced excess dividends tax. On the contrary, as I. S. Gulati says, this tax has introduced an inequity by taxing one type of capital gains (in the shape of bonus issues) and leaving the rest untouched. *Economic Weekly*, 8 December 1956.

issued by the Section 23A companies were simply treated as dividends for the following reasons :

1. Under the Income-tax Act accumulated profits for six years preceding the liquidation of the company are subject to supertax in the hands of the shareholders. If all previous accumulated profits were converted into bonus shares and the actual liquidation purposely delayed, the big shareholders would be able to escape the supertax.

2. If a 'private' corporation is allowed to issue bonus shares, it gains in two ways : (a) the amount available for distribution is reduced, and (b) the paid-up capital is also increased. Thus by a continuous process of issue of bonus shares, a company can indefinitely evade the application of Section 23A, whose very purpose is to check tax evasion by the big shareholders through the method of keeping money in the form of reserves in the private companies.

3. In the case of private companies owned by foreigners, a further advantage is gained. By getting bonus shares instead of dividends, the shareholder gets a marketable commodity which could be sold and the proceeds sent to the home country without incurring any tax. If, however, the amount is remitted in the form of dividends he will have to pay supertax on it.

Computation of Income

In our discussion of the various taxes affecting the income and profits of the corporations, we have been taking for granted the meaning of concepts like 'income' and 'taxable income' instead of getting lost in the labyrinthine recesses of legally perfect definitions. Income for income-tax purposes is but the net increase of economic power which is realised and which is capable of measurement between two points of time. This excludes additional investments and withdrawals of capital. The computation of gross income is, of course, comparatively easy ; it is the computation of assessable income that poses problems to both the assessor and assessees in the matter of company taxation.

WHAT IS NET INCOME ?

When we deduct from the gross income the costs incurred or involved in earning this gross income, we should arrive at the net income; this is but common-sense. But, for income-tax purposes, it is not enough that we know the net income of a company over a long period; it is the net income between two near points of time that has to be known, and this brings in most of the difficulties to be faced in the computation of income. As C. J. Gaa says, "If income were calculated for the entire life-span of an enterprise, there would be few difficulties to face".[40] The beginning and the end are there for all to see—the story is ended—and it is easy to strike the balance-sheet of success or failure: "The assets on the opening balance sheet could be evaluated, totalled, and compared with the money on hand after realising on all of the assets and after liquidating the liabilities. These figures could then be adjusted for the relative purchasing power of the capital originally invested as compared with that which remained after liquidation. The difference would be income...."[41]

Unfortunately, the tax-gatherer will not patiently wait—he cannot obviously afford to either—till the corporation has gone into liquidation. Normally, in accounting for income and deductions, the tax systems have always used a twelve-month calendar or fiscal year, and the Indian tax system is no exception to this practice. A twelve-month stretch does not at our bidding separate itself from the past and the future and permit autonomous scrutiny. Yet from such a narrow concentration of attention a conclusion is sought to be forced even though the conclusion is still in the process—will for many more years perhaps be in the process—of concluding. The whole confusion arises because the introduction of such a mechanical calculation at regular intervals makes it necessary for the accountant to remove parts of income and to match them with those parts of expenditure which are supposedly related to the inflow of income.

According to the Indian Income-tax Act, the total assessable income is calculated by deducting certain expenses from the assessee's receipts during the twelve-month period. These permissible deductions are set forth in detail in Section 10 of the Income-tax Act. Before 1918, there were no provisions in the Income-tax Act as to the method of computing business income, as this was governed mainly by rules and executive instructions. The provisions introduced in 1918 underwent considerable revision in 1939, and these

[40] *The Taxation of Corporate Income*, p. 22.   [41] Ibid., p. 22.

revised provisions, with but minor modifications, are still in force.

HEADS OF INCOME

The Act specifies various heads of income, and actually separate provisions exist for deductions and allowances for computing income under these several heads. Income can arise from

(a) interest on securities,
(b) income from property,
(c) income from sources other than (a), (b), (d) and (e),
(d) profits from business, and
(e) capital gains.

In the above list, profits from business occupy the central place in the taxation of corporations. As far as (a) above is concerned, while computing taxable income, any reasonable sum spent for realising the interest on securities could be deducted.

Income from property includes receipts by the owner from the users of any buildings or lands appurtenant to a building. Taxable income under this head is calculated after deducting from the bona fide annual rental the following:

1. one-sixth of the annual rental, for repairs;
2. the annual premium for insurance against damage;
3. interest on mortgages;
4. ground rent;
5. interest on borrowed capital invested; and
6. collection charges up to 6 per cent of the annual rental.

There is also an allowance for the period during which the house or property remains vacant.

Income from other sources, which include income from dividends, is computed after making allowances for any amount spent on earning the income, as opposed to capital expenditure.

While the Indian Income-tax Act does not define 'profits', it says however that certain deductions are permissible in the computation of income. The tacit assumption made by the Act is that profits will somehow be calculated. Generally, the gross profit depends upon the method of accounting regarding receipts, exclusion of receipts on fixed capital accounts, inventory, etc. But Section 13 of the Act specifies that "income, profits and gains shall be computed, for the purposes of Sections 10 and 12, in accordance with the method of accounting regularly employed by the assessee". While computing the gross income, capital receipts are distinguished from current receipts. There can, of course, be no single test to decide which is a capital receipt and which is income. However, certain broad tests have been evolved and laid down by the courts. In general, these various tests consider receipts to be capital in nature if they arise out of mere substitution or conversion of fixed capital assets, or arise from the replacement of a source of income by sale, exchange or transfer.

PERMISSIBLE DEDUCTIONS

Trading losses and capital losses are automatically deducted from the gross income. These are distinct from the allowed expenses. More caution is necessary in allowing expenses than in allowing trading losses because 'expense' implies a certain amount of willingness, whereas 'loss' comes from circumstances perhaps beyond control. Indian Income-tax law allows deductions in respect of rent and repairs for business premises, interest on capital borrowed, premium for insurance against risk of damage or destruction, current repairs for building, plant, machinery and furniture, land revenue, local rates or municipal taxes, reasonable amounts paid as bonus or commission to employees, bad and doubtful debts written off, and expenses on scientific research. This is by no means an exhaustive list. It is safe to assume that, all things considered, the Indian Income-tax law is very lenient in the matter of allowing expenses, and this will be brought home even more forcibly when we look at the list of items *not* admissible as deductions—for among these we find such perfectly obvious items as income-tax, supertax and surcharge; taxes and cesses levied by local authorities on the basis of profits and gains of business; salaries and interest payable outside India, if taxes are not deducted therefrom; and funds set apart for reserves against future contingencies like bad debts; etc., etc.[42] While calculating the taxable income, the above per-

---

[42] This list is not complete by any means, for it gives only the major items. There are 'minor' items which are also 'non deductible', flowing from judicial pronouncements or executive instructions.

missible expenses are first to be deducted; in other words, the items of current expenditure as distinct from the items of capital expenditure or depreciation allowances are to be deducted from the gross receipts, and thus the 'operating' gain or loss is to be ascertained. While the relevant Section of the Act lists most of the items that could be deducted as current expenses, judicial and administrative interpretations also determine certain other possible deductions. The question whether the Section is exhaustive or not does not arise because of the steam-roller clause (S 10, 2, xv), according to which "any expenditure (not being an allowance of the nature described in any of the clauses i to xiv inclusive, and not being in the nature of capital expenditure or personal expenses of the assessee) laid out or expended wholly and exclusively for the purpose of such business" is allowed as current expense. Actually, this wide and comprehensive clause sees to it that no current outlay is really left out. Even though the Section was originally intended to strengthen the hands of the authorities for disallowing spurious or superfluous deductions, it has now, in the words of Nicholas Kaldor, "actually come to serve the opposite purpose of ensuring that no type of expenditure which comes within the scope of this definition should fail to qualify."[43]

DEPRECIATION ALLOWANCES

Thus far about 'current' expenses. How, then, about the wearing out of the fixed capital? Everything wears out and dies in course of time: and provision should be made for this inevitable 'decline and fall' of fixed capital, which is alas! far from fixed. There are many provisions for depreciation allowances and obsolescence allowances in the Indian Income-tax Act.[44] As we saw in the first chapter, depreciation allowances are given for "the insidious and irreparable decay" of the machinery and other fixed assets, while obsolescence allowances are given against the machinery getting out of date, necessitating renewal for the very existence of the factory or unit of production on a modern competitive basis.

After the 1939 Amending Act, depreciation is being allowed on the basis of the written-down-value of an asset or group of

[43] *Indian Tax Reform*, p. 63 fn.
[44] "Liberal amount": such is the claim of the Central Board of Revenue in their *Income-tax for the Layman*, p. 28.

assets. The depreciation is calculated by taking the percentage rate of depreciation allowed for the asset against the original cost, deducting the appreciation allowed in the previous years. This method is advantageous because this accelerates the total depreciation allowable into the early years, as against the 'straight line' method, which allows depreciation at a uniform rate. Recommending this method, the 1936 Income-tax Enquiry Committee said: "The written-down-value basis automatically secures that the aggregate allowance can never exceed 100%. Moreover, the necessary calculations are simpler and more easily followed with a corresponding saving of time."[45] Of course, it is not always that the written-down-value is the better base for calculation; there are assets where the straight-line method is preferable; and hence the Indian Income-tax Act has some exceptions to the written-down-value method of computation (for example, ships plying in inland waters).

Normal and additional depreciation is allowed at percentage rates statutorily given in Rule 8. These rates are calculated after giving due consideration to the useful life of the asset, and these rates are classified under three categories, viz. (1) Plant and machinery; (2) buildings; and (3) furniture. The rates vary from 2.5 per cent to 40 per cent; the most common rates for items of industrial machinery vary from 9 per cent to 12 per cent. Rates have been fixed for single items as well as groups like the entire plant, etc.

Apart from the usual depreciation allowed on buildings, plant, and machinery, additional depreciation equal to the normal rate is allowed for the first five years. Thus, during the initial five years, the effective depreciation is double the normal rates. Some industries work on a shift system, and naturally machinery used by such establishments wear out quickly. Hence extra depreciation to the extent of 50 per cent of the normal rate is allowed to such corporations. Initial depreciation allowance is also given to new buildings, and new plant and machinery.

If, however, an asset is sold, demolished or discarded, the difference between its written-down-value and scrap value is allowed as a deduction from the income. On the other hand, if the sale proceeds are more than the written-down-value, the excess over the written-down-value is included in the taxable profits. There

[45] *Report*, p. 37.

is also the provision of a further allowance for safeguarding against a fall in the prices of the machinery used in the factory.

Even though all these depreciation allowances are cumulative, the sum-total is not allowed to exceed the original cost of the asset. Another salient feature of the Indian Income-tax law is that, even if there is not sufficient income in a year to absorb the depreciation charges (normal and additional, etc.), the deficiency can be carried forward indefinitely and set off against the profits of the subsequent years. Whether the company makes profits or not, the 'wear and tear' goes on remorselessly, and it is but proper that there should be this arrangement for the cumulative accounting of depreciation allowances over a period of years, should it become necessary. Under the Indian Income-tax law there is no fear of the depreciation allowances lapsing, as no time limit exists for this 'carry forward'.

DEVELOPMENT REBATE

In addition to such liberal depreciation allowances, a 'development rebate' also is provided by the Finance Act of 1955. This is really an allowance of 25 per cent of the cost of new machinery installed to replace battered old machinery with a view to augmenting the quality or raising the quantity of production. Such new machinery for which this development rebate is claimed must really be for the purposes of the business carried on by the company. In other words, the development rebate is intended, not for buildings, furniture, etc., but for new plant and machinery. Buying old plant and machinery at second-hand prices would not qualify for the development rebate: it is for new, which implies modernised, up-to-date plant and machinery, which alone could be expected to give a fillip to the business, that the development rebate is intended. We saw earlier that the total depreciation allowances could not go beyond 100 per cent of the cost of the asset. The development rebate is in addition to this: it is really a sort of bonus or special allowance over and above the normal recoupment of the cost of plant and machinery through depreciation allowances.[46] The advantage of this system is that the company can, not only get back through depreciation allowances the cost of the production unit, but also an extra 25 per cent of the cost of the new machi-

[46] See pamphlet on *The Taxation of Corporate Income in India* issued by the Central Board of Revenue, 1958.

nery secured to replace the old. There are also provisions for carrying forward that portion of the development rebate which cannot be fully set off against net operating income for the year in which the development rebate is allowed. The basic purpose in allowing the development rebate is, after all, to promote reinvestment in industry for effecting improvement and expansion, and hence the provisions in respect of the grant of this rebate are reasonably liberal. But anticipating misuse of these provisions, the Finance Act of 1958 has specified that certain conditions like the following must be fulfilled to qualify for the grant of the development rebate :

(i) An amount equal to $\frac{3}{4}$ of the development rebate must be debited to the profit and loss account of the relevant year and credited to a reserve account ;
(ii) This amount must be utilised by the company within ten years for the acquisition of assets for the purposes of the company or for investment in the company ; and
(iii) The asset on which the development rebate is allowable must not be sold or otherwise transferred by the company within ten years from the end of the year in which the new asset was first put to use.

If the above three conditions are not fulfilled, the development rebate will be disallowed for tax computation purposes. It is always a struggle between use and misuse, a two-pronged attack to extend help where help is really needed and withhold help where such help is misused, that is, used for other than the purpose intended. In the result, a simple provision tends to be more and more cluttered with qualifications, exceptions and penal clauses, thereby contributing yet further to the baffling complexity of the law and administration of Income-tax in India.

DEPOSITS

Another safety valve introduced in 1958 to prevent misuse and the frittering away—through doubtful speculation, etc.—of depreciation allowances and rebates is the provision for deposits. According to this scheme, companies have to deposit with the Central Government a prescribed amount calculated according to its undistributed profits and reserves. The deposits will carry interest at rates prescribed by the Government. The amount will, however, be refunded as and when the company requires funds for 'approved purposes', which mean legitimate capital expenditure. The penalty for not making the statutory deposit with the Government would be the cancellation of the permissible depreciation allowance or development rebate. This is yet another example of the Government trying to play the guardian to the corporations and keeping them 'straight' in spite of themselves. Ingenuity is met by greater ingenuity, and in the result some sort of balance in the health of the corporate sector is sought to be maintained.

CAPITAL GAINS AND LOSSES

Profits or gains of a capital nature arising from the sale, exchange, relinquishment or transfer of a capital asset are taxable under the head 'capital gains'; the evolution and the present state of the taxation of capital gains are discussed on a later page. When a loss, rather than a gain, is incurred under any of the five heads of income mentioned earlier (viz. interest on *securities*, income from *property*, profits from *business*, gains from *capital*, and income from *other sources*), the company is given the right to set it off against the income under any other head in the same year. This does not apply to loss under *capital*, for capital losses can be set off only against capital gains, not gains under any other head. In the case of a *business* loss (though not other losses) which is not absorbed in the first year, it can be carried forward indefinitely against future business income. This is subject to one condition, that is the business to which the original loss related should not in the meantime have changed hands or identity, or ceased to exist. Losses could be carried forward for only six years in the original Act. After 1954-55, the Government, accepting the recommendations of the Taxation Enquiry Commission,[47] extended the period indefinitely. But once again, in the Finance Act of 1957, the 'indefinite' period has been reduced to just eight years. Another instance of the legislative see-saw moving forth and back to meet the challenges and exigencies of changing times !

TAX HOLIDAY

It may not be out of place here to refer to the income-tax and

[47] *Report*, Vol. II, p. 70.

supertax holiday given to new industrial undertakings, and the exemption from corporation tax on dividends received from certain types of industrial undertakings. Since 1948, profits of new industrial companies are exempt from the payment of income-tax and supertax up to 6 per cent of the invested capital. It was, however, specified that such undertakings must not be those only notionally new, being formed by splitting up or reconstruction of any business already in existence. Dividends declared by a truly new industrial company out of its profits (these being exempt from tax according to the tax holiday concession) are also to be exempt from income-tax and supertax at the hands of the shareholders. Such relief is given even to non-residents who invest in the shares of newly established manufacturing undertakings.

With a view to encouraging intercorporate investments in certain basic industries it has been provided that dividends received by any of the Indian companies engaged in the manufacture and production of coal, iron and steel, petroleum, heavy chemicals, structural and electrical machinery, non-ferrous metals, paper, internal combustion engines, power pumps, automobiles, tractors, cement, electric motors, locomotives, rolling stock, machine tools, agricultural implements, ferro-manganese and dyestuffs, formed or registered after 31 March 1952, will be exempt from corporate tax. This applies also to fresh capital raised by public subscription by an Indian company after 31 March 1953, for increasing production or starting a new unit.

Other Taxes

Besides income-tax and supertax, which we have described so far, there are also other taxes that call for some scrutiny. These varied taxes have affected in the past or are still affecting, one way or the other, the finances of the companies in India. During the two decades since 1939, the following taxes have been levied on the companies for differing periods as indicated :

The Excess Profits Tax :	1940-46 ;
The Business Profits Tax :	1947-50 ;
The Wealth Tax :	1957-59 ; and
The Capital Gains Tax :	1947-48, and reintroduced in 1956.

THE EXCESS PROFITS TAX

The first tax on 'excess profits' was levied in India, surprisingly enough, in 1919, after a major war had just concluded. The tax was levied on abnormal profits made by certain businesses as a consequence of the First World War. Its belated imposition certainly reflected an almost Pickwickian financial policy, and it is not surprising that the tax was withdrawn the very next year after its first introduction.

The tax was again introduced during the Second World War, and came into operation in September 1940; and, after being in force for the duration of the war, it ceased to apply to profits made after 31 December 1946. Even though the tax was thus a short-lived one, it had its own quota of annual amendments and usual modifications. As we saw in the first chapter, the excess profits tax is a means of extracting money from those who make enormous profits in war time, taking easy advantage of the abnormal conditions prevailing then. The Government also wanted to soak the "rich-because-of-the-war", as is evidenced by the references to what is euphemistically termed as the principle of "priority taxation" made by the then Finance Minister, Sir Jeremy Raisman, in his Budget speech as well as his speech in the Legislative Assembly on 6 February 1940. "Priority taxation" means that the burden of the additional defence measures should be borne, in the first instance, by those who during the war find themselves in a better economic condition than previously. As originally introduced, the excess profits tax was levied at the rate of 50 per cent on any excess profits earned by any trade, commerce, manufacture or vocation (except where the profession or vocation depended wholly or mainly on personal qualifications) over "standard profits" earned in the pre-war years. "Standard profits" was thus loosely equated with the profits earned in 'normal' times. However, a workable method was devised that could be applied without much difficulty or hardship to businesses which were started either before 1936 or after 1936. The method combined elasticity and ready utility, and proved acceptable on the whole to the parties concerned.

METHOD OF COMPUTATION

As regards companies started before 1936, five options were

available to them to choose from for settling their 'standard periods':

1. Profits during 1935-36 ;
2. Profits during 1936-37 ;
3. The average of the profits during 1935-36 and 1936-37 ;
4. The average of the profits during 1936-37 and 1937-38 ; and
5. The average of the profits during 1937-38 and 1938-39.

Further, it was stipulated that none of the above could be less than 9 months for consideration as the 'standard period'.

With regard to the businesses started after 1936, the 'capital standard' was adopted. During the debates in the Legislative Assembly, a member unsuccessfully tried to extend the 'capital standard' to the old firms also, but the Finance Member vetoed it on both equity and administrative grounds. In the case of new companies, a statutory percentage of 8 per cent of the capital invested in the case of companies and 10 per cent in the case of individuals was considered the standard rate of profits. The Excess Profits Tax was levied only on excess profits over and above Rs. 36,000 per year. This was to offset the deleterious effects on partnerships, and also to reduce administrative problems.

COMPULSORY SAVING

The 50 per cent rate was, in effect, maintained only for one year. The rate was increased to 66⅔ per cent in the second year of the currency of the Excess Profits Tax, and this rate remained in force till the withdrawal of the tax in 1946. In 1941, the 'standard profits' for new industries was fixed at 12 per cent of the employed capital. In March 1942, the Government introduced a novel scheme, inspired by J. M. Keynes's proposal for deferred payments : "The first provision in our radical Plan is, therefore, to determine a proportion of each man's earnings which must be deferred ;— withdrawn, that is to say, from immediate consumption and only made available as a right to consume after the war is over".[48] The same point has also been made by another writer, Frank G. Moult : "The prime object of the Government in introducing this scheme for a post-war credit was to alleviate the bad effects of the 100

[48] *Readings in Fiscal Policy* (Ed. by American Economic Association), p. 180.

per cent rate and to placate the businessmen somewhat with the assurance of a little jam tomorrow even though the pill must be swallowed in all its bitterness today".[49] The essence of the scheme in India, known as the scheme of compulsory deposits, was as follows :

1. The Excess Profits Tax rate would be $66\frac{2}{3}$ per cent ;
2. In addition, the assessee would deposit one-fifth of the amount of the tax with the Government ; the percentage thus leaving the hands of the assessee would be $66\frac{2}{3}$ per cent *plus* $13\frac{1}{3}$ per cent equal to 80 per cent ; this deposit of one-fifth was raised to $\frac{19}{64}$ (i.e. almost one-third) in the 1944 Finance Act, leaving practically nothing of the excess profits in the hands of the assessee ;
3. The Government would repay the deposit a year after the end of the War, and the deposit would further carry interest at 2 per cent ;
4. The Government would also, at its convenience, return to such of those assessees as had participated in the scheme of compulsory deposits, one-tenth of the excess profits tax paid already : in other words, the net tax rate would be reduced from $66\frac{2}{3}$ per cent to 60 per cent ; and
5. The amount so repaid and returned would be deemed as taxable income.

This scheme of compulsory saving was intended to curtail civil consumption during the war and increase civilian demand in the immediate post-war years when the War demand would naturally diminish. This scheme also enabled the industries to build up reserves, and served as an incentive to increased production and economical management in war time. As M. H. Gopal has pointed out, "The Government very clearly exploited the businessman's plea of the need for reserves and attempted to prevent evasion by wasteful expenditure ... the compulsory deposit was, in fact, a compulsory reserve available to the depositor after the war .... This was a very clever scheme which, if completely successful, could achieve many objects."[50] All financial policy flows, in the

[49] *The Economic Consequences of the Excess Profits Tax*, p. 68.
[50] *The Theory of Excess Profits Taxation*, pp. 305-6.

ultimate analysis, from the high plateaus of common-sense, and has often to negotiate the difficult passage between the opposing rocks of necessity and equity; to vary the metaphor, the tax-gatherer has to collect as best as he can as many golden eggs as he can without killing the goose itself that lays the eggs. If the Excess Profits Tax was an aggressive way of collecting the eggs, the Deposits Scheme made some attempt also to sustain and feed the goose both for present and for future advantage.

THE END OF THE TAX

Hardly had the War come to a close at long last than the Excess Profits Tax also was abolished. In his now famous "farewell" Budget of 1946, Sir Archibald Rowlands said: "The only justification for the Excess Profits Tax as a tax is the emergency which called it into being. By all the canons of taxation doctrine it is a thoroughly bad tax. It is rough and ready in its operation; it is unfair in its incidence and beyond a certain point, it is a direct inducement to inefficiency. Except that I, as tax gatherer-in-chief, cannot refrain from casting a longing, lingering look behind it at its high yield, none of us will, I think, mourn the passing of the Excess Profits Tax." The business community was naturally very enthusiastic over the outright abolition of the tax, but otherwise the prevailing view was rather that, although the war had ended, conditions were far from normal, and the tax might as well have continued a little longer. Inflationary pressures had been accentuated by the scarcity of goods, and there was witnessed both increased money supply and the release of the pent-up demand for consumer goods. It was accordingly still possible for manufacturers to capitalise the situation and try to make excessive anti-social profits. Many therefore viewed the abolition of the Excess Profits Tax as being hasty and premature. There was the further plea that funds were needed for the urgent tasks of reconstruction. As M. R. Masani said in the course of the Budget debate in the Legislative Assembly on 22 March 1946: "The relief in direct taxation and the complete abolition of the Excess Profits Tax was not justified. I am arguing on the basis of a smaller reduction of direct taxation which would have left the Honourable the Finance Member of the Government with larger funds. I am suggesting that a part of these could have been given to certain positive purposes." People who thought along these lines should have derived great comfort from the now 'notorious' Budget for the next year, presented by Liaquat Ali Khan; but that went too far in the opposite direction, and was to face even greater criticism.

THE BUSINESS PROFITS TAX

In the Budget for 1947-48, the newly partnered Congress-League Provisional Government introduced a Business Profits Tax, which was on the face of it somewhat of a variant of the now defunct Excess Profits Tax. This new tax was imposed on profits as from the 1st of April 1946 (that is to say, immediately following the termination of the earlier tax); and like the earlier tax, this tax too was closely modelled on similar legislation in the United Kingdom.

The Business Profits Tax was really like a special income-tax levied at the rate of $16\tfrac{2}{3}$ per cent on business profits exceeding Rs. one lakh. Business included any trade, commerce, or manufacture, or any profession or vocation, the profits of which are chargeable according to Section 10 of the Income-tax Act. Apart from the flat figure of Rs. one lakh as abatement, the Business Profits Tax fixed different criteria of abatement for different classes of assessees. For example, in the case of a company "not being a company deemed for the purposes of Section 9 to be a firm", the abatement was 6 per cent of the 'capital' of the company on the first day of the said period, or Rs. one lakh whichever was greater. Here 'capital' meant paid-up capital and reserves in so far as they were not allowed in computing profits under the Income-tax Act. Thus only a part of the invested capital was taken into account, whereas in the earlier tax assessment, the arrangement was far more equitable. The procedure in the new tax was simpler but less equitable than in the older tax, which was both more complicated and more reasonable. The Business Profits Tax was also much more broad-based than the earlier Excess Profits Tax, and the Finance Member, Liaquat Ali Khan, even claimed besides (though not with much justification) that it was much fairer in its incidence as well.

It is necessary to point out that, appearances notwithstanding, the Business Profits Tax was no mere repetition of the war-time Excess Profits Tax, although the similarities between the two are obvious enough. The new tax was on profits generally, on prosperity *per se*, whereas the earlier tax was on the "excess arising out of present (abnormal) conditions", in other words on the portent of abnormal prosperity. The aim of the Excess Profits Tax was to collect money for promoting the war-effort, whereas the ostensible aim of the Business Profits Tax was to correct the inequalities in the distribution of wealth. The Excess Profits Tax was clearly war-effort oriented, the Business Profits Tax was professedly general-welfare oriented. The Finance Member himself claimed, replying to the debate on 1 April 1947 in the Legislative Assembly, that the Business Profits Tax was an easy tax to assess and an easy tax to collect and that it would not fall heavily on the industry.

In the very next year (1948-49), the rate of the Business Profits Tax was reduced from $16\frac{2}{3}$ per cent to 10 per cent, and the abatement allowed was also raised from Rs. 1 lakh to Rs. 2 lakhs or 6 per cent of the capital, whichever was higher. Thus the rigours of the tax were softened a good deal. Finally, in the 1950 Budget, the tax itself was abolished. Rightly or wrongly an odium had attached itself to the tax from the very beginning, and hence hardly anybody regretted its complete withdrawal.

THE TAX ON CAPITAL GAINS

Apart from the Business Profits Tax, another tax too was the creation of the Liaquat Ali Khan Budget. This was the tax on capital gains, which has since had an interesting history. We have seen that, before 1947, income tax was levied on revenue gains, as opposed to capital gains. In 1947, following the practice in the United States, Liaquat Ali Khan included capital gains in the total income for computing the income-tax. This new tax was payable on profits arising out of the sale, exchange or transfer of any capital asset. Capital asset was defined as property (but excluding agricultural land) held by an assessee, whether or not connected with his business, profession or vocation. Stock-in-trade and personal effects were not included in the capital assets. Further, capital gains were taxed only if they exceeded Rs. 15,000, and no supertax was levied on the capital gains. Again, the tax was not payable in respect of any profits arising out of the sale, exchange or transfer of a capital asset (property) the income of which was chargeable under Section 9 and which had been possessed by the assessee or his parent for not less than 7 years before the date on which the sale, exchange or transfer took place. Here a peculiar problem was presented: Could a joint-stock company have a 'parent'? R. K. Dalal writes, however, offering a plausible affirmative answer to the question: "To summarise, the corporation is an assessee. If the assessee is an individual, he can also take the benefit of the words 'or a parent of his'. Cannot the corporation take the benefit of these words and contend that it is entitled to tack on the previous possession of his predecessor? There is nothing in the Section to preclude the corporation itself from being an assessee."[51] Since metaphorically we talk of a "parent institution", by analogy there should be nothing wrong in talking of a "parent corporation" as well!

If, instead of capital gains, only a loss was sustained under this head, this loss could not be set off, except against any profits and gains falling under this head; besides, such losses could be carried forward for six years.

ABOLITION OF THE TAX

This Capital Gains Tax too was abolished in the 1949-50 Budget presented by John Matthai, who said by way of explanation and justification: "At the time this tax was introduced, it was expected to yield a large revenue, but it synchronised with a period of falling values and the yield from this tax has in consequence been small. Its psychological effect on investment has, however, been markedly adverse, and it has had the effect of hampering the free movement of stocks and shares, without which it is hardly possible to maintain a high level of industrial development. In the present circumstances, I consider the retention of the tax ill-advised." This sealed the fate of the tax for the time being, and for some years to come. The Taxation Enquiry Commission also did not favour the introduction of the tax, and declared emphatically: "The reasons then given for the abolition of the capital gains tax still hold good today."[52] Even though the Taxation Enquiry Commission thus rejected the claims of this tax for a place in the fiscal system, Nicholas Kaldor who came to India about two years later to study

[51] *Business Profits Tax and Capital Gains Tax*, p. 131.
[52] *Report*, Vol. I, p. 164.

the tax system here and suggested reforms, recommended the introduction of a capital gains tax.[53]

RE-INTRODUCTION IN 1956

Taking his cue from the distinguished Cambridge economist, the new Finance Minister, T. T. Krishnamachari, revived in 1956 the taxation of capital gains. While piloting this Bill, he felt that the justification for such a tax was the expectation of capital appreciation in a phase of rapid development of the economy in which the public, as represented in the Government, must have a good share. Introducing the Bill in Parliament on 30 November 1956, he said: "For a developing economy like ours, it is necessary to take early action, as the implementation of our programme is certain to create conditions in which assets of all kinds will appreciate. It is only fair that the Exchequer should get a proportion of these incomes when realised in the form of capital gains." It is an interesting commentary on the whirligig of politico-economic taste that what was poison when proposed by Liaquat Ali Khan became medicine, or even tonic, when proposed by T. T. Krishnamachari only a few years later. Besides, of course, Nicholas Kaldor had come to the Finance Minister's help—verily, a Daniel come to judgment! The tax gatherer-in-chief needed money to meet the growing needs of Defence and to sustain the planning effort of the nation, and all was grist that came to the mill. Necessity, not equity, was the prime justification for the imposition of the new taxes, including this revival of the tax on capital gains. Now as before, the tax is imposed on *realised* capital gains only, and the capital gains are computed after deducting from the sale price the actual cost of the asset to the seller and any expenditure incurred in connection with the sale or any other operation giving rise to the capital gains.[54]

It is clearly provided that both individuals and companies are liable to pay the tax on capital gains. The exemptions (namely, agricultural lands and personal effects) are the same in both cases; and also exempt from the purview of the tax are any gains arising

[53] *Indian Tax Reform*, p. 92.
[54] Choice of two methods is provided for the calculation of capital gains: (i) the excess of the sale price over the original cost price; and (ii) the excess of the sale price over the estimated market value.

from the transfer of a capital asset by a parent company to its wholly owned subsidiary, the subsidiary of course being resident in India and registered in India under the Indian Companies Act. No exemption limit is available for companies regarding capital gains taxation; in the case of other assessees, however, no tax is payable if the amount of capital gains is less than Rs. 5,000 or if the capital gains *plus* the other taxable income is less than Rs. 10,000. Companies have to pay only income-tax on the capital gains, and unlike the previous tax which allowed losses to be carried forward for six years, this tax allows the losses to be carried forward generously for as many as eight years. Assessees other than companies can carry forward the losses only to the limit of Rs. 5,000, but no such limit is prescribed for the companies.

This tax, though it owes its present lease of life to Kaldor's inspiration and authority, is not quite the same tax as the one that he proposed in the larger context of Indian tax reform. The tax as it now stands exempts capital gains which are passed on through gratuitous transfers, although Kaldor would have liked these to be taxed as well. This is an important point because it is now possible to postpone the payment of the Capital Gains Tax indefinitely. Besides, Kaldor suggested a much higher than the present tax rate. But, then, it would not be proper to isolate one item alone from Kaldor's proposals and institute any rewarding comparison with a parallel item in the prevalent tax system.

THE WEALTH TAX

Another novel tax measure suggested by Kaldor in his Report to the Government of India on Tax Reform was the wealth tax. This tax also was introduced, along with the tax on capital gains, by T. T. Krishnamachari in the 1957-58 Budget. Kaldor, while suggesting a direct wealth tax on individuals, wanted the corporate property to be taxed only through its shareholding. But the wealth tax, as implemented, taxed corporate property both directly as well as through the shareholdings, thus involving double taxation. Gulati, of course, dismissed this objection glibly: "But this sort of differentiation is not more indefensible than the differentiation which exists at present in charging companies to a non-refundable tax (corporation tax) on their profits".[55] But it is

[55] *Capital Taxation in a Developing Economy (India)*, p. 199.

surely a matter to be considered whether the currency of one doubtful differentiation by itself justifies a repetition of the possible wrong, or whether merely because double taxation has been (rightly or wrongly) in force for a long time there is equal validity for what may almost be called quadruple taxation.

The wealth tax, so long as it was alive, was an annual tax on joint-stock companies (whether public or private, Indian or foreign) as separate units. Generally speaking, in the case of an Indian or a resident corporation, all its wealth, whether held within or without India, was chargeable to this tax. In the case of a foreign company not resident in India, only the Indian wealth was liable to be taxed. The wealth tax as liable to companies was levied at the rate of $\frac{1}{2}$ per cent on net wealth over and above Rs. 5 lakhs. The net wealth of companies was calculated by deducting the aggregate value of debts from the aggregate value of all assets belonging to the company. Normally, balance-sheet values were adopted; it was an annual tax, and was computed on the net wealth as on the last day of the accounting period of the assessee. In the matter of granting exemptions, the tax was reasonably liberal:

1. New industrial undertakings were exempted for the first five years;
2. Inter-corporate investments were exempted from the tax;
3. Companies which had incurred net losses and which had not declared any dividend on their equity capital were also likewise exempted;
4. Banking, insurance, and shipping companies were also exempted, as also were Government institutions for the promotion of art and culture;
5. The wealth tax holiday was given, not only to new companies, but also to new industrial units of existing companies; and
6. If the profits made by a company in any year were less than the wealth tax due for the relevant assessment year and it had not declared any dividend, the tax payable would be limited to the amount of profits.

While introducing the tax in the Indian Parliament, the Finance Minister merely said that the peculiar economic structure of India necessitated the inclusion of companies within the purview of the wealth tax. He did not—perhaps he found himself unable to—elaborate the point. Did he mean by his reference to the "peculiar economic structure of India" that there was a tendency on the part of the wealthy to evade taxes by means of the formation of private limited companies and that the wealth tax would be a necessary corrective to it ? On the whole, his speech seemed to lack conviction, and at times he fell back on the Maginot Line of a mere financial defence of the tax. Not since the Liaquat Ali Khan Budget has any new bunch of taxes provoked as much opposition as T. T. Krishnamachari's in the 1957-58 Budget. The new measures of taxation, including the wealth tax, were assailed from the Right as well as from the Left. The Rightists thought that the wealth tax was unduly harsh, while the Leftists thought that it was half-hearted and not harsh enough. The Communist Member, Nagi Reddi, said in Parliament that the wealth tax and expenditure tax were ornaments that only glittered: "scrape them", he said, "and you will find that they are not gold".[56] But G. D. Somani said : "I am afraid that so far as internal finances available to the companies . . . this tax will encroach on them very severely";[57] and M. R. Masani said even more emphatically : "The policy of applying this Bill to limited companies is a policy of grab . . . this seems to be the only justification".[58] Outside the Parliament, too, there was little support. It was one thing to get the measure through the Parliament with the overwhelming strength of the ruling Party, but it was a very different thing to carry the real consent of the people. The National Council of Applied Economic Research recorded the finding : "There have been strong reactions from both Indian and foreign companies to the imposition of the tax".[59] Meantime an unsavoury and unexpected jerk in the political kaleidoscope led to the resignation of T. T. Krishnamachari as Finance Minister. His successor, Morarji Desai, wisely withdrew the tax in the 1959-60 Budget, and the exit of this tax was accomplished with remarkably little fuss.

THE GIFT TAX

Under the gift tax (yet another of the taxes tracing their paren-

[56] 26 August 1957. [57] 26 August 1957. [58] 28 August 1957.
[59] *Taxation and Foreign Investment*, p. 89.

tage to Kaldor and Krishnamachari), which came into force from April 1958, private companies and closely controlled public companies have to pay a tax on the value of the gifts paid by them. The rates of the tax vary from 4 per cent on the first slab of Rs. 50,000 of taxable gifts to 40 per cent on gifts totalling over Rs. 50 lakhs. Normally it is the giver who is taxed ; but if the tax cannot be recovered from the giver, then the 'taker' will be taxed. A modern Portia might well have remarked :

> The taxation of gifts is not to be restrained :
> It touches him that gives, and failing there,
> It touches him that takes with equal ease.

The gift tax is, in a way, the logical outcome of the new taxes on capital gains and wealth. If the validity of the other taxes should be accepted, then this too would be defensible, for certainly it may be expected to facilitate the prevention of the avoidance of estate duty, income-tax, wealth tax, expenditure tax, etc. It may even be argued, in defence of the gift tax, that in levying it the Government had in mind, not so much the netting in of much revenue, but rather the minimisation of the evasion of the other taxes.

Conclusion

The above rapid survey is an attempt to present a conspectus of all the taxes that at one time or another have been—or are being— paid by the companies during the past two decades and more. It must be abundantly clear even from this summary that it is only in the post-freedom period that revolutionary tax-changes have come about. The desire to check evasion is always there, no doubt ; but the real, the overwhelming reason behind the fiscal revolution is the Government's insatiable desire for more and more funds for developing the economy, and for meeting the ever-expanding civil and military expenditure. The socio-economic policies that flow partly from the objectives of the Constitution and partly from the economic and political predilections of the ruling Party (the Congress) have brought about a certain tempo of national expenditure, and funds on an ever-growing scale are needed to meet it. The Finance Minister in Free India, and especially Planning India, is not a free agent; no Finance Minister wholly is. He is obliged willy-nilly to put his hands into as many pockets as possible and hand over the money so diligently and adroitly gathered by him to the spending Departments of the Government. India has been served well, on the whole, by a succession of able Finance Members and Finance Ministers. But they have had a difficult, an almost impossible, task to discharge. The problem really has always been the necessity to tax a relatively backward economy to find the funds to run a comparatively modern (which means, in effect, an expensive) administration. It is easy to cavil and carp, and it is easy to be wise after the event. But taking a total view of it all, it must be conceded that the British Finance Members and our own Finance Ministers have on the whole made the best of what has always been a bad job.

A VICIOUS CIRCLE

India is a large country—it is verily what is often called 'a sub-continent'. There is a Central Government and there are several Provincial or State Governments. The tax system in such a country cannot hope to achieve the neat clarity and simplicity of a small country with a unitary Constitution. It is an incontrovertible fact that Indian taxes are heavily cumbersome to administer. Avoidance and legal evasion on the one hand and checks and more rigorous checks on the other create a vicious spiral of increasing cumbersomeness and complexity. First a loophole is found, and it is carefully plugged; the remedy starts a new disease, with new complications; and this chain reaction goes on. A noted industrialist is said to have remarked: "A few intelligent men in New Delhi impose the taxes; they forget that there are many more and far more intelligent men outside to find loopholes in the taxes"! It is thus an unending struggle between the Government on the one hand and the very clever evaders of taxes on the other, and the marks of the struggle are visible clearly on our complex, cumbersome and almost baffling tax system.[60]

---

[60] In fact, this leads to increasing complexity in the business organisation also. As R. K. Hazari says, intercorporate investment and similar complex intra-business arrangements have arisen in India due to high rates of taxation. "Ownership of Capital", *Economic Weekly*, Dec. 10, 1960, p. 1801.

The Five Year Plans have introduced fresh problems for the tax system, for the Plans having been decided upon, they have to be financed somehow. New taxes have had to be hurriedly brought into existence and administered with the help of a Service that is proving increasingly unequal to these heavy additional responsibilities. New taxes mean new legislation, and, under present circumstances, hasty legislation. The Income-tax Act has had to be amended with alarming frequency. Either these amending Bills are introduced and enacted in a hurry, or the Annual Finance Acts are made to do duty for effecting amendments to the provisions in the Income-tax Act. In fact the Direct Taxes Administration Enquiry Committee, headed by Mahavir Tyagi, complained that "changes were being effected in the tax laws rather too frequently ... if such frequent changes were not effected in the tax laws, it would add to the efficiency of the administration... frequent changes in the statutes should be avoided."[61] An eminent authority has roundly declared that this habit of amending the Income-tax Act by having recourse to the Finance Act is "a very unhealthy development".[62] Another authority likewise points out that "many important measures do not even go to a Select Committee. The present tendency to introduce important amendments in income-tax and other existing laws by means of the Finance Bill, which never goes to a Select Committee, is deeply to be deplored."[63] All too often the Government is only too ready to take the line of least resistance, relying with too much complacency on the steam-roller majority in the Parliament. This is very far from being a satisfactory or healthy state of affairs.

EVILS OF HASTY LEGISLATION

Such hasty legislation in the matter of tax laws suffers from three main drawbacks :

(i) loose and bad drafting ;
(ii) ill-conceived provisions ; and
(iii) too much technicality.

[61] *Report*, pp. 2-3.
[62] A. C. Sampath Iyengar, *The Indian Income-tax Act*, p. 4.
[63] N. A. Palkhiwala in "Crushing Burden of Taxation" (*The Hindu Survey of Indian Industry*, 22 November 1958).

Thus the whole income-tax structure has now become a veritable tangled web of all sorts of clauses and provisions and qualifications and exceptions. It is fatally easy for the unwary law-abiding citizens to trip and fall into the quagmire of legal subtleties and severe penalties. It is not surprising that Kaldor, after a careful study of our tax system (or want of system) with regard to the corporations, found it a "perfect maze of unnecessary complications, the accretion of years of futile endeavour to reconcile fundamentally contradictory objectives".[64] And he found a very important Section of the Indian Income-tax Act dealing with companies "a peculiarly badly drafted piece of legislation".[65] The vicious circle goes on, and the tax expert and the tax consultant run a permanent race, each trying to outwit the other.

Apart from the legal aspect of correct and efficient drafting and clean and expeditious administration, there is the economic aspect of the right and proper use of the tool of taxation for achieving the right social ends. The vacillation of policies in the past has to a great extent been responsible for the complexity and confusion of the legislation and administration of taxes relating to companies. Tax systems must ultimately be judged by the following basic criteria: adequacy, equity, administrative efficiency, and economic and social effects. It will be our task in the next chapter to examine the evolution and structure of corporate taxation in India in the light of these canons of taxation, and also evaluate the effects of corporate taxation on the various sectors of the economy.

---

[64] *Indian Tax Reform*, p. 85.
[65] Ibid., p. 87.

CHAPTER IV

EFFECTS OF CORPORATE TAXATION

Expenditure rises to meet income ... the public revenue is regarded as limitless and expenditure rises eternally to meet it.

C. Northcote Parkinson

Introduction

IN the second chapter we saw that the corporate sector showed signs of rapid growth only after the late thirties, and we saw in the third chapter that the taxation of companies underwent a thorough overhaul in 1939. This applies also to the economy as a whole. It has been often said, and with no small justification, that it was only after the second world war that Indian economy began to change from a predominantly agricultural to an increasingly industrial one. Before the second world war there was doubtless some partial industrialisation, mainly the production of semi-manufactures. As P. S. Lokanathan says, "Progress was far from adequate and was mainly confined to consumers' goods industries. Even these could not expand owing to the lack of purchasing power on the part of the large agricultural population; thus industrialisation was in the danger of coming to a halt unless rooted in the prosperity of the rural population".[1] But the war came and gave an impetus to the growth of industries, and the industrial sector consequently played its part magnificently.[2] The present writer has had occasion to say elsewhere that "whatever its attendant evils—and they are numberless—War is a hustler, and under its pressure much hectic activity is usually witnessed, especially in the industrial sphere. In times of war, many an industry is started to feed the ravenous war machine, and when the war is over, such industries are turned to the tasks of a peace-

---

[1] *Industrialisation*, pp. 8-9.
[2] See *Fiscal Commission Report* 1949-50, p. 20 *et seq*, and also A. C. Sampath Iyengar, *Role of Private Enterprise in India*, p. 5.

time economy."[3] To a certain extent this is what happened in India during the second world war and the years immediately following.

Changing Structure of the Tax System in India

PRE-WAR PREPONDERANCE OF INDIRECT OVER DIRECT TAXES

With a major war to be fought, the Government had necessarily to face the problem of wartime financing. While the traditional sources of revenue in India were mainly customs and land revenue, the Indian financial system betrayed all the characteristics of a regressive tax system imposed on a backward economy. The chief feature, of course, was the preponderance of indirect taxes over direct taxes—progressive direct taxes playing but a very minor role in the fiscal system. The only direct tax of any importance was the income-tax, but the receipts from this tax represented no more than a comparatively small percentage of the total public revenue of India. Land revenue, though a direct tax, still exhibits

TABLE I

PERCENTAGE REVENUE OF SOME IMPORTANT HEADS

(*Percentage of Total Receipts of Union and Provincial Governments*)

Year	Customs	Taxes on Income	Salt	Land Revenue	Excise	Stamps	Railways
1921-22	18.5	11.9	3.4	18.7	9.2	5.8	8.2
1922-23	20.9	9.2	3.4	17.9	6.8	6.0	13.6
1923-24	18.7	8.7	4.7	16.4	9.1	6.0	15.4
1924-25	20.9	7.4	3.3	16.3	8.9	6.0	15.6
1925-26	21.6	7.3	3.3	16.1	9.0	6.1	15.6
1926-27	21.7	7.3	3.0	15.9	9.0	6.0	15.1
1927-28	21.8	7.0	3.0	16.8	8.9	6.1	17.5
1928-29	22.3	7.7	3.4	15.0	9.0	6.2	17.1
1929-30	22.5	7.5	2.9	14.2	8.3	6.1	16.8
1930-31	22.5	7.8	3.2	14.5	8.0	3.0	18.8
1931-32	22.6	8.5	4.2	16.1	7.2	5.8	16.4
1932-33	23.7	8.5	4.8	14.7	7.0	6.1	15.9
1933-34	23.3	8.4	4.4	14.8	7.4	6.0	16.3
1934-35	24.1	8.4	3.6	14.7	6.8	5.5	14.8
1935-36	25.7	8.1	4.0	15.3	7.2	5.6	15.2

[3] *A Grammar of Indian Planning*, p. 49.

most of the inequitable characteristics of an indirect tax because it affects the landholders equally, irrespective of their income, and thus tends to be regressive in its ultimate incidence. Even if we included land revenue as a direct tax, the Indian financial system before the War would be found to be mainly dependent upon indirect taxes, as TABLE [14] will show.

The table clearly shows that the two direct taxes (income-tax and land revenue) were together able to muster only about 25 per cent of the total receipts. During the period between 1921 and 1936, we see that actually the proportion has been reduced to a certain extent. In 1921-22, the two taxes together contributed 30.6 per cent of the total revenues, whereas in 1935-36 their share was only 23.4 per cent. In the above table the receipts of the Central as well as the Provincial Governments have been taken into account. If the Central finances alone are taken into consideration, then the percentage share of taxes on income would be much higher as may be seen in TABLE II.[5]

TABLE II

TAXES ON INCOME AS PERCENTAGE SHARE OF UNION REVENUES

Year	Taxes on Income as percentage of Union Revenues
1921-22	28.9
1922-23	24.9
1923-24	24.5
1924-25	21.3
1925-26	20.5
1926-27	20.6
1927-28	19.7
1928-29	21.1
1929-30	20.9
1930-31	21.5
1931-32	22.8
1932-33	21.6
1933-34	22.4
1934-35	21.7
1935-36	20.7

[4] Source : Z. A. Ahmed, *Public Revenue and Expenditure in India*, p. 14.
[5] Ibid.

Even so, the percentage share only ranges roughly between 20 and 30 per cent, whereas it ranges between 7 and 12 per cent when the Central and Provincial finances are together taken into account.

Excise duties are levied on manufactured goods locally made whereas customs duties are taxes levied on imported or exported goods. We see that the percentages of receipts from excise taxes are low compared to the high yield from customs. This shows, firstly, that considerable manufactured goods were imported, and secondly, that the production of manufactured goods was low in India.

WARTIME SHIFT TO INCREASING DIRECT TAXATION

Out of sheer necessity, the Government felt the need to get out of this rut during the war and rely more and more on direct taxation. Such a shift in emphasis was also facilitated by the other structural changes that were fast taking place in the economy. The growth of the corporate sector consequent on large-scale industrialisation and the increase in the personal incomes, coupled with the drastic abridgement of imports and a corresponding increase in national production, brought about considerable changes in the Indian financial system. The main result was an increase in the percentage of direct taxes to the total income. TABLE III[6] gives the growth of the gross total tax revenue and the growth of taxes on income (including the corporation tax).

We can now see clearly the gradual growth, firstly of the total revenue, which has increased seven-fold in the course of two decades; secondly, of the taxes on income, which have increased over twenty times; and thirdly, of the percentage share of taxes on income, which again increased from 22.5 per cent in 1937-38 to 62.7 per cent in 1943-44, and has since declined to 32.4 per cent in 1958-59. The vicissitudes within the 22-year period notwithstanding, there has been a total increase in the gross revenue as well as revenue from the taxes on income, and a total rise in the percentage share of the latter in the former.

An interesting conclusion that emerges from the figures is that while, after the War, the percentage of the taxes on income to the total revenue fell (from the wartime maximum of 62.7 per cent

[6] Sources: *Statistical Abstract of India* (Relevant years) and *Annual Reports on Currency and Finance* issued by the Reserve Bank of India.

TABLE III

THE GROWTH OF CENTRAL TAX REVENUE

Year (1)	Gross Total tax Revenue (2)	Taxes on Income (3)	(3) as % of (2) (4)	Customs (5)	Excise (6)
1937-38	82.41	18.58	22.5	43.11	7.66
1938-39	81.87	20.23	24.7	40.51	8.66
1939-40	90.27	21.80	24.1	45.88	6.52
1940-41	86.77	27.72	31.9	37.30	9.49
1941-42	112.11	46.66	41.6	37.89	13.15
1942-43	151.66	92.60	61.0	25.12	12.79
1943-44	229.23	143.72	62.7	26.57	24.94
1944-45	357.90	210.72	58.9	39.76	38.14
1945-46	387.27	201.15	51.9	73.61	46.37
1946-47	344.85	192.22	55.7	89.22	43.03
1947-48	332.19	152.61	45.9	127.47	24.38
1948-49	385.18	203.10	53.0	126.50	50.63
1949-50	389.01	190.73	49.0	124.71	67.85
1950-51	444.91	211.98	47.6	157.15	67.54
1951-52	505.07	187.60	37.1	231.69	85.78
1952-53	442.01	185.23	41.9	173.75	83.03
1953-54	418.07	164.38	40.0	158.71	94.98
1954-55	452.67	159.59	35.3	184.87	108.22
1955-56	480.35	168.40	35.0	166.70	145.25
1956-57	566.58	202.92	35.8	173.23	190.43
1957-58	673.44	219.83	32.7	179.99	273.62
1958-59	698.27	226.34	32.4	170.00	301.93

in 1943-44 to 35 per cent in 1955-56), the actual yield from these taxes did not register any steep fall. The record percentage of 62.7 in 1943-44 was the result of a yield of only Rs. 143.72 crores, whereas the much smaller percentage of 32.4 in 1958-59 was the result of a yield of Rs. 226.34 crores. The reason for this decline in the comparative importance of the direct taxes must be mainly attributed to the phenomenal growth of the yield of Central excise duties. While the yield from customs and the taxes on income shows but moderate growth, the yield of Central excise shows a rapid and steep rise as may be observed from the table given above.

WARTIME SHIFT FROM CUSTOMS TO EXCISE DUTIES

Before the War, customs was the main source of revenue for the Central Government. The yield of customs was 52 per cent of the total revenue in 1937-38, and 54.8 per cent in 1938-39. With the beginning of the War, large-scale imports became impossible. This drastic reduction in imports gave an impetus to the Indian producers to increase their efforts. This double action shifted the importance from customs duties to Central excise as TABLE IV clearly indicates.

TABLE IV

Year	Percentage Share of Customs in the Total Revenue	Percentage Share of Central Excise in the Total Revenue
1939-40	56.9	8.1
1940-41	48.4	12.3
1941-42	38.7	13.4
1942-43	20.9	10.2
1943-44	15.5	14.5
1944-45	15.7	15.0

Another reason for the growth of excise duties was the increased number of items hit. Before the War, excise duties were levied by the Central Government only on sugar, matches, kerosene, motor spirits and steel ingots. But every year during the War, new items were added, while there was a simultaneous increase also in the rates of the duties on the items already taxed.

POST-WAR DEVELOPMENTS

The point should not thus be overlooked that a decline in the rate of increase of revenue from the direct taxes is also due sometimes to regressive indirect taxes. After the War came to an end, the yields of both customs and excise have risen considerably, thus relegating the yield of direct taxes once more to a secondary place. The forces behind this development may be indicated as follows:

1. Increased domestic production of both articles already being manufactured and of the products of the newly established industries has resulted in a greatly increased yield of Central excise duties. TABLE V gives the index numbers of industrial production from 1939, which clearly shows a steady upward trend in industrial production.

TABLE V

INDICES OF INDUSTRIAL PRODUCTION[7] (1939 = 100)

Year	Index
1939-40	110.3
1940-41	114.2
1941-42	123.2
1942-43	125.5
1943-44	126.8
1944-45	121.7
1945-46	120.0
1946-47	105.0
1947-48	105.9
1948-49	115.9
1949-50	109.5
1950-51	104.5
1951-52	115.4
1952-53	121.4
1953-54	121.8
1954-55	151.9
1955-56	163.0
1956-57	170.2

2. The increased imports of capital goods for the development and reconstruction of Indian industry have also swelled the income from customs. For instance, TABLE VI gives the amounts spent

[7] Source: Records and Statistics of *Eastern Economist*, July 1957.

on machinery and on iron and steel imported into India from 1949 to 1954, compared to the imports of the same categories of goods in 1938-39 and 1946-47 :

TABLE VI

Year	Imports of Machinery & of Iron and Steel (in crores of rupees)
1938-39	25.63
1946-47	34.48
1949-50	121.33
1950-51	108.06
1951-52	122.90
1952-53	108.87
1953-54	107.37

The increase in these imports naturally gave a boost to the yield of import duties also. The increase in the customs revenue in the early fifties must also be ascribed in no small measure to the 'liberalisation of imports policy' unwisely followed by the then Union Minister for Commerce and Industry, T. T. Krishnamachari.

3. A certain amount of incentive taxation and certain tax concessions for the industrial class resulted in the reduction of possible yields from direct taxation. We shall look into this aspect more in detail later in the course of the chapter.

Pattern of Corporate Taxation in India

INCOME AND CORPORATE TAXES

In spite of the abolition of certain taxes like the Excess Profits Tax for encouraging capital formation and even in spite of the surgical partition of the country in 1947 with its attendant sudden diminution of revenue, the revenue from income and corporation taxes has remained more or less constant. The revenue from the income and corporation taxes has not shown any major variations during the last fifteen years, and has ranged only between Rs. 143.72 crores in 1943-44 to Rs. 226.34 in 1958-59. On the other hand, the relative part played by the corporation tax began to assume on the whole a greater importance in the early years as may be inferred from TABLE VII.[8]

TABLE VII

THE RELATIVE IMPORTANCE OF THE CORPORATION TAX

Year (1)	Taxes on Income Including the Corporation Tax (in crores of rupees) (2)	Corporation Tax inclusive of E.P.T. & B.P.T. (in crores of rupees) (3)	Index of Corporation Tax Yield (Base=1939) (4)	(3) as per cent of (2) (5)
1937-38	18.58	2.14	79.3	11
1938-39	20.23	2.50	92.6	13
1939-40	21.80	2.70	100	14
1940-41	27.72	4.28	158.5	15
1941-42	46.66	11.95	442.6	26
1942-43	92.60	33.98	1259.3	37
1943-44	143.72	58.23	2156.7	40
1944-45	210.72	93.68	3469.6	45
1945-46	201.15	95.18	3525.1	47
1946-47	192.22	77.21	2859.6	40
1947-48	152.61	46.37	1717.4	30
1948-49	203.10	62.26	2306.0	31
1949-50	190.73	39.53	1464.0	21
1950-51	211.98	40.49	1499.6	19
1951-52	187.60	41.41	1533.7	22
1952-53	185.23	43.80	1622.2	25
1953-54	164.38	41.54	1538.5	26
1954-55	159.59	37.33	1382.6	23
1955-56	168.40	37.04	1371.9	22
1956-57	202.92	51.18	1895.6	25
1957-58	219.83	56.13	2078.9	25
1958-59	226.34	54.33	2012.2	24

[8] Source: For 1937-48, *Statistical Abstract*; for 1948-59, Annual Budgets.

The yield from the corporation taxes has thus increased considerably during the last twenty years. From a mere Rs. 2.14 crores, it reached the peak of Rs. 95.18 crores in 1945-46, and the yield in recent years has ranged between Rs. 50-60 crores. The index, again, rose from the base of 100 in 1939-40 to 3525.1 in 1945-46 and, after a more or less steady decline during the next decade or so, has touched 2078.9 and 2012.2 in 1957-58 and 1958-59 respectively. Although the actual yield has thus increased phenomenally, the part played by the corporation tax in the total scheme of taxes on income has somewhat diminished in importance after 1947. In 1937-38, the yield of the corporation tax was 11 per cent of the total yield of the taxes on income; in 1945-46, it was 47 per cent; but, in recent years, the share of the corporation taxes is seen to be oscillating between 22 and 25 per cent of the total taxes on income.

In the above paragraph we took into consideration only the taxes paid by the companies in the form of the corporation tax. But the companies also pay the income-tax in addition to the corporation tax. It would be possible to gauge the extent of the corporate contribution to the treasury if we examined their joint contribution to the treasury as shown in TABLE VIII.[9]

TABLE VIII gives the annual receipts from companies in the form of taxes to the Central Government. The figures in the table, being taken from the annual combined Revenue Accounts of the Central and State Governments and representing as they do the actual amounts received, will not tally with the earlier figures taken from the Budgetary Memoranda. According to the table, the contribution made by the companies to the national exchequer has increased more than fourteen times since 1939-40. From Rs. 8.44 crores in 1939-40, it has grown to Rs. 122.34 crores in 1958-59. We saw earlier that the contribution from the corporation tax alone has grown by nearly twenty times by 1958-59. For purposes of comparison, the smaller combined index is better than the higher index relating to the corporation tax alone, because in the base year (1939-40) the corporation tax structure had not grown sufficiently and hence the collection was very poor, so much so a certain

[9] Source: *Combined Finance and Revenue Accounts of Central and State Government of India from* 1937-38 *to* 1958-59. (Taxes include Excess Profits Tax and Business Profits Tax.)

TABLE VIII

CORPORATE CONTRIBUTION TO THE TREASURY
(in crores of rupees)

Year (1)	Income-tax Paid by Companies (2)	Total Income-tax Revenue (3)	(2) as per cent of (3) (4)	Corporation Tax (5)	Total Tax Paid by Companies (6)	Index of Column (6) (Base = 1939-40) (7)
1937-38	4.44	14.89	22	1.88	6.32	75
1938-39	5.65	16.38	35	2.04	7.69	92
1939-40	6.06	16.49	46	2.38	8.44	100
1940-41	6.54	18.50	35	4.14	10.68	127
1941-42	8.64	22.27	39	11.66	20.30	242
1942-43	13.00	31.26	42	31.40	44.40	529
1943-44	13.83	38.19	36	51.28	65.11	775
1944-45	17.75	47.38	38	83.65	101.40	1207
1945-46	14.76	45.26	33	84.06	98.82	1176
1946-47	26.91	76.44	35	59.22	86.13	1025
1947-48	26.82	59.92	45	32.18	59.00	702
1948-49	32.79	96.76	34	62.08	94.87	1177
1949-50	33.82	93.29	36	37.16	70.98	845
1950-51	40.66	98.79	41	39.33	79.99	952
1951-52	37.63	100.20	38	40.75	78.38	933
1952-53	50.38	110.82	45	42.98	93.36	1111
1953-54	45.13	102.27	44	40.19	85.32	1016
1954-55	36.04	115.62	31	36.45	72.49	859
1955-56	37.93	122.56	31	36.52	74.45	882
1956-57	43.46	151.19	29	50.40	93.86	1112
1957-58	48.92	164.61	30	55.66	104.58	1239
1958-59	68.82	172.78	40	53.52	122.34	1447

inflation in value became possible. But income-tax on the companies was a settled affair even in 1939-40, and hence there is not much scope in that regard for exaggeration in the index. The percentage share of companies in the income-tax revenue has remained more or less stationary after an initial increase from 22 per cent in 1937-38 to 46 per cent in 1939-40. In absolute terms, it has increased from Rs. 6.06 crores in 1939-40 to Rs. 68.82 crores in 1958-59. Apart from the fact that rates were being increased gradually, this phenomenal increase in the yield of corporate taxation only reflects the growth of the corporate sector itself.

THE PRINCIPLE OF 'GROSSING'

Objections could be raised against considering the income-tax paid by the companies as ultimate contributions to the treasury. This is because of the principle of 'grossing' which remained in force till the 1959-60 Budget. According to this principle, the income-tax paid by the companies was refundable to shareholders in some measure and under certain conditions described already in the third chapter. It may be argued that, after all, the shareholders constitute the company, and if the income-tax taken from the company is paid back partly or wholly to the shareholders, it doesn't to that extent involve any net burden on the company or, ultimately, on the shareholders. But this argument will prove to be more apparent than real if the whole system of 'grossing' is properly examined.

Now, according to this principle, when the companies declare dividends out of their taxed profits, the shareholders receive credit in their personal income-tax assessments for the income-tax paid by the companies. Here the point to be carefully noted is that this advantage applies only to the amount actually distributed, for the undistributed profits will still have to bear the whole burden of the income-tax. In the second chapter we saw, after taking into account the C.B.R. statistics and the Reserve Bank of India survey of the Indian company finances, that Indian companies plough back nearly 50 per cent of their profits. Hence we can conclude without more ado that at least 50 per cent of the income-tax paid by the companies did not go back—did not have even a chance of going back whether partly or wholly—to the shareholders.

Even where the profits were distributed, it was not possible for shareholders to get back either as refund or as credit the whole of the income-tax paid by the company. The following illustration will make this point clear :

Let us suppose that a company earns a taxable income of Rs. 100. According to the income-tax and supertax rates prevailing in, say, 1958-59, Rs. 51.50 (Rs. 31.50 as income-tax and Rs. 20 as supertax) will go to the treasury, thus leaving Rs. 48.50 for dividend distribution or ploughing-back. Even if the whole of this amount is distributed, the grossed up dividend will come to only Rs. 70.80, according to the formula which we have already examined in the previous chapter. Thus the Government anyhow retains Rs. 29.50, 'grossing' or no 'grossing'. Hence the maximum that the shareholders can expect to get back works out to be slightly over 70 per cent of the income-tax paid by the company (i.e. Rs. 22 out of Rs. 31.50). If we can assume further that only Rs. 25 (out of the available Rs. 48.50) is actually distributed—and this is the approximate proportion under Indian conditions—only Rs. 11.50 (i.e. 36.50 per cent) is got back from the amount paid by the company as income-tax. In the 1959-60 Budget, the 'grossing' system was abolished, which was at once a sensible and bold step. Although the 'grossing' system was supposed to have solved the vexed problem of double taxation, it created more difficulties than it solved. The process being a little cumbersome, it is not unreasonable to assume that many people did not claim rebates at all and so failed to benefit by the provision of 'grossing'. Furthermore, the rates were kept unconscionably high since the bait of 'grossing' was also dangled before the taxpayer, which was rather a deceptive situation as above explained. It is gratifying, therefore, that 'grossing' has been given up for good.[10]

Another point too : after all, the modern joint-stock company *is* in some unique way distinct from the individual shareholders. In fact, as we saw in the previous chapter, Indian judicial opinion itself favours this view. In modern times, the division of the functions of management and ownership in the corporate form of enterprise is almost complete, though not as yet in India. Actually, the shareholders of big corporations are now-a-days no better than bond-holders. Hence, whether they receive any monies back from the tax-gatherer or not under the system of 'grossing', it is all the same to the corporation itself. As far as the corporation is concerned, it will worry only over the taxes that are to be paid by

---

[10] Out of the Rs. 68.82 crores of Income-tax paid by Companies, the shareholders received only Rs. 13.90 crores by way of refund either in cash or set off against their tax liability in 1958-59 (information given by Mr. A. K. Roy, Secretary of the Finance Ministry). *Economic Weekly*, March 7, 1959.

it,—the taxes being just an item of costs. Taking note of all these factors, we shall not be very wrong if we treat the income-tax paid by the corporations on a par with the corporation tax, at any rate for our analytical purposes.

GROWTH OF THE CORPORATE SECTOR

TABLE IX indicates the growth both in the number of assessees and in the total taxes paid by the companies. It is clear that both are showing an unmistakable upward trend. It is, however, necessary to see whether the growth of these is commensurate with the growth of the corporate sector itself and the growth in the net profits of the corporate sector.

From 11,372 in 1940, the number of companies working in India increased to 27,479 in 1959, which means a net increase of 16,107 companies. The number of assessees who pay corporate taxes has increased only by 6,308. In 1959, out of 27,479 companies in existence, only 10,777 paid taxes. Thus, nearly two thirds of the companies operating do not pay any tax. This may mean either that these companies are sustaining losses, or that their profits are being eaten up by depreciation allowances, development rebates, etc., or that they are enjoying a tax holiday, or again, simply, that they are somehow accomplishing 'plain evasion'. Profits and taxes, after registering a rapid rise till 1946, are both showing a slow, if also erratic, upward movement. Whereas the taxes paid by the companies have increased by nearly fourteen times, the net profits during the same period have increased only by about six times. In short, the companies paying taxes have increased by about $2\frac{1}{2}$ times, profits by 6 times, and taxes by 14 times. There is thus ample justification for the contention that, as matters stand, too few companies bear too heavy a tax burden.

CORPORATE PROFITS

Profits, especially in the Indian context, depend mainly upon the demand for goods, and profits have naturally been growing because of the phenomenal demand during the years 1940-46. After 1946 we find that the profits are more or less steady, and in 1950-51 the profits are seen to have actually fallen, while in the next year they have gone up again. This could be mainly attributed to the situation with regard to the external demand. In

TABLE IX
GROWTH OF THE CORPORATE SECTOR

Year	Growth of corporate Sector (number of companies)	Number of Assessees	Net Profits	Percentage Increase or Decrease over Previous Year	Taxes Paid (Inclusive of E.P.T. & B.P.T.)	Percentage Increase or Decrease over Previous Year
(1)	(2)	(3)	(4)	(5)	(6)	(7)
1939-40	11,372		37.03	—1	8.44	+10
1940-41	11,638	4,469	47.39	+28	10.68	+27
1941-42	12,049	5,467	56.48	+18	20.30	+90
1942-43	12,770	5,606	97.68	+73	44.40	+119
1943-44	13,689	5,962	134.50	+38	65.11	+47
1944-45	14,859	6,397	168.76	+25	101.40	+94
1945-46	17,343	6,754	169.44	+.4	98.82	—3
1946-47	21,853	6,561	148.38	—12	86.13	—13
1947-48	22,675	6,257	157.92	+6	59.00	—31
1948-49	25,340	7,500	169.47	+7	94.87	+61
1949-50	27,558	7,349	185.60	+10	70.98	—25
1950-51	28,532	8,519	145.92	—21	79.99	+13
1951-52	29,223	10,761	199.99	+37	78.38	—2
1952-53	29,312	9,700	201.40	+1	93.36	+19
1953-54	29,528	9,933	219.96	+9	85.32	—9
1954-55	29,625	9,455	197.54	—10	72.49	—18
1955-56	29,874	10,261	188.14	—5	74.85	+3
1956-57	29,357	10,780	235.94	+25	93.86	+26
1957-58	28,280	10,989	219.70	—7	104.58	+11
1958-59	27,479	10,777	265.93	+21	122.34	+17

1949-50, the various war-ravaged countries recovered from the war-effects and were much more effectively competing with India.

But the Korean War, which started in June 1950, gave a stimulus to Indian exports, and this enabled the profits to rise by 37 per cent in 1951-52 over the figure for 1950-51.

The growth of the tax yield, however, is dependent not only upon the profits but also on the tax policy of the Government. In the war-years, the tax yield had increased more than the profits. For example, in 1941-42, profits increased over the previous year's by 18 per cent, but the tax yield rose by 90 per cent. In the following years up to 1945, this was roughly the position: on the one hand, profits were increasing, which naturally brought in more revenue through taxes; and, on the other hand, the tax rates also were rising at a pretty rapid rate. How an increase in profits and tax rates jointly influences the tax yield could be shown in the post-war years also. Even though profits remained steady after the war, the tax yield began to fall, mainly because of the 'easy' post-war Budgets. But, again, the yields increased in 1948-49, because of the higher taxation measures proposed in the 1947-48 Budget. Subsequent less 'troublesome' Budgets have again reduced the yield. The rise in the tax yield in 1957 was mainly due to the increased tax measures proposed in 1956. As for the reverse side of the effects of the tax yield on company profits, it obviously depends upon the 'coincidence of taxes and profits', and we shall discuss this problem at a later stage.

HIGHER TAX RATES IN THE POST-WAR PERIOD

We have seen above that the tax yield has increased at a faster rate than the increase of profits in the corporate sector. The main reason for this is naturally the higher tax rates enforced after the commencement of the second world war. The following table gives the percentage of profits that a public company had to pay as income-tax and corporation tax in effective rates at various levels of income. It is assumed that the dividends distributed during the relevant taxable years came to less than 6 per cent of the paid-up capital. Taxes like the Excess Profits Tax and Business Profits Tax are omitted from the purview of this table because they were, after all, of a temporary nature and, besides, they affected only a segment of the profits.

We find from TABLE X how the rates (that is, rates of income-tax and corporation tax affecting the corporations) have more than doubled during the past twenty years : from 22.0 per cent to 46.5 or 51.5 per cent.

TABLE X

PERCENTAGE OF CORPORATE TAXES ON CORPORATE PROFITS

Year	For Companies with Profits up to Rs. 25,000	For Companies with Profits over Rs. 25,000
1939-40	22.0	22.0
1940-41	23.2	23.2
1941-42	27.1	27.1
1942-43	32.8	32.8
1943-44	38.5	38.5
1944-45	46.9	46.9
1945-46	48.4	48.4
1946-47	37.5	37.5
1947-48	43.8	43.8
1948-49	28.1	43.8
1949-50	37.5	43.8
1950-51	34.4	40.6
1951-52	37.2	43.4
1952-53	37.2	43.4
1953-54	37.2	43.4
1954-55	37.2	43.4
1955-56	37.2	43.4
1956-57	37.2	43.4
1957-58	46.5	51.5

If we include the Excess Profits Tax to the rates prevailing in 1940-45 and also the Business Profits Tax to the rates prevailing in 1947 to 1950, then the percentage tax liability of the corporations in relation to their profits would be as shown in TABLE XI[11].

TABLE XI

CORPORATE TAX LIABILITY OF CERTAIN INCOME GROUPS
(*Expressed in terms of percentage*)

Year	Income in Rupees						
	25,000	50,000	100,000	200,000	300,000	500,000	1,000,000
1940-41	24.0	34.1	47.9	54.8	57.1	58.9	60.3
1941-42	29.2	42.4	59.4	67.5	70.7	73.0	74.7
1942-43	32.8	45.3	61.1	69.5	72.2	74.4	76.0
1943-44	38.5	50.0	64.7	72.1	74.6	76.5	78.0
1944-45	46.9	56.8	69.6	75.9	78.1	79.8	81.0
1945-46	48.4	58.0	70.4	76.6	78.7	80.3	81.6
1947-48	43.8	43.8	43.8	48.5	50.1	51.3	52.3
1948-49	43.8	43.8	43.8	43.8	45.7	47.2	48.3
1949-50	37.5	43.8	43.8	43.8	45.7	47.2	48.3

The peak years are understandably enough, 1944-45 and 1945-46, the percentage tax liability rising in the highest income-brackets to 80 and over.

It has been pointed out by David Walker that "company taxes bring in large sums of money comparatively painlessly. They are difficult to avoid or evade, and as they do not obviously or directly reduce the standard of living of voters, politicians are under a great temptation to increase them."[12] Gerhard Colm also feels that corporation taxes are almost "ideal from the point of view of the politician. There is no other tax which brings in so much money while making so few voters mad".[13] Company taxes do not *directly* take anything from people as income-tax does (for it immediately reduces the disposable income), or as indirect taxes like

---

[11] Source: 'Income-tax Rates Compared' (1955), issued by the Association of Indian Trade and Industry.
[12] 'Some Economic Aspects of the Taxation of Companies', (*Manchester School*, January 1954, p. 34.)
[13] 'The Corporation and the Corporation Income Tax', (*A.E.R.*, May 1954, p. 494.)

sales tax or excise duties do (for they immediately increase the prices of commodities). On the other hand, the popular sentiment against the so-called 'money-making rich' is satisfied in some measure by any tax imposition on the companies.

Effects of Corporate Taxation in India

Any tax which hits a particular section of the economy and reduces the available means is bound to have certain repercussions. The tax might or might not be shifted, but either way some effects must ensue because the existing allocation of resources has been upset by the tax to a greater or a lesser extent. Thus it may be taken as axiomatic that the many discriminatory aspects of corporation taxes must make them other than neutral in their effects.[14]

As we saw in the first chapter, the *effects* of corporate taxation —the *effects* of almost any taxation measure, in fact—can be ambiguous and uncertain in the extreme. It is not possible to relate with utter certainty and precision causes and consequences in the economic sphere. The cause-effect relationship, although we know that nothing happens but has its originating cause or causes, cannot be clearly stated in every instance, and this applies particularly to corporate taxation and its effects. The problem acquires a further complexity in war-time, post-war and independent India, because Indian economy during this period has been in the throes of economic growth, and it is not possible to assess the effects of taxation in an expanding economy because of the frequent shifts in the very "underlying economic conditions".[15] Even if certain broad trends could be ascertained, *accurate* statistical demonstrations must be practically impossible.

Nevertheless, it must be still worth while to study the effects of corporate taxation in India because, as we saw in the second chapter, the corporate sector, though confessedly small as yet, occupies an increasingly important place in the economy of the country. Only a careful study of the effects of corporate taxation

---

[14] See Harold M. Somers, *Public Finance and National Income*, pp. 231-2. What Somers says about the discriminatory nature of American Corporate Taxation is applicable to the Indian counterpart also.

[15] See J. K. Butters, 'Taxation, Incentives and Financial Capacity', *A.E.R.*, May 1954 p. 507.

in India can provide the necessary clues to help us to devise ways and means of improving the corporate tax structure and making it serve best the national economy. Taxation as a tool in the hands of the State can be useful only if it achieves what it is intended to achieve, what it is proper for it to achieve ; and to know whether it has performed the needed functions, a study of the effects of taxation in the past and the present becomes very necessary, however fraught with difficulties such a study may be.

PSYCHOLOGICAL EFFECTS

It is a truism to say that taxes have both psychological and physical effects. The psychological effects are those which affect the "intentions, motivations, and behaviour of business managers, capitalists, workers and consumers".[16] These effects are different from the purely economic or physical effects of tax changes on the flow of funds and on demand and costs. In the ultimate analysis, perhaps, there is not much difference between the two species of effects, but in the short run certain changes in the tax structure, without actually changing either the flow of funds or cost or demand, can nevertheless cause irritation or jubilation, which are the psychological effects, in varying degrees. In the long run, irritation or jubilation will lead to changes in the economic behaviour also. Feeling is father to the thought which, in its turn, issues in action. In other words, some taxes are apt to "burden the mind of the business more than lighten its purse".

Psychological effects may have, after all, no rational foundation, but may rather be based on fear, suspicion, false scare or blind prejudice. Richard Goode rightly says that such subjective reactions of corporate officials and shareholders are "based on all degrees of ignorance and information, of rationality and irrationality. They are conditioned by the prevailing state of optimism or pessimism, by international tensions, and perhaps by political pique or gratification".[17] In spite of such irrationality, psychological effects (or shifts in mental attitude) are very important, for as M. H. Gopal truly says, "the psychological factor *may* induce people to shy away from risky enterprise, or distort the direction

---

[16] Gerhard Colm, 'The Corporation and the Corporate Income Tax', op. cit., p. 492 fn.
[17] *The Corporation Income Tax*, p. 139.

of investment, or keep executives from shifting to more productive jobs or reduce personal effort going into production".[18]

Granting, then, that the psychological factor *is* important, how are we going to evaluate it ? From the very nature of the problem, it is obvious that statistical or quantitative measurement of these 'shifts in mental attitude' is impossible. Consequently we are forced to limit our scrutiny to the various pronouncements by people in the know (or in a favoured position to judge) or to rely on certain general indicators. For example, there are broad statements like the one which the *Hindu* made in the course of a leading article : "The psychological consequences of the new tax pattern (the post-1955 tax pattern is here referred to) have been more damaging perhaps than even its actual incidence".[19] A similar statement was made by G. N. Noel-Todd, Chairman of the Madras Chamber of Commerce, at the Chamber's annual meeting in 1958 : "In short, I would say that practically every taxation measure recently introduced has had the effect of restricting or altogether removing the incentive of profit-making, both from the corporation and the individual". Such statements revealing representative psychological reactions to particular taxation measures could easily be multiplied.

TREND OF SECURITY PRICES

However, to judge even if only in a very general manner the impact of fresh taxation on the minds of the investors, recourse must be had to an examination of the trend of security prices. The value of the share generally reflects the financial position of the company, though this is only a broad long-run tendency.[20] It is sometimes seen that the valuation of companies lags a good deal behind the increase in their earning power. For example, in 1942-43, when the War was still in an unpredictable stage, people could not form a correct view of the intrinsic worth of many of the companies operating in India. As the *Investor's Year Book* remarked in its Preface, "it is not untrue to say that the share prices have not, taking an average of the year's differing levels, reflected fully the

[18] 'Towards a Realistic Tax Policy for India', *Indian Economic Journal*, January 1959, p. 294.
[19] Issue dated 13 March 1958.
[20] See Kaldor, *An Expenditure Tax*, p. 143.

increased dividend-earning capacity in most branches of industry ... the share prices are, on the whole, rather below, and in some cases well below, the intrinsic value of the scrips concerned".[21] But at any specified time the market value of any particular share depends more on the current dividend paid rather than on the intrinsic worth of the company. Corporate taxation is *prima facie* more likely to be shifted to the shareholders (at any rate, in the short run), with the result that security prices *are* affected. Normally, once the new tax proposals are announced, there will be witnessed the Pigovian 'announcement effects' which, in the context of stock exchange operations, may thus succinctly be described in the words of George Barrell: "Operators learn of the new imposition, and before any balanced judgement can be formed about its long-term effects, speculators have rushed in, investors have taken fright, and the prices of shares affected have fallen sharply".[22] Some time later, and after the play of balanced judgement about the new tax proposals, "when the speculative covering has finished, and every bargain-hunting investor has been satisfied, the price of the share gradually falls back to the level at which its yield and future prospects, not of the new tax, dovetail in with the general pattern of the market".[23] If there were no psychological effects on risk-taking and enterprise, due either to taxation or to any governmental measure, the share price will be exactly like the old one with minor adjustments flowing from the discounted value of the tax change.

Now, what we have said above would be all right if the tax changes were few and far between. But if there are numerous tax measures embodying frequent changes in tax-coverage and rates-structure, the capital market must inevitably be in a chronic state of uncertainty and suspicion—a condition that by itself must sharply affect the prices of securities. We could take for our study the index of the average prices of some representative securities compiled by the Reserve Bank of India, and it would be an interesting, and even a rewarding, task to study the indices in relation to the tax measures from time to time.

---

[21] Twenty-ninth Edition, p. xxxi.
[22] 'Stock Exchange and Taxation Policy', in *The Stock Exchange: A Symposium*, edited by A. K. Sur, p. 51.
[23] Ibid., p. 51.

TABLE XII

INDICES OF VARIABLE DIVIDEND SECURITIES

Year & Month	Index of Securities Base: 1927-28	Tax Changes & Other Remarks
1939		
January	105.4	
February	103.6	
March	100.8	
April	97.6	The Income-tax Amendment Bill passed; Slab system introduced; exemption limit of Rs. 50,000 for the corporation tax abolished.
May	100.8	
June	106.4	
July	100.0	
August	98.5	
September	111.4	
October	111.9	
November	124.7	
December	130.7	
1940		
January	120.9	
February	121.6	
March	122.1	
April	123.0	E.P.T., 50% of the 'excess profits' over 'standard profits'; excise duty on sugar raised from Rs. 2 to Rs. 3 per cwt.; duty on motor spirit raised.
May	115.6	
June	(not available)	
July	111.7	
August	109.5	
September	110.6	
October	114.2	
November	119.8	
December	119.3	

Year & Month	Index of Securities Base : 1927-28	Tax Changes & Other Remarks
1941		
January	121.2	
February	122.9	E.P.T. increased to 66⅔%;
March	123.8	Central surcharge of 25%
April	118.1	on income-tax and super-
May	119.2	tax raised to 33⅓%; excise
June	123.9	duty on matches doubled;
July	129.2	specific import duty on art
August	129.0	silk & yarn raised; new
September	136.2	excise duty on tyres and
October	138.8	tubes.
November	151.6	
December	132.1	
1942		
January	128.5	
February	121.7	A slight increase in income-
March	119.6	tax surcharges; emergency
April	119.1	surcharges over the whole
May	122.8	field of import duties =
June	124.3	one-fifth of existing duties;
July	126.8	excise & import duties on
August	127.4	motor spirit increased; ex-
September	136.3	cise duties on kerosene &
October	140.0	silver = import duties.
November	149.2	
December	143.7	

Year & Month	Index of Securities Base: 1927-28	Tax Changes & Other Remarks
1943		
January	152.7	
February	158.3	
March	162.8	
April	174.5	Surcharge on income-tax & rates of supertax & corporation tax raised; new Central excise on tobacco & Vanaspati; control of capital issues instituted.
May	170.7	
June	174.8	
July	168.8	
August	170.9	
September	176.3	
October	183.1	
November	188.9	
December	186.8	
1944		
January	200.1	
February	196.2	
March	195.3	Rise in surcharge on income-tax, and in supertax & corporation tax rates; surcharge on basic customs duties raised from 20% to 50% for tobacco & spirits; fresh excise duties on betel nuts, coffee & tea.
April	190.7	
May	197.2	
June	198.9	
July	203.6	
August	194.3	
September	187.7	
October	191.2	
November	196.1	
December	202.8	

EFFECTS OF CORPORATE TAXATION

Year & Month	Index of Securities Base year: 1927-28	1938	Tax Changes & Other Remarks
1945			
January	200.8		
February	204.6		
March	199.9		
April	199.8		Increased surcharge on income-tax; differentiation between earned and unearned income introduced.
May	202.2		
June	207.3		
July	217.0		
August	212.6		
September	213.3		
October	214.9		
November	225.3		
December	232.4		
1946			
January	238.6	231.6	E.P.T. discontinued; rates of income-tax slightly raised; import duties on raw materials reduced; special depreciation & obsolescence allowances: 10% on new buildings, 20% on new machinery; allowances for research; income-tax & corporation tax reduced from 7¾ annas to 6 annas in the rupee; demonetisation of high denomination rupee notes.
February	236.7	230.2	
March	249.7	236.9	
April	259.8	242.5	
May	267.3	249.6	
June	280.9	262.5	
July	303.8	278.4	
August	314.9	286.1	
September	282.0	266.7	
October	265.5	259.1	
November	264.6	251.2	
December	252.6	237.9	

Year & Month	Index of Securities Base year: 1927-28	1938	Tax Changes & Other Remarks
1947			
January	256.3	237.8	
February	239.3	226.9	Salt duty abolished; B.P.T. @ 25% on all business profits over Rs. 1 lakh (rate later reduced to 16⅔%); capital gains tax (Rs. 15,000 & over); corporation tax doubled from 1 to 2 annas in the rupee.
March	235.6	217.1	
April	217.7	208.4	
May	215.2	202.4	
June	200.3	195.8	
July	197.9	187.8	
August	189.7	182.7	
September	182.4	176.6	
October	178.5	171.6	
November	176.5	167.5	Rupee de-linked.
December	192.4	178.6	
1948			
January	192.2	177.0	B.P.T. lowered to 10%; tax on undistributed profits lowered to 4 annas; income-tax on companies (with income less than Rs. 25,000) halved; corporation tax raised by 50%; rebate of 1 anna to companies declaring dividends in India; Industrial Policy Resolution (6 April).
February	181.7	168.3	
March	178.0	160.9	
April	170.8	151.3	
May	173.3	147.1	
June	168.9	143.6	
July	164.9	138.9	
August	167.3	139.1	
September	163.0	136.4	
October	162.6	135.5	
November	158.1	132.6	Dividend Limitation Ordinance (29th October).
December	157.9	130.8	

EFFECTS OF CORPORATE TAXATION 211

Year & Month	Index of Securities Base year: 1927-28	1938	Tax Changes & Other Remarks
1949			
January	156.7	128.9	Capital Gains Tax abolished; income-tax reduced; withdrawal of some export duties; relief in respect of customs on raw materials for industry; depreciation allowances doubled on new plant & machinery; 'Tax Holiday'; Control of Industries Bill (23 March); Rupee devaluation.
February	153.3	126.8	
March	152.0	125.9	
April	145.8	120.9	
May	141.2	116.7	
June	135.5	112.9	
July	131.1	109.7	
August	138.2	112.2	
September	143.1	117.0	
October	140.2	116.9	
November	137.1	112.1	
December	144.2	115.9	
1950			
January		118.8	B.P.T. abolished; company income-tax reduced from 5 to 4 annas; corporation tax enhanced by ½ anna; dividend limitation allowed to lapse.
February		116.3	
March		115.1	
April		115.3	
May		118.9	
June		117.9	
July		118.8	THE KOREAN WAR
August		126.0	
September		125.0	
October		124.2	
November		124.7	
December		126.7	

Year & Month	Index of Securities Base year: 1938	1949-50	Tax Changes & Other Remarks
1951			
January	130.9		
February	129.8		Corporation tax raised from
March	132.8		2½ to 2¾ annas & a sur-
April	138.0		charge of 5% was levied
May	138.8		on income-tax supertax;
June	138.6		a general increase in in-
July	131.9		direct taxes.
August	127.9		
September	127.9		
October	126.7		Increase in the Bank Rate.
November	124.5		
December	121.5		
1952			
January	121.6		
February	122.2		
March	115.5		
April	109.8	96.2	No significant changes in the
May	109.9	96.3	tax structure or rates.
June	110.1	96.5	
July	109.1	95.6	
August	107.8	94.5	
September	107.5	94.2	
October	106.8	93.6	
November	107.1	93.9	Collapse of the Korean War
December	104.9	91.9	boom.

Year & Month	Index of Securities Base year: 1938	Index of Securities Base year: 1949-50	Tax Changes & Other Remarks
1953			
January	103.7	90.9	
February	104.5	91.6	
March	107.0	93.8	
April	106.1	92.9	Personal income-tax exemption limit slightly raised; exemption from corporate tax on dividends invested in new undertakings in some industries.
May	107.2	94.0	
June	107.9	94.4	
July	106.4	93.3	
August	105.5	92.6	
September		91.6	
October		93.0	
November		96.0	
December		98.1	
1954			
January		98.2	
February		102.0	
March		102.6	No material changes in the tax structure or rates; publication of the RBI Report on Finance for the Private Sector.
April		103.8	
May		104.0	
June		106.9	
July		110.6	
August		117.4	
September		120.9	
October		118.2	Recommendations of the Taxation Enquiry Commission.
November		116.0	
December		113.7	

Year & Month	Index of Securities Base year : 1949-50	Tax Changes & Other Remarks
1955		
January	114.9	
February	114.2	
March	115.4	
April	115.4	Increase in income-tax rates; provision for development rebate; unlimited carry-over of losses permitted.
May	112.9	
June	113.1	
July	117.9	
August	122.7	
September	122.7	
October	124.5	
November	129.9	
December	130.6	
1956		
January	125.7	
February	121.0	
March	122.4	Surcharge on railway freight. Tax on bonus shares & dividends; enhancement of supertax on personal incomes; reintroduction of capital gains tax. Industrial Policy Statement (30 April).
April	123.1	
May	123.8	
June	125.1	
July	125.1	
August	127.4	
September	126.9	
October	124.9	
November	122.9	
December	117.4	

Year & Month	Index of Securities Base year : 1949-50	Tax Changes & Other Remarks
1957		
January	113.7	
February	113.6	
March	111.1	
April	106.9	Increase in the rates of cor-
May	104.5	poration & bonus share
June	102.6	taxes; Wealth Tax and
July	105.5	Expenditure Tax (15 May).
August	103.1	
September	99.3	
October	97.4	
November	98.7	
December	97.2	
1958	Base year : 1952-53	
January	121.1	
February	123.3	
March	124.2	
April	127.9	
May	127.2	
June	130.6	
July	136.7	
August	140.0	
September	143.4	
October	142.9	
November	142.0	
December	137.7	
1959		
January	137.5	
February	138.5	'Grossing' abolished; Wealth
March	144.6	tax on Companies removed.
April	149.0	
May	150.8	

The period between 1939 and 1959 could be divided into three parts, viz. (I) 1939-45 : The War period ; (II) 1946-50 : The Transitionary Period ; and (III) 1951-59 : The Plan Period.

I. 1939-45 : THE WAR PERIOD

During this period, every year the tax rates were being raised to meet the requirements of the War, but the tax rates did not have much influence on the minds of the investors or on the security prices. Before 1943, owing to the Allied reverses, the general uncertain conditions and the imposition of the Excess Profits tax, the prices of securities were very low. As the *Investor's Year Book* puts it, "Indian market psychology is notoriously mercurial, and as one depressing event succeeded another, its effect upon share and commodity prices was allowed full play".[24] After 1943, the Allies began slowly recovering lost ground and pushing forward, and consequently the breeze of optimism began to blow with steadily increasing force. Even the little influence the taxation measures had on the investors' minds thus disappeared after 1943. Although the rates rose and the rules were tightened, these failed to have any marked effect on the share prices. As A. K. Sur says, "people no longer judged securities from the income-earning standpoint. The idea that dominated both investors and speculators was capital appreciation in the near future rather than dividend prospects".[25]

II. 1946-50 : THE TRANSITIONARY PERIOD

In 1946 one could see the full effect of the taxation measures on the minds of the investors. The many tax reliefs and depreciation allowances enthused the investors, and accordingly the prices of securities rose considerably. A similar effect of the taxes on the psychology of investors was witnessed in the very next year, but in the opposite direction. The severity of the 1947-48 Budget presented by Liaquat Ali Khan made so violent an impact on the minds of the investors that a leading article in the weekly journal, *Commerce*, declared : "Never in one's living memory did a Budget of the Central Government hit the Stock Exchange so hard as the

[24] Twenty-sixth Edition, p. xxxvi.
[25] 'History of the Stock Exchange' in *The Stock Exchange : A Symposium*, Ed. by A. K. Sur, p. 18.

Budget of 1947-48 has done. The blow has been so heavy, indeed, that the markets have been unable to stand it."[26] From 226.9 (the base being 1938) in February 1947, the index fell to 217.1 in March, and by July it was as low as 195.8 and it continued thus to decline, clearly exhibiting the repressive psychological effects of the Budget proposals—the main new impositions being the Business Profits Tax and the Capital Gains Tax. Even the substantial watering down of the original proposals before they became law failed to restore the confidence of the investors who seemed indeed to have received almost a knock-out blow. War-time tax measures had seemed reasonable enough, but these peace-time heavy imposts had a different complexion altogether and the investor became confused and nearly panicky.

Although the 1948-49 and the 1949-50 Budgets tried hard to reverse the trend in the security market, they could not fully succeed; the damage was beyond complete repair. Though the investors were not as depressed as they were after the 1947-48 Budget, yet they were very far from recovering the optimism of 1946. While as a whole the tax policy of the Central Government during 1947-50 was one aimed at encouraging industry through incentives, there were many other factors which continually nurtured fear and suspicion in the minds of the business community. Apart from the many contradictory statements issued by the ruling party about nationalisation, ceilings on income, etc., Governmental measures like the Industrial Policy Resolution (April 1948), the Dividend Limitation Ordinance (October 1948), and the Control of Industries Bill (March 1949) worked in the opposite direction to reduce—or even to neutralise—the effectiveness of the tax measures in encouraging the investors.

In the latter half of the year 1950, owing both to the relaxed tax policy and the Korean War, the security prices began to rise. Even though there was an increase in tax rates in the 1951 Budget, it did not seem to have any appreciable effect on the Stock Exchange; as a matter of fact, the prices actually increased, exhibiting a favourable impact on the business community. This favourable turn was mainly due to the statement made by the Finance Minister, in his Budget Speech for the year 1951-52, regarding the necessity of relief to the direct taxpayers: "I know that

[26] Issue date 8 March 1947, p. 411.

there will be some criticism that the entire burden next year has been thrown on the taxpayer and that in distributing this burden the direct taxpayer has been let off more lightly than the indirect taxpayer". Meeting this possible criticism he affirmed that "a fair amount of the bruden has necessarily to be laid on the community by means of indirect taxes".

III. 1951-59 : THE PLAN PERIOD

With the bursting of the Korean War boom, the prices of securities began to fall. In the 1952, 1953 and 1954 Budgets, there were practically no changes that could affect the psychology of the investors adversely. The tax system being thus largely neutral, certain other factors like the progress of the first Five Year Plan and the publication of the Shroff Committee's Report injected an optimistic note into the capital market which resulted in a steady, though small, rise in the security prices. Even though the 1955-56 Budget increased the excise taxes and the personal income-taxes, it did not affect the stock market adversely, probably because of the provision for development rebate. It is interesting to see that the Bombay stock market was affected much more than the Calcutta market because operators at Bombay reacted violently to the tax changes falling on the backbone of the stock markets, namely the middle class within the Rs. 7,500—10,000 range. But the position stabilised itself soon.

Contrary to the usual apprehensions, the 1956-57 Budget (harsh though it was from the point of view of the investor) failed to impress the market. But this was not because the stringent tax measures had no reactions on the minds of the investors. The real reason was that the market had already discounted the Budget well in advance, as may be seen in the drop from 130.6 in December 1955 to 121.0 in February 1956 on the eve of the presentation of the Budget. Actually, it may seem strange that security prices should increase *after* such a Budget had been presented. What had happened was that the Budget proposals had been preceded by the most frightening rumours about the possibility of a Wealth Tax, a low ceiling for industrial incomes, an Expenditure Tax, rationalisation of the sales tax through the introduction of heavy excise duties, direct control of dividends, a straight steep rise in the corporation tax, etc., and the Budget reality, bad as it was,

was rather better than the grim forecasts and gloomy apprehensions. The tax payers had indeed been prepared for the worst ; but when the tax proposals were made known, harsh though they doubtless appeared, they were yet almost a relief to the stock market. "It might have been much worse", the investor and the speculator thought, and almost felt a sigh of relief !

The prices were slowly getting stabilised at the lower levels, but the introduction of new taxes in November 1956, coupled with "recurrent provocative statements" from the Finance Minister, presently reversed the trend, with the result that from 122.9 in November 1956 the index gravitated to 106.9 in April 1957. As the commentator in the Annual Number (1956) of the *Indian Finance* says, "The fundamental outlook for the market in terms of the implications of the Second Five Year Plan is, no doubt, healthy even in the face of increased taxation ; but there has been a complete reversal of sentiment on account of apprehensions of further heavier taxation". These fears were more than justified because, in May 1957, the Wealth Tax and the Expenditure Tax were introduced which further accentuated the fall of security prices and the diminution of the enthusiasm of the investors. But there was a bullish market in 1958-59 due to an increased confidence owing to the presence of a 'rightist' Finance Minister and not many unfavourable tax measures.

The above description of the stock market movements during the twenty years between 1939 and 1959 reflects only one aspect of the picture : it gives an indication of the vicissitudes in the mental state of the investing class. But, then, many factors affect security prices, and the factors that affect most are the fiscal and monetary policies of the Government. The reason for this is obvious : modern industry is so complex that at every phase of the production and distribution of goods, Business and Government meet each other. Consequently the actions of the Government exercise a great influence over the whole province of industrial organisation. One must not therefore attribute too much importance to tax measures alone in judging the psychology of the business class. Tax measures naturally reflect the social philosophy of the ruling Party, and hence the psychological reactions of the businessmen to tax increases must be viewed against the background of the general economic and social policies of the Government.

...CAL EFFECTS

...he repercussions of a tax increase or decrease on the psychological outlook of the investor are important only in so far as it affects his actual economic actions. Thus the psychological effects of taxation measures make but an indirect impact on the economy. But tax changes and tax increases have certain direct effects as well. In other words, the direct physical effects on the flow of funds, and on demand and supply, have a primary place in the discussion on the effects of taxation. The fundamental question is: What are the economic consequences of the decrease or increase in the flow of funds—as taxes from the corporate sector of the economy—to the Government? Here we are not taking into account the mental reactions of investors to tax changes, and hence our concern here is to examine how the increase or reduction brought about by taxation in the net disposable profits of the corporations reacts upon the economic actions of the corporate sector, not to mention the effects of such increase or reduction in the economy itself as a whole.

THE PROBLEM OF 'SHIFTING'

It is very seldom that one comes across a completely neutral tax. Each tax has its own unique range of repercussions, even if it apparently falls on all. But the position is accentuated if the tax hits only a particular section—a comparatively small section—of the community. There is bound to be at least some shift in the motivations and economic behaviour of the people concerned due to the imposition or withdrawal of the tax. These repercussions will vary, of course, according to the actual persons who are ultimately required to bear the burden of the tax. As we saw in the first chapter, the theory of public finance is yet unable to formulate a definitive answer to the question: Who ultimately bears the burden of the corporation tax? Is there 'shifting' at all, and if there is, on whom is the tax shifted? However, it was also seen that, according to the economists in general, the corporation tax cannot be shifted in the short run. But this will hold good only if profit is considered as a reward for the entrepreneurs. In actual practice—and this is more so in India than elsewhere—such is not the case. Not the pure 'economic' profit, but the accounting profit, is reckoned for tax calculations. And yet it is very rarely that corporations charge the highest possible price, for what Carl Shoup says about the U.S.A. is also applicable to India : "The larger part of the corporation income-tax is paid by corporations that (a) are engaged in monopolistic competition ... (b) do not charge prices that are as high as they would charge if they were consolidated into one firm".[27] The reason why the corporations will not charge the maximum possible price is the desire to maintain the goodwill of the people, even if this should mean diminished profits ; as Frank Bower said, in his evidence before the Royal Commission : "A businessman ... just does not charge the maximum price of the market. He values his connection rather than his today's profit".[28]

We are unable, then, to come to the definite conclusion that, in the short run at any rate, corporation taxes could be shifted. But this is not all. A heavy tax or a big rise in the tax rate is a very different proposition from a small tax or a small rise in the tax rate. Besides, the long-run effects may be different from the short-run effects. As Harold M. Somers says, "A tax which might theoretically be imposed on pure business profits would not be shifted in the short run, but the taxes which are actually imposed on business income do impinge on elements other than pure business profit and therefore can be shifted".[29] If the tax rise is very small and entails very little sacrifice, the tax might not be shifted on somebody else's shoulders. But the taxes will definitely be shifted—at least attempts will be made in that direction—if the taxes make serious inroads into the profits or involve actual deficits.

In case a corporation decides to shift the tax burden, it can do so in three ways, viz. shift it to labour by cutting down the wages ; to the consumers by raising the prices ; or to the shareholders by slashing the dividends. We shall now consider these three possibilities one by one in the Indian context.

1. CUTTING DOWN WAGES AND SHIFTING TO LABOUR

It may be stated at once that normally it is not possible to shift

---

[27] 'Incidence of the Corporation Income Tax' (*National Tax Journal*, 1948) ; reprinted in *Readings in the Economics of Taxation*, p. 329.
[28] Quoted by Paul Streetan, 'Some Problems Raised by the Report of the Royal Commission on the Taxation of Profits and Income' (*Bulletin of the Institute of Statistics*, November 1955, p. 324).
[29] *Public Finance and National Income*, p. 216.

taxes to labour by cutting down wages because of labour union pressures and Governmental regulations concerning minimum wages, etc. Statistics of the earnings of factory workers are collected by the Labour Bureau of the Union Government and are published in the *Monthly Abstract of Statistics*, and TABLE XIII, based on these statistics, gives the annual average earnings of factory labour. The data given in the table relate to the factories covered by the Payment of Wages Act of 1936, and comprise the perennial industries which account for more than eighty per cent of the total factory employment in India and, again, cover only those who get less than Rs. 200 per month inclusive of bonuses and other allowances.

TABLE XIII

AVERAGE EARNINGS OF FACTORY LABOUR IN INDIA

Year	Earnings in Rupees	
1939	287.5	
1940	307.7	
1941	324.5	
1942	Not available	
1943	525.0	
1944	586.5	
1945	595.8	
1946	619.4	
1947	737.0	
1948	889.7	
1949	985.9	
1950	966.8	
1951	1035.6	
1952	1112.2	
1953	1110.9	
1954	1111.3	
1955	1173.5	
1956	1208.1	
1957	1233.9	
1958	1295.2	(excluding Kerala, Mysore and Madras)
1959	1333.3	(Excluding Madras, Mysore, and the Punjab)

TABLE XIII shows that the wages have been rising steadily, except in 1950 when a slight decrease was witnessed. The maximum rises have taken place between the years 1940 and 1944, and between 1946 and 1949. We have already noted that during the entire period, 1939-59, both taxes paid by the corporations and corporate profits have risen in spite of the increased wages of the workers. This leads us to the conclusion that the tax burdens could not have been shifted to the labourers. In fact, the taxation policy might have itself influenced to some extent the rise of the worker's wages during 1940-44. One of the common charges levelled against the Excess Profits Tax was that it led to extravagant expenditure on the part of the corporations.[30] During the two war-periods, and especially during 1940-45, the import of capital goods was not possible to expand the productive apparatus. Consequently the employers might have increased the wage-packet in order to gain a good name from the labourers and perhaps also to 'spite' the tax gatherer. It is also possible, on the other hand, that the corporations, whether they liked it or not, were compelled (because of the fear of trade union action) to raise wages in response to the increased war-time cost of living as shown in TABLE XIV.

TABLE XIV

ALL INDIA CONSUMER PRICE INDEX[31]

Year	Index (1939=100)
1940	97
1941	107
1942	145
1943	268
1944	269
1945	269
1946	285
1947	323

[30] See J. R. Hicks, U. K. Hicks and L. Rostas, *The Taxation of War Wealth*, p. 43 ff. See also M. H. Gopal, *The Theory of Excess Profits Taxation*, pp. 223-5.

[31] Source: *Indian Labour Gazette*, October 1955, p. 249

It is, of course, possible that the employers raised the wages more as a natural reaction to the Excess Profits Tax than in anticipation of possible trade union action. For one thing, trade union activity was not so very much pronounced then as it is now; and, secondly, Government too was not favourably disposed towards labour. On the other hand, the reason for the 1946-49 spurt in wages should be mainly ascribed to the widespread agitation for increased wages carried on then by the labouring class.[32] It seems reasonable to conclude, therefore, that apart from the indirect influence of the Excess Profits Tax during the war-period already referred to, corporation taxes have had no appreciable effect or influence on the wages of Indian industrial labour.

II. RAISING PRICES AND SHIFTING TO THE CONSUMERS

Broadly speaking, the course of price level in India in the recent past has passed through distinct phases. From 1939 to 1951 was the first phase, and it was characterised by a steady upward trend. From 1951 to 1959 was the second phase, and it was characterised by an initial fall, accompanied by a rising trend, as indicated in TABLE XV[33] of the general index of wholesale prices of manufactured goods in India.

The taxes paid by corporations also show a similar upward trend, though some fluctuations are noticed after 1947.

The coefficient of correlation of the tax collections and the index of the wholesale prices of manufactured goods works out to be $+.7756$. This is a pronounced positive correlation and suggests that both have moved together. In other words, this leads us to the conclusion that the taxes were largely shifted to the consumers. But, then, are we justified in coming to this conclusion by merely looking at this high correlation?

It is commonly conceded that the price level at any time is influenced by the supply of goods and services and the effective demand for them. Demand for goods in a community could be gauged by the money supply with the public, and there are many factors besides taxation that affect the community's demand and supply.

[32] See S. L. N. Simha and K. N. R. Ramanujam, 'The Present Price Situation in India', (*RBI Bulletin*, May 1948, p. 286).
[33] Source: C.S.O., *Statistical Abstract of India* (relevant years).

TABLE XV
INDEX OF WHOLESALE PRICES OF MANUFACTURED GOODS IN INDIA

Year	Index of Wholesale Prices of Manufactured Goods (Base 1939)
1939-40	132
1940-41	120
1941-42	155
1942-43	190
1943-44	252
1944-45	258
1945-46	240
1946-47	259
1947-48	288
1948-49	346
1949-50	347
1950-51	354
1951-52	402
1952-53	371
1953-54	367
1954-55	377
1955-56	373
1956-57	385
1957-58	380
1958-59	391

THE FIRST PHASE, 1939-51 : A SELLERS' MARKET

It has been pointed out by D. Bright Singh that "increase in effective demand and relative deficiency in supply were the main forces behind the general rise in prices upto 1951".[34] During the second world war period, it was the abnormal war demand that first sent up the prices, but thanks to the control policy of the Government, prices were relatively more stable after 1943. In

[34] *Inflationary Price Trends in India since* 1939, p. 228.

spite of the large concessions granted to the industry in the 1946-47 Budget, prices registered no decrease but, on the contrary, continued to rise, mainly due to the post-war release of considerable suppressed demand. We may say that, due to a sellers' market prevailing during the period up to 1951, the producers were able to shift the taxes. However, this view does not quite carry conviction. During this period the profits of the corporate sector were steadily swelling, and reduction or enhancement of tax rates apparently made no difference to the continually rising price level as also the steadily mounting profits. Hence we can safely conclude that prices would anyhow have risen, whether there was any tax or not, and whether the tax rates were high or not. Another aspect which is relevant here is the rise in the production costs. The cost both of labour and of raw materials was increasing more and more during this period, as TABLE XVI[35] shows:

TABLE XVI

Year (1)	Indian Labour Bureau's Index of Labour earnings (2)	Index of Cost of Raw Materials (refers to the financial year) (3)
1939	100	100
1940	105.3	118.8
1941	111.0	121.5
1942	129.1	146.9
1943	179.6	165.9
1944	202.1	185.0
1945	201.5	206.0
1946	208.6	210.0
1947	253.2	235.3
1948	304.0	254
1949	340.3	444.8
1950	334.2	471.7
1951	356.8	523.1

[35] Source: For column (2), *Indian Labour Gazette*, October 1955, p. 249; for column (3), relevant Annual Reports of Currency and Finance of the Reserve Bank of India. For the years 1949-51, the index refers only to the industrial raw materials with the base as 1939 = 100.

Thus we see that demand had gone up, the cost of production had gone up too, and the taxes also had gone up. It is no wonder that the price level, as a result of this triple impulsion, also pursued an irresistible upward trend. In such a situation, how can we categorically say that taxes only, taxes alone, have caused the high prices ? However, because of the inefficiently administered control measures, goods go to the black market ; controls generally try to achieve too much and actually accomplish too little, sometimes causing more harm than good to the community at large, especially in an extensive backward country like India. The official index figures, it has been perceptively pointed out, "substantially understate the war-time increase in prices, because, during periods of price control, official prices are used and no allowance made for black market transactions, which were generally of considerable importance".[36] In the light of these factors, all that we can say is that producers had no doubt every chance of shifting the corporation tax ; but if we are further to decide whether they did actually shift the tax or not, we shall have to narrow down our enquiry and take up only particular industries.[37]

THE SECOND PHASE, 1951-59

The price situation between 1951 and 1957 was more complex than the price situation prior to 1951, a period marked as we have seen by a fluctuating upward trend. In the 1951-59 period, as may be seen from TABLE XVII, the chief features were a fluctuating price level of manufactured goods, a steadily rising trend in industrial production, and an initial fall of money supply followed however by a steep increase.

The rising trend in industrial production has helped to reduce the inflationary pressures generated by the increased money supply in the economy. A fall in the external demand followed by an adverse balance of payments position has further reduced the inflationary pressures. The supply position has become better,

---

[36] A. J. Brown, *The Great Inflation*, p. 186.

[37] G. N. Arora, after analysing five major industries in India for the period 1947-51, has come to the conclusion that "total taxes were mostly borne by the consumers" (*Taxation of Industry in India*, p. 134). His conclusions cannot, however, be accepted because his method of analysis is open to serious drawbacks.

TABLE XVII

INDICES OF INDUSTRIAL PRODUCTION AND PRICE OF MANUFACTURED GOODS AND MONEY SUPPLY[38]

Year	Index of Industrial Production	Price-index of Mfgd. Goods (August 1939=100)	Money Supply as in March of the Year under Reference (Rs. crores)
1951	100	395.5	1965.87
1952	103.6	377.5	1792.84
1953	105.6	367.0	1750.96
1954	112.9	375.5	1844.80
1955	122.4	373.4	1980.90
1956	132.6	381.9	2184.31
1957	137.3	389.6	2312.89
1958	139.7	388.0	2388.83
1959	151.9	390.8	2498.75

and demand as represented by money supply has slightly decreased. The result is a more or less steady price level. During this period profits as well as taxes paid have been growing; and it is pertinent to note that the profits of the corporate sector have increased maily due to increased production rather than inflated prices. Once again it would appear that higher tax collections are the result of increased profits and higher rates coupled with the introduction of new taxes.

A BUYERS' MARKET

The demand having fallen and the market being transformed from a sellers' to a buyers' market, there is not even the slightest suspicion of tax-shifting as we had in the former period (1939-51); and this is amply demonstrated by the low correlation coefficient, $+.172$, of the index of taxes paid by the corporate sector and the index of the wholesale prices of manufactured goods.

[38] Source: *Statistical Abstract*: 1958-59 and the *Annual Reports on Currency and Finance* of the Reserve Bank of India.

III. SLASHING DIVIDENDS AND SHIFTING TO THE SHAREHOLDERS

Our conclusion from the foregoing discussion would be that the taxes might have been partially shifted during the boom period between 1939 and 1951, but might not have been shifted during the period after 1951 ; and this summary statement also conforms to the views expressed by Richard A. Musgrave in the context of the conditions prevailing in the U.S.A. : "Probably the corporation income-tax is shifted in part, although little is known about the exact extent of shifting. It is perhaps more extensive during a war boom or a period of high excess profits taxation, and less extensive under other conditions, as in depression periods when there is no sellers' market and the rates are lower. Such evidence as is available, however, suggests that under ordinary conditions a substantial—probably the larger—part of the tax is not shifted."[39] Musgrave, however, suggests that it is reasonable to assume that about two-thirds of the tax at least must fall on corporate profits. In other words, the taxes must either come from the company direct, which means a reduction of the amount ploughed back into the business, or from the shareholders of the company, which means a slashing of the dividends. Either a fall in retained profits, or a cut in the dividends, or both : such must inevitably be the main result of corporate taxation.

IMPACT OF COMPANY TAXATION ON THE LEVEL OF CORPORATE SAVINGS

David Walker rightly says that "it is not possible for any statistical study to tell the whole story about the effects of company taxation on the levels of prices and investment".[40] While statistical analysis cannot help us to arrive at any definite or final conclusion about the effects of company taxation on the willingness of entrepreneurs to invest, it is possible to examine the impact of company taxation upon the level of corporate savings. To put in the form of a question : What are the effects of corporate taxation

---

[39] In his article on 'Federal Tax Reform' in *Public Finance and Full Employment*, p. 47 ; see also R. A. Musgrave, *A Theory of Public Finance*, pp. 286-7.

[40] 'Some Economic Aspects of the Taxation of Companies' (*The Manchester School*, January 1954, p. 12).

on the availability of funds to carry out investment?

Naturally, this problem is closely related to the problem earlier discussed, i.e. whether the corporate sector is or is not able to shift its tax burden to the consumers in the form of prices. It was found that taxes were probably shifted to the consumers in part during 1939-51, and thereafter, during 1951-59, the burden of the taxes was borne by the companies themselves. The related subject of investment possibilities could also be studied in two stages.

VICISSITUDES OF CORPORATE SAVINGS : FIRST PHASE, 1939-51

In India data are not available for all the corporations in the manner in which they are presented in *National Income and Expenditure : 1946-51 for Britain*. Consequently we have to be content with samples instead of the corporate sector as a whole. Here, for the period between 1939 and 1951, we have taken six industries. TABLE XVIII[41] gives particulars regarding the finances of six leading Indian industries, viz. cotton textiles, jute textiles, cement, paper, sugar, and iron & steel, for selected years from 1939 to 1951.

It would be seen that internal finances have risen from Rs. 19.49 crores in 1939 to Rs. 78.27 crores in 1951. Of this amount, dividends declared rose from Rs. 7.56 crores to Rs. 17.81 crores, and tax payments rose from Rs. 3.99 crores to Rs. 28.08 crores. The gross capital formation increased likewise from Rs. 25.97 crores to Rs. 89.56 crores. The table clearly shows how the corporate sector was unable to find resources for expansion internally and was forced accordingly to resort to outside capital for expansion every time it was needed.

Between 1939 and 1951, while the net profits had increased by four times, tax payments rose by seven times; and the retention of corporate profits nearly kept pace with the increase in profits, increasing from Rs. 5.49 crores to Rs. 20.76 crores. This does not quite mean that the taxes have been shifted to the shareholders, as we suspected earlier; what has actually happened is that the dividends, although they have more than doubled, have not increased commensurately with the four-fold increase in the net profits and the retained profits. While profits have increased four-fold,

[41] Source : Compiled from the consolidated balance sheets published in the various publications of the Association of Indian Trade and Industry, Bombay.

TABLE XVIII

COMPANY FINANCES AND CAPITAL FORMATION IN SIX INDIAN INDUSTRIES

(in crores of rupees)

Receipts	1939	1942	1944	1946	1948	1950	1951
Net Profits	14.00	76.31	93.95	49.59	67.51	40.47	57.51
Depreciation	5.49	12.49	9.26	9.45	11.95	17.75	20.76
Total	19.49	88.80	103.21	59.04	79.46	58.22	78.27
Payments							
Dividend	7.56	16.00	13.88	14.50	14.39	15.33	17.81
Tax payments	3.99	46.79	68.44	25.09	34.42	20.72	28.08
Gross investment	25.97	65.58	14.75	34.95	107.39	57.63	89.56
Total	37.52	128.37	97.07	74.54	156.20	93.68	135.45
	—18.03	—39.57	+6.14	—15.50	—76.74	—35.46	—57.18
Increase in paid-up capital over previous year	3.46	3.80	5.15	12.18	22.16	8.75	5.90

taxes have increased seven-fold; since the tax-gatherer has taken more than his proportionate share and the company has retained its usual share, the shareholder has had to be content with a smaller share of the increased profits. It is thus appropriate to conclude, as Musgrave has done, that a sizeable part of the tax burden was really borne by the shareholders. It may be called a negative rather than a positive loss, but it was a loss all the same.

This conclusion is further strengthened if we examine gross profits, taxes, dividends, and retained profits *plus* depreciation as percentages of the total gross income as shown in TABLE XIX.

TABLE XIX

GROSS PROFITS, TAXATION, DIVIDENDS AND RETAINED PROFITS + DEPRECIATION AS PERCENTAGES OF THE TOTAL GROSS INCOME[42]

	1939	1942	1944	1946	1948	1950	1951
Cotton-Textiles							
Gross profits	7.2	29.0	23.1	14.4	14.6	7.9	8.3
Taxation	.8	16.4	16.8	6.4	6.7	3.2	3.2
Dividend	2.4	4.0	2.2	3.0	2.2	2.0	1.7
Retained profits + Depreciation	4.0	8.6	4.1	5.0	5.7	2.7	3.4
Jute Textiles							
Gross profits	11.4	17.8	14.3	11.1	4.2	8.6	5.0
Taxation	3.6	10.5	10.0	5.3	2.3	2.9	2.1
Dividend	4.3	4.5	2.8	3.8	1.6	2.5	1.6
Retained profits + Depreciation	3.5	2.8	1.5	2.0	.3	3.2	1.3
Cement							
Gross profits	17.7	28.8	23.5	21.0	20.9	20.9	23.7
Taxation	2.0	6.6	8.1	6.8	9.2	5.1	6.6
Dividend	6.5	10.2	6.5	7.0	5.1	5.6	5.9
Retained profits + Depreciation	9.2	12.0	8.9	7.2	6.6	10.2	11.2
Paper							
Gross profits	11.9	34.3	24.5	20.4	12.9	16.4	19.1
Taxation	1.9	17.2	14.0	8.6	4.8	4.4	5.4
Dividend	4.4	5.9	4.7	5.1	3.9	4.0	4.3
Retained profits + Depreciation	5.6	11.2	5.8	6.7	4.2	8.0	9.4

[42] Source : As for Table XVIII

	1939	1942	1944	1946	1948	1950	1951
Iron and Steel							
Gross profits	30.2	34.2	31.9	23.3	15.1	16.3	18.7
Taxation	8.0	14.3	11.9	9.4	4.6	5.1	6.0
Dividend	15.5	10.4	8.2	6.0	4.2	4.4	4.2
Retained profits + Depreciation	6.7	9.5	11.8	7.9	6.3	6.8	8.5
Sugar							
Gross profits	16.5	20.3	12.3	9.2	12.3	7.9	10.4
Taxation	2.0	4.7	4.9	2.2	3.6	2.4	2.9
Dividend	4.3	5.6	3.2	2.7	1.9	2.3	2.2
Retained profits + Depreciation	10.2	10.0	4.2	4.3	6.8	3.2	5.3
All Industries							
Gross profits	15.8	27.4	21.6	16.6	13.3	13.0	14.2
Taxation	3.1	11.6	11.0	6.5	5.2	3.9	4.4
Dividend	6.2	6.8	4.6	4.6	3.2	3.5	3.3
Retained profits + Depreciation	6.5	9.0	6.1	5.5	5.0	5.7	6.5

Gross profits as percentages of total sales fell from 15.8 per cent in 1939 to 14.2 per cent in 1951. Even though taxation increased from 3.1 per cent to 4.4 per cent of the total gross income (or sales), undistributed profits *plus* depreciation remained at 6.5 per cent of the total sales. It is now quite clear that the main reason for this position is the considerable reduction in the percentage of income distributed as dividends, that is, reduction from 6.2 per cent in 1939 to 3.3 per cent in 1951.

From a scrutiny of TABLE XX it can be seen that gross capital formation had more than trebled during this period (i.e. increased from Rs. 25.97 crores to Rs. 89.56 crores), whereas the net savings available for investment (retained profits + depreciation allowances taken together) showed a four-fold increase, (i.e. from Rs. 7.94 crores to Rs. 32.40 crores). In monetary terms it will be clear from TABLES XIX and XX how insufficient funds from internal sources were. Thus in real, though not in monetary, terms, there was a small increase. Whereas retained profits *plus* depreciation registered an increase to 408 per cent, the index of prices of manufactured goods also rose to 354 per cent, both compared with the 1939 base of 100 :

TABLE XX

NET COMPANY SAVINGS[43]

Year	1939	1942	1944	1946	1948	1950	1951
Retained profits (in Crores of Rs.)	2.45	13.52	11.54	10.00	18.80	4.42	11.64
Depreciation (in Crores of Rs.)	5.49	12.49	9.26	9.45	11.95	17.75	20.76
Total	7.94	26.01	20.80	19.45	30.75	22.17	32.40
Index	100	328	262	245	387	279	408
Gross investment	25.97	65.58	14.75	34.95	107.39	57.63	89.56
Index of wholesale prices of manufactured goods	100	155	252	240	288	347	354

We can say this much, then, that tax payments have caused a certain strain on the financial resources of the corporate sector. It is true that, even if all the taxes were abolished, the corporate sector's need for funds will not be met from internal resources alone. Especially in the post-independence years, we find that outside capital brought into the corporate sector is much higher than the amounts paid as taxes. Because it was—at any rate after 1947—a time when the corporate sector was expanding, taxation by taking a part of the income which could otherwise have been ploughed back into the business must definitely have hampered the growth of the corporate sector. The amount saved through the reduction of taxation might not necessarily have been distributed as dividends because companies would have ordinarily

[43] Source : As for TABLES XVIII & XIX.

availed themselves of the concessions open to them when the profits were reinvested. Hence higher taxation must have resulted in a certain diminution in the flow of internal funds for investment.

VICISSITUDES OF CORPORATE SAVINGS : SECOND PHASE, 1951-59

For analysing the effects of corporate taxation in the period between 1951 and 1959, we may conveniently use the data collected by the Research and Statistics Division of the Reserve Bank of India regarding the finances of 750 joint-stock companies for 1951-55 and of 1001 companies for 1956-59. These data are not strictly comparable to the data used for discussing the effects for the earlier period. Whereas we took only six industries with more or less complete coverage for that period, the present analysis is based on representative samples from as many as 31 industrial groups. But both procedures seem to lead to roughly the same conclusions regarding the basic tendencies governing the divers components of the corporate sector.

During this period not many changes in the basic structure or rates of corporate taxation took place, for the combined effective rates of income and corporation taxes remained constant. The new taxes like the Wealth Tax, etc. did not play any notable part, excepting for the controversies they ignited at the time ; and some measures like the Development Rebate were introduced during the early years of this period to encourage corporate investment. TABLE XXI[44] gives the percentage share of the various items, viz. gross trading profits (profits *before* tax + depreciation), tax provision, dividends, and retained profits, in the total gross receipts of the corporate sector.

The percentage share of gross trading profits to total receipts was fairly constant, except for minor fluctuations owing mainly to the current conditions. For example, in 1952, the ratio suddenly fell, obviously because of the crash of the Korean War boom. Again, in 1957, with the slowing down of the rate of increase in industrial production and with slackness in certain sectors of industry (prominent among them being cotton textiles) the rate of increase in total receipts slowed down and profits recorded a steep fall. Barring such fluctuations, the prices relative to costs remained

[44] Source : Calculated from data given in *RBI Bulletin*, September 1957, August 1959 and September 1961.

TABLE XXI

	1951	1952	1953	1954	1955	1956	1957	1958	1959
Gross trading profits	10.2	7.8	9.6	10.4	11.4	11.2	9.2	9.6	11.2
Taxation provision	3.1	2.3	2.7	3.1	3.3	3.7	3.0	3.0	3.0
Dividend	2.4	2.3	2.6	2.8	2.7	2.7	2.4	2.5	3.2
Retained profits + Deprecn.	4.7	3.1	4.2	4.5	5.4	4.8	3.8	4.0	5.0
Retained profits	2.3	0.7	1.3	1.6	2.3	1.8	0.6	1.0	2.0

reasonably constant. Tax provision too steadily kept pace with gross trading profits and remained constant, allowing, of course, for the increase or decrease in the taxable profits.

But the most striking feature is the remarkable constancy of the dividends declared. They have remained steady, impervious even to the decline or rise in the ratio of gross trading profits to the total receipts.

With the tax provision and dividends thus remaining constant, it had fallen to the lot of retained profits to accommodate the rise or fall in the prices relatively to the costs.[45] The correlation coefficient of these two variables actually works out to be $+.678$, which is a very significant positive correlation. In the earlier period, it was the dividend which was suffering attenuation to offset any tax increases. But the dividend had by 1951 already fallen considerably from the 1939 rate, and hence any further attenuation

[45] The position is not different with closely controlled corporations. The following table gives the figures for 333 private limited companies, (Source: *RBI Bulletin*, January 1956 and November 1961):

as % of total gross receipts	1955	1956	1957	1958	1959
Gross trading profits	7.2	7.2	7.3	8.0	8.6
Taxation Provision	2.6	3.0	3.5	3.7	3.4
Dividends	1.7	1.7	1.7	2.0	2.4
Retained profits	1.1	0.7	0.2	0.5	1.1

Here it is crystal clear that increased taxation has adversely affected the level of retained profits, leaving the other items practically unaffected one way or the other.

was rightly viewed with grave apprehension; it has accordingly remained more or less constant during 1951-59, as indicated by TABLE XXII which shows dividends as percentage of net worth for the period under consideration.

TABLE XXII

Year	Dividend (in percentage)	
1951	5.0	(for 750 companies)
1952	4.5	do
1953	4.6	do
1954	5.0	do
1955	5.1	do
1955	5.2	(for 1001 companies)
1956	5.2	do
1957	4.9	do[46]
1958	5.1	do
1959	6.6	do

It would appear, then, that the practicable minimum dividend rate (about 5 per cent) having been reached, the extra tax burden has had to be borne by others than the shareholders. Thus taxation or any other factor that causes the costs to rise will in the short run have to be borne by the company itself in the form of reduced retained profits, or even in the form of negative retention, as has happened in industries like jute textiles in 1952, 1955, 1956 and 1957; in cotton textiles in 1952, 1953, 1954 and 1957; agricultural and allied industries in 1952 and 1957; and coal mining in 1956.

TABLE XXIII shows the percentage of tax provision to gross trading profits (i.e. profits + depreciation) and the net trading profits (*minus* depreciation).

The tax provision ranges roughly between 40 and 50 per cent of the net distributable profits, but, as we saw in an earlier table, the taxation provision has more or less stood constant at about 3 per cent (actually ranging between 2.6 to 3.5 per cent during

[46] Source: *RBI Bulletin*, September 1957, August 1959 and September 1961.

TABLE XXIII

	1951	1952	1953	1954	1955	1956	1957	1958	1959
Tax as % of gross trading profits	30	30	29	30	29	33	33	31	26
Tax as % of net trading profits	40	44	41	42	39	46	49	46	37

1955-57) of the total gross receipts. Even though in absolute terms the amounts involved may be considerable, relatively this 3 per cent represents but a small part of the total gross receipts. Thus, excepting for causing slight marginal changes in the total receipts, taxation will have little influence on the gross income of the companies. Thinking of conditions in the U.S.A., H. Dewey Anderson says that Taxation "tends to follow changes in income rather than to cause such changes, and it seems fairly clear that taxes are incidents in business rather than determiners of business activity and income".[47] By and large this applies to conditions in India as well: taxation but follows income, it does not play the part of an antecedent determiner or controller.

This conclusion is further strengthened if we consider the present "buoyant business conditions" in India, when the economy as a whole and the corporate sector in particular are expanding rapidly.

We have seen already that dividends become as it were 'sticky' at a particular level, and that the only variable factor that remains is the amount of retained profits which must necessarily diminish as the tax load increases. Thus the only legitimate conclusion concerning the effects of corporate taxation on free reserves that we can venture is that retained profits will most probably *not* rise as rapidly as they would have done in the absence of that taxation; on the contrary they might even decrease. But profits are determined independent of the volume and rate of taxation. It is, after all, the volume and rate of profit rather than the volume and rate of taxation that finally determine the amount that is ploughed back into the business.[48] The absence of corporate taxa-

[47] *Taxation, Recovery and Defence* (TNEC Monograph), p. 209.
[48] See Taxation Enquiry Commission 1953-54, *Report*, Vol. I, p. 127,

TABLE XXIV

	1951	1952	1953	1954	1955	1956	1957	1958	1959
Receipts									
Gross profits	85.16	55.70	65.63	78.46	97.36	128.76	104.45	120.92	161.48
Depreciation	27.71	26.80	28.62	30.20	35.34	47.45	53.43	56.80	65.37
Total	112.87	82.50	94.25	108.66	132.70	176.21	157.88	177.72	166.85
Payments									
Dividend	26.99	24.46	26.07	29.22	32.22	42.31	41.98	46.85	64.06
Tax provision	33.61	24.67	27.03	32.66	37.81	58.80	51.26	55.95	59.11
Gross capital formation	124.09	32.26	49.33	101.03	136.09	256.47	235.16	152.82	122.54
Total	184.69	81.39	102.43	162.91	206.12	357.58	328.40	255.62	245.71
plus or minus	—71.82	+1.11	—8.18	—54.25	—73.42	—181.37	—170.52	—77.90	—78.86

tion might have left more funds with the corporate sector for business expansion, but this circumstance would not by itself have solved the problem of the need for additional funds for expansion, as TABLE XXIV clearly shows.[49]

Except for one year (1952), every year external resources have had to be tapped: Rs. 71.82 crores in 1951, Rs. 54.25 crores in 1954, Rs. 181.37 crores in 1956, Rs. 170.52 crores in 1957, Rs. 77.90 crores in 1958 and Rs. 78.86 crores in 1959.

EFFECTS OF COMPANY TAXATION ON THE GROWTH OF THE CORPORATE SECTOR

The main conclusion to emerge from the foregoing tortuous discussion is that in recent years, by and large, corporate taxes are *not* shifted—not to the labourers in the form of lower wages, not to the consumers in the form of higher prices, nor yet to the shareholders in the form of diminished dividends; the brunt of the corporation tax is borne by the companies themselves in the form of reduced retained profits. If this were so, how does it react on the progress of the corporate sector?

The essential requirement for the healthy growth of joint-stock companies is the willingness of individuals to supply effort and imagination to increase production. These pioneering individuals will naturally require capital to carry out their programmes of production. The more there is of such risk-taking, the more must be the demand for capital: hence the second essential requirement, namely the readiness of capital to flow into the hands of the risk-taking individuals who are ready and eager to put forth the necessary imaginative effort for the realisation of their programmes of production. In other words, good entrepreneurship and adequate flow of capital are the two factors that ensure the progress of the corporate sector. There must be the demand for funds from enterprising risk-takers and the ready supply of capital from investors to meet this demand. The conjunction of the two alone can create a healthy climate for corporate development. Now, corporate taxation obviously affects both the supply of funds and the demand for funds, as we shall now proceed to show more in detail.

[49] Source: *RBI Bulletin*, September 1957, August 1959 and September 1961.

SUPPLY OF CAPITAL FOR INVESTMENT

Investment in the corporate sector is done out of either internal or external funds. Internal resources are the depreciation allowances and the profits retained after the payment of dividends. The prevailing tax laws can affect the quantum of internal resources available for corporate expansion in two ways: (1) Depreciation and amortisation provisions which determine what the taxable profits shall be, and (2) the level and variety of taxation which determine the amount of disposable profits left over after the payment of taxes.

DEPRECIATION ALLOWANCES

We have seen in the third chapter that the Indian income-tax law has made liberal provisions for depreciation allowances. It has also been authoritatively held that the current depreciation law "has not militated against significant rising production from equipment which, in an accounting sense, must be deemed to be steeply declining in value".[50]

However, business interests feel that replacement has been made difficult because of the high and rising prices of manufacturers' goods. Their contention is that the producer who installed his machinery in the thirties and the early forties is the worst hit of all. As J. R. D. Tata, Chairman of India's leading steel producers, said at the annual meeting of TISCO in 1951: "The problem of adjusting the rates of depreciation for income-tax purposes to the present inflated costs of machinery remains unsolved and that, in so far as the rates of depreciation allowed for tax purposes are insufficient to meet replacement costs, the taxation of profits amounts in reality to the taxation of capital". In other words, it is implied that when corporate profits are calculated without making any adjustment for the additional cost involved in replacing old machinery, the result will be erosion through taxation of industrial capital. It has been calculated that, owing to the overvaluation of net profits, the iron and steel industry has been overtaxed in the period between 1937-51 to the tune of about Rs. 25 crores, which represent the capital erosion in that industry.[51] Likewise

---

[50] *Quarterly Economic Report* (April 1954), issued by the Indian Institute of Public Opinion.

[51] *Financial Trends in Iron & Steel Industry*, p. 40.

the capital erosion in the paper industry has been estimated at Rs. 2.50 crores between 1937 and 1953.[52] In the sugar industry the capital erosion has been estimated at Rs. 10.43 crores between 1938 and 1954 ;[53] and in the cement industry, the figure is Rs. 10.75 crores between 1938 and 1951.[54] These figures are calculated on the basis of a 300 per cent rise in the cost of replacing old worn-out machinery—by no means an unreasonable basis for calculation. Such 'capital erosion' is the result, it is said, of the 'faulty' practice of calculating the depreciation allowances for income-tax and price-fixing purposes on the basis of the historical cost, instead of the actual replacement cost.

But even if what the business interests say about the total depreciation allowances being insufficient to cover replacement requirements is correct, the case for tax relief will not be complete and unanswerable. After all, nothing prevents the companies from using at least a part of the taxed profits or even borrowing funds for the purpose of replacement. Besides, the nature of the administration of the depreciation funds by Indian companies is such that the replacement funds of the companies are often mixed up with other reserves and freely used as working capital. Hence the Balance Sheets maintained by Indian companies do not give the 'precise relation' between the depreciation allowances annually made and the actual amounts spent periodically on replacement. Hence, too much importance should not be given to results based entirely on consolidated Balance Sheets as the Association of Indian Trade and Industry have done.[55] Indeed, the position in India is not as hopeless as it is sometimes made out. Actually, as the Taxation Enquiry Commission says after a sample survey of the corporate sector : "On the whole, the companies were able to undertake a gross fixed assets formation ... at a significantly larger rate than the estimated average rate of requirement for replacement".[56]

[52] *Financial Trends in Paper Industry*, p. 38.
[53] *Financial Trends in Sugar Industry*, p. 16.
[54] *Financial Trends in Cement Industry*, p. 11.
[55] See a study based on questionnaires received from selected industries in India (N.C.A.E.R., *Replacement Cost in Indian Industry : A Report*, p. 17).
[56] *Report*, Vol. II, p. 77. See also *The Second Five Year Plan*, p. 390, where it is said with reference to the first Plan period (1951-56) : "As

Hence, if past performances are taken into account, it appears that replacement has not been such a difficult problem as is made out by the captains of business and industry.[57] To alleviate any real hardship in this regard, the income-tax law was amended in 1948 to allow industries to write off depreciation on fixed assets acquired in that year and after at a much higher rate than the usual rate. This method of accelerated depreciation has proved to be of inestimable value to the industry and has greatly helped the growth of the corporate sector during the last decade. "Without this relief", says H. T. Parekh, "it would have been impossible at the present cost of capital goods to implement any capital plan".[58] It is, however, true that some companies which own assets that have a long life and have created specific capital reserves like Government securities or an insurance policy will be particularly hit by the rising prices. But such difficulties faced by a few companies are a minor matter considering the overall high level of earnings and general prosperity of the corporate sector as a whole during the past decade and a half. As for the effect of corporate taxes on retained profits, we have already seen that the volume of profits ploughed back depends much more on the rate and quantum of profits than on the tax rate or the tax yield.

DELETERIOUS EFFECTS OF CORPORATE TAXATION

The *Economist* once declared that "if 'soaking the rich' is the order of the day, then the best way to do it is by means of death duties. The second best is by a wide margin in the income-tax

regards investment on replacement and modernisation programmes, on the whole, except in case of the sugar industry, progress was satisfactory".

[57] It is noteworthy that the Royal Commission also rejected the 'erosion of capital' argument of the Federation of British Industries for tax concessions in the matter of depreciation allowances as they felt that the whole case depends upon improbable assumptions. *Report*, p. 105, paragraph 354. Even the Shoup Commission, although they recommended a revaluation of all business assets, found it necessary to say that "we do not favour replacement cost depreciation as a general rule. But when a monetary unit has sunk almost to 1/200th of its former value, depreciation based on historical cost can have little significance, and some way of relating depreciation to current price level becomes necessary". *Report*, Vol. II, p. 126. See also Vol. III, Appendix C.

[58] *The Future of Joint Stock Enterprise in India*, p. 38.

between earned and unearned income. The worst of all—worst in equity and worst in its effects on enterprise—is a tax on profits as such."[59] Corporate taxation in India is a tax on profits, and consequently it must also have deleterious effects on enterprise, and consequently on the growth of the corporate sector. Enterprise is reflected on the investment made in the corporate sector. If it is found that corporate taxation affects investment adversely, then what the *Economist* says becomes a grim reality : equity is thrown to the winds, and enterprise languishes.

Corporate taxation can affect investment in one of three ways:

1. It can affect business costs and thus reduce the profitability of the concern : that is, corporate taxation, by increasing the costs, raises the standard of profitability to which new investment projects should conform if they are to be launched;
2. It can reduce the return on investment that accrues to the shareholders, and thus drive them away from corporate investment ; and,
3. It can affect investment by depriving the firms of a large part of their working funds.

As long as the capitalistic principle of free enterprise is accepted, the profit motive has to be the main spring of economic development. We saw earlier that, by and large, Indian industry had itself borne the tax burden without shifting it. It is reasonable, therefore, to suppose that corporate taxation has acted somewhat as a damper to higher investment. But it is not possible to measure in precise statistical or quantitative terms the extent of this effect. The period between 1940 and 1959 has been one of rising economic activity. Both the number and the total paid-up capital of the companies have been growing during this period. The various incentive measures—taxation and other—operating in the climate of a growing economy have on the whole helped to neutralise as far as possible the deleterious effects of corporate taxation.[60]

[59] Issue dated 8 February 1947, pp. 225-6.
[60] But we do find a reduction in capital formation in the corporate sector in 1958 and 1959 which is rather surprising considering the bouncing nature of the economy. This slackening might be due to certain bottle-

EFFECTS OF CORPORATE TAXATION

The principal effect of corporation income-tax in an expanding economy with plenty of business opportunities and favourable business expectations is more the reduction of the supply of available funds (both with the corporations and outside) for new investments than the diminution of incentives to invest. Conversely, in a contracting economy, the situation is likely to be reversed, with investment incentives undergoing relatively greater impairment than the supply of available funds.[61] In present-day India, we can safely say that, because of the expanding nature of the economy, there is no question of a lack of incentives.

A glance at the annual consents for capital issues by the controller of capital issues (TABLE XXV) shows us that there is no lack of enterprising producers and promoters to float new companies[62]:

TABLE XXV

Year	Number of New Companies	Capital (in crores of rupees)
1948	375	126
1949	326	63
1950	263	75
1951	343	60
1952	254	40
1953	232	81
1954	220	111
1955	289	125
1956	297	230
1957	345	153
1958	282	423
1959	264	203

necks like the difficulty of obtaining bank capital as evidenced by the low percentage of borrowed capital to the total capital used by the corporate sector in 1958 and 1959. But, perhaps, the tax measures had also some effect. In fact, the finance minister, T. T. Krishnamachari, introducing the Budget in the Lok Sabha on May 15, 1957, anticipated such a slackening. He said, "These measures are not intended to curtail genuine investment in the private sector, though it would not be unreasonable to assume that a slight *slowing down for a short period will not, in the present circumstances, be undesirable*". Speeches, pp. 27-28.

[61] See James K. Hall's discussion of the problem (*A.E.R.*, May 1954. p. 542).

[62] Source: Relevant issues of RBI *Report on Currency and Finance,*

There are, of course, the usual year-to-year fluctuations due to the immediate economic conditions. The question now is whether it was corporate taxation that by itself slowed down the rate of increase of corporate investment?

INVESTMENT RISKS

Dividends are the obvious reward for risk-taking. A person who invests in a joint-stock company is obliged to assume three kinds of risks: these are, firstly, the risk of losing the capital altogether, secondly, the risk of a fluctuating and uncertain income, and, thirdly, the risk of not being able to take back the capital if he wants to use it in any other way. If taxation reduces the reward for such risk-taking, the investors will go in for less risky investments like gold, real estate, Government securities, etc. (This was written, of course, before the 'Emergency' caused by Communist China's

TABLE XXVI

Year	Difference between Total Net Receipts and Total Payments (in crores of rupees)	Paid-up Capital
1939	—18.03	3.46
1942	—39.57	3.80
1944	6.14	5.15
1946	—15.50	12.18
1948	—76.74	22.16
1950	—35.46	8.75
1951	—57.18	5.90
1951	—71.82	7.05
1952	1.11	3.30
1953	—8.18	5.76
1954	—54.25	3.62
1955	—73.42	11.35
1956	—181.37	21.87
1957	—170.52	27.49
1958	—77.90	20.41
1959	—78.86	27.00

aggression and the promulgation of the Gold Control Rules in 1963.) The existence of high taxation thus drives even the little available capital away from the corporations and they are compelled to explore sources other than equity capital for funds. In India, during the period under review, an interesting feature is that the paid-up capital of newly registered firms constitutes but a fraction of the increased paid-up capital of all existing corporations.[63] Because of the risks involved in investing in new firms, people are evidently contented with investing in the older and better established corporations.

TABLE XXVI shows how much the extra capital formation is financed by equity capital.[64]

Evidently the tendency is increased plough-back and increased loan capital to finance expansion, rather than increased equity capital.[65] TABLE XXVII[66] shows clearly how increasingly loan capital is being used.

TABLE XXVII

Year	Loan Capital as % of Total Capital Used
1950	39.6
1951	42.5
1952	41.2
1953	39.9
1954	42.1
1955	40.2
1956	45.2
1957	49.2
1958	26.0
1959	3.6

[63] See Chapter II above, Table xiv, p. 112.

[64] 1939-1951 data for 6 leading industries; 1951-54 RBI data for 750 companies; and 1955-59 RBI data for 1001 companies.

[65] This is because enterprises in the non-Government sector are finding it increasingly difficult to raise equity capital. (See *The Case for Relief in Direct Taxation*, p. 3.)

[66] Source: Calculated from the relevant issues of the *RBI Bulletin*.

This tendency has become very marked only recently i.e. since 1955-56 and 1956-57. The reason for this is not far to seek. The rate of interest has increased from 3.89 per cent in 1956 to 4.55 per cent in 1957, whereas the net rate of return on capital has fallen from 9.53 to 7.37 per cent in the same period. However, because of the name and fame of the established corporations, which give ample security to the investor, they are less dependent upon borrowed capital. A recent study by the Research Division of the Company Law Administration, for example, shows that bigger companies tend to depend much less on borrowing than the smaller companies.[67] But again due probably to the Government absorbing a lot of available savings, the Corporate sector has to use very limited amounts of loan capital.

Actually, what we notice in India now is a downward trend in the risks involved in investment. The risk of losing the capital itself is, of course, the most serious risk which the investor faces. The other two risks mentioned earlier could be reduced considerably by sufficient loss-offsets and a healthy stock exchange. Hence the investor who boldly takes the risk must get an economic rate of return on his corporate investment. This economic rate of return is the minimum return which he can anyhow get (for instance, in Government securities) *plus* the reward for actually taking the risk. And the reward for the risk taken must naturally depend upon the risk itself, its nature and its volume.

In his *Enterprise, Purpose and Profit*, D. H. Macgregor has calcu-

---

[67] See Raj K. Nigam and N. D. Joshi, *Trends in Company Finances*, pp. 7-8. G. Balakrishnan of the Gokhale School of Economics also came to the same conclusion for the years 1950-52 after examining the financial experience of 269 small companies (i.e. with paid-up capital less than Rs. 5 lakhs) and 408 big companies. See G. Rosen, *Some Aspects of Industrial Finance in India*, pp. 39-41; also, G. Balakrishnan, *Financing Small-Scale Industries in India*, 1950-1952 (Bombay, 1962). A Reserve Bank of India study has revealed that bigger companies (in terms of total capital employed) plough back a higher proportion of profits into the business, as compared to the smaller companies; thus the bigger companies are able to grow rather faster with the aid of this relatively higher proportion of internal financing than the smaller companies. Higher corporate taxation must thus, to some extent at least, stand in the way of corporate growth, and this applies more to the bigger than to the smaller companies. See 'Profits in Relation to Size of Companies', *RBI Bulletin*, March 1959.

lated the risk factor in investment by taking into account the companies that went into liquidation. It is assumed by him that investors get practically nothing out of the liquidated companies. Now in India, the statistics of companies which have ceased to operate may with even greater justification be taken as an indicator of the loss of investment, because there are few cases of amalgamation or absorption; and it is reasonable to expect that most of the paid-up capital of the corporations which ceased to work relates actually to companies completely wound up on account of inefficiency and/or fraud.[68] The capital lost by the investors as a percentage of the paid-up capital at work represents the overall risks in the long run. In India, both during the War and after, investment activity was pretty high. While examining the psychological effect of corporate taxation we saw how, especially after 1944 up to 1947, there was a mad rush for buying shares of any floatation whatsoever. We shall now examine the risk factor in the post-independence period[69] (TABLE XXVIII).

TABLE XXVIII

Year	Paid-up Capital at Work	Liquidated Capital	Risk Factor
1947-48	569.6	9.01	1.6
1948-49	528.3	7.90	1.5
1949-50	723.9	8.58	1.2
1950-51	775.4	9.06	1.2
1951-52	855.8	9.15	1.0
1952-53	897.6	11.31	1.3
1953-54	944.9	8.81	0.93
1954-55	969.6	8.81	0.90
1955-56	1024.2	12.74	1.2
1956-57	1077.6	7.59	0.70
1957-58	1306.3	12.51	0.96
1958-59	1509.8	12.72	0.84

[68] See B. R. Kishore, *Indian Economic Review*, February 1952, pp. 39-40.
[69] Source: *Monthly Bluebook of Joint-Stock Companies*, relevant issues.

It is clear that the trend of the risk factor is low, and hence there seems to be no appreciable disincentive.

The foregoing analysis has led to the conclusion that (1) there is no dearth of incentives for the growth of the corporate sector; (2) the risk factor is low and is tending to decrease still further; and (3) fresh equity capital is still comparatively scarce.

WHO ARE THE INVESTORS?

Investment in corporate ventures depends upon the investment decisions of the investors. Who, then, are the investors? How has taxation affected their investment policies and decisions?

If we take into account the small income groups, their main interest will only be the maintenance of their capital, and hence they will be inclined as a rule to play 'safe'. They will not care (or dare) to invest in new and risky enterprises; their preference will be for investments in gold, Life Insurance, Banks, and certain 'safe' corporations. Moreover, the Indian Income-tax Law, by exempting from the levy of income-tax amounts invested in either small savings or Life Insurance, affords a great incentive to people to divert their savings to those channels of investment. Consequently, people with small incomes, being inveterately security-conscious, will invest their moderate savings only in such perfectly safe institutions.

Thus it is only the higher income people who can afford to take sufficient risks in the hope of getting a high rate of return for their investments. This will be clear from the income-tax statistics of the Central Board of Revenue, from which it will be seen that dividend income is concentrated in the high income groups, that is, people with incomes above Rs. 15,000 per annum. The concentration is not as pronounced in the income from securities as in dividend income, whereas income from property may almost be said to be concentrated in the low and middle income groups.

Assessees with an annual income of Rs. 15,000 or below accounted for Rs. 5.46, 6.54, 6.59 and 7.99 crores respectively of dividend income in the first four years specified, whereas assessees with an annual income exceeding Rs. 15,000 accounted for Rs. 21.31, 24.10, 24.60 and 28.86 crores respectively—roughly four times

EFFECTS OF CORPORATE TAXATION

TABLE XXIX
TABLE OF INCOME ASSESSED[70]
(amount in Rs. crores)

Year-Income-range	1955-56	1956-57	1957-58	1958-59	1959-60
TABLE OF DIVIDEND INCOME					
0-15,000	5.46	6.54	6.59	7.99	8.95
15,001-25,000	3.09	3.84	3.77	4.34	4.74
25,001-100,000	9.52	11.20	11.67	14.22	13.63
Over a Lakh	8.70	9.06	9.16	10.30	9.18
TABLE OF SECURITIES INCOME					
0-15,000	0.93	1.13	1.13	1.27	1.35
15,001-25,000	0.44	0.57	0.59	0.56	0.59
25,001-100,000	0.94	1.11	1.20	1.29	1.18
Over a Lakh	0.61	0.67	1.20	.68	.55
TABLE OF PROPERTY INCOME					
0-15,000	10.31	11.74	12.08	13.58	14.92
15,001-25,000	3.42	4.20	4.08	4.49	4.44
25,001-100,000	5.30	6.21	6.16	6.89	6.53
Over a Lakh	2.12	2.02	1.93	2.08	1.55

in every instance.[71] The distribution is less grossly uneven with regard to income from securities, and even more so with regard to income from property.

The above conclusion is confirmed if we examine the percentage of distribution of the market value of shareholdings by various groups. In the absence of all-India figures, we have to refer to sample studies. For example, a sample study conducted by the Reserve Bank of India in the Bombay City revealed the following figures,[72] which are of course very suggestive.

---

[70] Source: Central Board of Revenue, *All-India Income Tax Revenue Statistics* (relevant years).

[71] The remarkable increase in the dividend income in the under 15,000 group lends support to the contention that shares are being purchased by lower income groups increasingly. See p. 275 below.

[72] Source: *RBI Bulletin*, February 1955.

TABLE XXX

Income range (rupees per annum)	Market Value of Shares Held (in crores of rupees)
0-4,000	8.8
4,001-8,000	17.6
8,001-15,000	9.2
15,001-30,000	38.2
Over 30,000	28.1

Thus we find strong support for the conclusion that corporations must look mainly to an insignificant percentage of the population for any ready willingness to assume the risks of corporate ownership, especially in new enterprises.[73]

The slowing up of the rate of growth in equity capital could be ascribed to the reduced profitability ratio caused by corporate taxation. The effects of the steeply progressive personal income-tax and supertax cannot be overlooked either. But more than all these, the disappearance of the princely houses and the Zemindars, who were at one time among the important investors, has caused a serious shrinkage in the rate of growth of equity capital.[74] On the other hand, investment by individual investors is being increasingly replaced by institutional investment, that is, investment by Banks, Insurance firms, and joint-stock companies. The current tendency is for more and more companies to invest in corporate securities, and this their new role as investors is a significant development.[75]

[73] See also H. Venkatasubbaiah, *Indian Economy Science Independence*, pp. 147-8 and L. C. Gupta, 'An Inquiry into the Ownership Pattern of Industrial Shares in India', *Indian Economic Review*, August 1959. See for another study of the problem *RBI Bulletin*, May 1962. The same condition prevails in the U.S.A. See Butters, Thompson and Bollinger, *Effects of Taxation : Investment by Individuals*, p. 27.

[74] See R.B.I., *Report of the Committee on Finance for the Private Sector*, p. 23. See also N. Das, *Industrial Enterprise in India*, p. 160 and A. Sur in *The Stock Exchange : A Symposium*, p. 24.

[75] See, for example, *The Eastern Economist* (Article on 'Growth Pattern of Companies'), 1 April 1960. But more recent events show that once again individuals are coming to the fore as investors. See below, p. 277.

INVESTMENT FOR CAPITAL GAINS

Besides return in the shape of dividends that the investors expect, investments are undertaken also (and perhaps more frequently) for possible capital gains. This is the usual tendency all the world over; and in India too, a survey conducted by the Indian Institute of Public Opinion in 1954 has confirmed this surmise. The survey has established that "both corporate and individual investors have tended more and more to invest because of rising stock values, based on higher dividend anticipations and larger allocations to reserves".[76] This tendency is generally very pronounced in times of rapid economic development, when business expectations are likely to be very favourable.

On the other hand, if a tax like the Capital Gains Tax were introduced, it would certainly affect the growth of corporate enterprises by hitting exactly the very thing which most goads the investors to invest in the corporate sector. We saw earlier that the first tax on capital gains was levied in the Budget for 1947-48. The effect of that tax on business enterprises could be seen from the steep drop in the applications for capital issues:

TABLE XXXI

Year	Number of Applications	Amount (Rs. in lakhs)
1948	480	168
1949	387	73
1950	320	85
1951	410	68
1952	326	152

Even though the tax was abolished in the 1949-50 Budget and notwithstanding the Korean War boom, the confidence of the

[76] *Quarterly Economic Report*, July 1954. This has been confirmed by NCAER's Survey (1960) based on interviews and questionnaires. 70 per cent of the replies received from investors from the high income groups indicated that they invested in shares with the objective of capital appreciation rather than that of earning high incomes. But middle income groups are not *so* definite. *Taxation and Private Investment*, p. 75.

entrepreneurs could not be restored till 1952 and the developing new climate for planning and corporate expansion.

SOCIO-POLITICAL EFFECTS OF CORPORATE TAXATION

One of the basic public policies in modern countries—even in countries where a capitalist form of economy prevails—is a movement towards the achievement of a reasonable degree of economic equality among all sections of the people. In other words, the socio-political ideal of equality involves the attempt to reduce existing inequalities as far as practicable. Many thinkers like Adolf Wagner have been urging from time to time that the instrument of taxation should be used mainly to achieve this purpose.[77] To reduce the existing tax burdens of the poor (by slashing the customs and excise duties, for example) is not possible in developing countries because of the continuing need for finance for programmes of development. The other course, namely heavy taxation of the richer sections of the community, is therefore resorted to so that the egalitarian objective may be sought to be achieved in the fulness of time.

We have seen—on an earlier page—that it is the shareholders who bear the main brunt of the taxation of corporate income (this was, of course, more pronounced in the 1939-51 period than in the 1951-57 period). Since the dividend recipients are concentrated in the upper income groups, is not the high rate of corporate taxation justified from the socio-political point of view?

Sufficient data are not available to give a complete picture of the nature of the dividend income distribution among various— high, middle, and low—income groups. But an attempt can at least be made to show the nature of the dividend distribution for the years between 1955-56 and 1959-60 with the data published by the Central Board of Revenue.

The total income assessed at the hands of individuals for personal income taxation came to Rs. 605.0 crores in 1957-58, Rs. 692.4 crores in 1958-59 and Rs. 743.6 crores in 1959-60. The dividend income of individuals assessed during 1959-60 was Rs. 36.50 crores. Thus only 4.9 per cent of all incomes received by individuals in 1959-60 was dividend income. The

[77] See Fagan's article in Musgrave and Shoup, *Readings in the Economics of Taxation*, p. 50.

figure is 5.3 per cent for 1958-59 and 5.2 per cent for 1957-58. Out of the Rs. 36.50 crores of dividend income in 1959-60, assessees with incomes over Rs. 25,000 (who were 18.3 per cent of the people with dividend income and who were also the supertax payers) accounted for more than 62 per cent. TABLE XXXII shows at a glance how the dividend income is lumped heavily in the top income groups.[78]

TABLE XXXII

RELATIVE SHARES OF DIVIDEND INCOME
(all in percentage)

Income Range	1955-56 Ass.	Amt.	1956-57 Ass.	Amt.	1957-58 Ass.	Amt.	1958-59 Ass.	Amt.	1959-60 Ass.	Amt.
0-15,000	64.1	20.4	63.6	21.3	63.9	21.1	65.0	21.7	65.7	24.5
15,001-25,000	15.6	11.5	16.8	12.5	16.2	12.1	15.7	11.8	15.1	13.0
25,001-100,000	17.9	35.6	17.5	36.6	17.9	37.4	17.5	38.6	16.8	37.3
Over 100,000	2.4	32.5	2.1	29.6	2.0	29.4	1.8	27.9	1.5	25.2

THE CORPORATE TAX SYSTEM PROGRESSIVE AS A WHOLE

Having seen above that dividend income is heavily concentrated in the high income groups, we can now safely conclude that the tax system *as a whole* is progressive. The corporate tax may fall unequally upon persons with the same total income, and it does hit some with lower incomes more heavily than others with higher incomes. But on a total view, however, the corporate tax may be claimed by the socio-political scientist to introduce an element of progressiveness in the tax system because taxes on corporate income by reducing dividends brings about a 'proportionately greater reduction in large disposable incomes than in small disposable incomes'.

But there is another factor, too, namely the progression in individual income-tax rates, which operates sometimes in the opposite direction. In the words of Richard Goode, "A reduction of dividends received is partly offset by a reduction in individual tax liabilities. The higher the individual income-tax, the smaller

[78] Source: Calculated from data in the *All-India Income Tax Revenue Statistics*.

is the reduction in the stockholder's disposable income resulting from a decrease in the total amount of dividends received by him."[79] A high personal income-tax absorbs the progressiveness of the corporate tax. The higher the progression in the individual income-tax, the lesser the overall progression of the corporate taxes on income. Of course, in absolute terms again, no serious harm is done. For individual assessees who pay either a high personal tax or bear the corporate tax through the holding of stocks, no reduction of the actual amount of the tax paid takes place due to such shifts in progression; and hence, in absolute terms, even by increasing the personal rates, a blow is struck for reducing the inequality of incomes in the community.

Conclusion

At the risk of repetition we have to say that taxes are but one of the many factors that affect the growth of the corporate sector. For example, a Government of India brochure lists *sixteen* Government measures that affect "investment in India", and taxation is just one among the sixteen.[80] The Shroff Committee, appointed by the Reserve Bank of India in 1953 to examine why investment in the private sector had not reached the level envisaged by the first Five Year Plan and how increased finances could be made available to this sector, pointed out that in India willingness to invest is affected by

(1) the threat of nationalisation,[81]
(2) procedural uncertainties and difficulties,[82]

[79] *The Corporation Income Tax*, p. 91.
[80] *Governmental Measures Affecting Investment in India* (1950), especially Chapter II.
[81] N. Das says that "private enterprise is in practice tolerated than accepted as a instrument of development.... Frequent references to the statutory power of nationalisation by Government spokesmen have increased rather than allayed the fears of potential investors and entrepreneurs." (*Industrial Enterprise in India*, p. 158.)
[82] G. Rosen says that in India, and especially in the Punjab, "the red tape of corporate legislation (embodied in Company Acts) discourages extension of the public limited form of organisation, and even those firms desiring to raise capital were unwilling to become public corporations to do so." (*Industrial Change in India*, p. 151).

(3) labour policy and legislation, and
(4) varying forms of control and regulation.

It is well known that these factors could be more effective dampers to investment than even taxation. Hence, apart from taxation, these factors too may be said to have influenced the level and quantum of corporate investment. There are other factors, besides the ones mentioned by the Shroff Committee, that have also played a significant part in lowering the level of corporate investments. These factors are :

(1) Increased labour costs and increased prices of machinery ;
(2) Inflation along with high personal taxation, which has reduced the capacity of fixed income earners like Government servants, teachers, etc., to save and to invest ;[83]
(3) The disappearance of the ruling classes like the Rajahs and the Zemindars who used to invest heavily in the corporate ventures ; and
(4) The heavy borrowing programmes of the Governments (Union and State),[84] which siphon off the savings of the public, thereby leaving less and less with possible investors to support corporate floatations.

The operation of these many factors makes it impossible for us to isolate the effects of corporate taxation alone on either the willingness or the capacity of people to invest in corporate enterprises. Again, if we take the tax structure as a whole, the disincentive part (like high rates, the nuisance taxes, etc.) is more or less neutralised by the various tax provisions intended as a positive incentive to industry (for example, the development rebate, the tax holiday, etc.).

If a general statement has to be hazarded in flat terms, the striking fact seems to be that, by and large, the corporate tax

[83] N. Das says : "Before World War II, shares in joint stock-companies were a common form of investment by middle-class families. Since the end of World War II, the number of such investors has gone down considerably." *Industrial Enterprise in India*, p. 160 fn. See also George B. Baldwin, *Industrial Growth in South India*, p. 323.

[84] For example, on 29 July 1960, twelve State Governments alone announced the issue of loans at 4 per cent per annum for amounts aggregating Rs. 75 crores.

structure has had only a relatively minor impact on both the investment incentives and the actual investment. The corporate tax structure would appear to have neither unduly discouraged nor uneconomically over-encouraged the corporate sector.

CHAPTER V

CORPORATE TAXATION AND ECONOMIC DEVELOPMENT IN INDIA

When we lay down a pattern of taxation, it does not mean that we are evolving a philosophy.

The Finance Minister in the
Rajya Sabha, September 5, 1957

Introduction

INDIA is a typical underdeveloped country, exhibiting all the peculiar characteristics of a backward economy. The main problem, however, could be put in plain 'Malthusian' terms as a perpetual race between population-growth and production per capita. To emerge out of the mire of backwardness and underdevelopment India must necessarily solve the crucial problem of low productivity in the context of terrific population pressure. There is but one solution to this problem, namely rapid economic progress. But economic progress is no rigid and static thing like a stick or a cart which can be secured easily and preserved safely; the very idea of 'progress' involves the principle of dynamism, and 'economic progress' is thus a process which is evolutionary in nature.[1] The economy must go on advancing and expanding, for, as the old German proverb says, "He who goes not forward goes backward".

Economic Development and Underdeveloped Countries

DETERMINANTS OF ECONOMIC PROGRESS

By and large, the three major determinants of this evolutionary process, besides of course the basic factor of natural resources, are the trend of population-growth, the state of technology, and the level of capital accumulation. All three tend to grow during

[1] See S. H. Frankel, *The Economic Impact of Underdeveloped Societies,* p. 56.

the period of a country's economic development, and act and react upon one another with results that are neither uniform nor are clearly foreseeable. Apart from these, there is another basic factor, without which all else can do very little : this is the psychological phenomenon of changing human attitudes to economic progress, and unless there reigns "a social attitude receptive to new fields and new methods of production, institutional arrangements that encourage enterprise and investment, and technical and managerial skills that make new methods of production effective",[2] the right climate for economic progress will not develop. This social dynamism could be described, indeed, in the pithy Rostowian terminology, as "the propensity to seek material advance",[3] the desire and the determination to seek and to achieve such economic progress. But, then, it is hardly possible to measure this 'propensity' in strictly quantitative terms.

THE PROBLEM OF POPULATION

Population pressure would cease to be a problem in underdeveloped agricultural countries like India if the surplus agricultural labour were diverted to industries through deliberate large-scale industrialisation. But how is this to be brought about ? Now, industrialisation requires heavy capital investment. It has been calculated that the amount of capital required per head in these countries is roughly equal to four years' income per head ; hence, the expected rate of population-growth multiplied by four should give us the percentage of the national income "which has to be invested in order to provide employment of the same average kind as now exists, for the increasing population".[4] For achieving economic progress, however, the rate of investment must *exceed* the rate of population growth multiplied by four.[5] On the other hand, Bauer and Yamey think that, owing to many factors like the improved status of women, etc., population growth tends to slow down as a country progresses economically.[6]

[2] E. M. Bernstein & Others, *Economic Development with Stability*, p. 3.
[3] *The Process of Economic Growth*, p. 11.
[4] Colin Clark, *Population Growth and Living Standards*, p. 18.
[5] See B. Dutta, *The Economics of Industrialisation*, p. 145 ; and also U.N.O., *Methods of Financing Economic Development in Underdeveloped Countries*, p. 60.
[6] *The Economics of Underdeveloped Countries*, p. 64.

THE STATE OF TECHNOLOGY

As for the factor of technology, the underdeveloped countries may now be said to be in a somewhat favourable situation because they can, if they so desire, utilise all the existing knowledge—scientific and technical—to increase their productivity. Kuznets has pointed out that the major capital stock of a country is not the sum of the physical assets but rather "the body of knowledge amassed from tested findings and the capacity and training of the population to use this knowledge".[7] The underdeveloped countries can now utilise all the impressive volume of scientific knowledge and technical skill that the advanced countries have already accumulated, for, after all, knowledge knows no barriers, and skill can be either acquired or hired. Underdeveloped countries can thus have personnel trained abroad, and whenever absolutely necessary, they may also import foreign technicians. On the other hand, there are economists like Yale Brozen who argue that given inventions, while they may be economic for some resource situations, may not be equally so for others. He accordingly makes the plea that the underdeveloped countries should think more in terms of raising the technological possibilities of the respective areas than of the mere importation of technical know-how developed abroad with specific reference to conditions obtaining there.[8] However sound this argument may appear to be, it is an argument against total and blind borrowing, not against the adaptation of skills and techniques which promise fair to meet an immediate economic challenge. It cannot, after all, be gainsaid that the present-day underdeveloped countries are not where the advanced countries of today were in their underdeveloped periods in respect of technical knowledge. Whereas they had to explore unknown possibilities, developing techniques through a process of trial and error, the underdeveloped countries today have only to decide on ways and means of adopting Western science and technology to their own pressing needs. To take a concrete example, such resourceful adaptation was among the main causes of Japan's phenomenal economic growth since 1868. "All stages of technological maturity and complexity," writes W. W. Lockwood, "tend to develop side

[7] Quoted in U.N.O., *Processes and Problems of Industrialisation in Underdeveloped Countries*, p. 5.
[8] 'Invention, Innovation and Imitation', *A.E.R.*, May 1951, p. 255.

by side in the greatest variety. But it is easier to introduce those innovations which do not break radically with the past. They generally require no large accumulations of capital or advanced technical skills. And in the aggregate such lesser adaptations and improvements were of immense importance in Japan."[9] The urge for economic progress must come from within, as a positive spurt of the social attitude, as a pointed propensity to advance materially. For the realisation of this urge, both existing skills and newly acquired or borrowed skills and techniques will come handy ; not blind borrowing but intelligent and judicious adaptation will best serve the purpose.

CAPITAL ACCUMULATION

Now remains the third factor, viz. capital accumulation. For the underdeveloped countries, capital accumulation is a pressing need, for without it there can be no large-scale industrialisation. Indeed rapid capital formation holds the key to higher productivity per man, rising levels of income, full employment, increase in consumer goods and services, etc. Increased investment can also promote agricultural productivity. It is not surprising, therefore, that the underdeveloped countries are engaged in increasing their capital stock by all possible means.

We mean here by 'capital' savings that could be invested in buildings, factories, plant, machinery, tools, etc. In the words of Bauer and Yamey, capital is the "accumulated stock of resources which contributes to a larger flow of goods and services through time, or which serves as a reserve sustaining a higher level of consumption at a time of more urgent demand or need than would otherwise be possible".[10] 'Put money in thy purse' is the urgent exhortation which the underdeveloped countries can ignore only at the risk of continuing to wallow in their present backwardness ; and money, once accumulated, is turned into the channels of increasing production and flow of goods and services, which are the visible criteria of economic progress. Investment means, among other things, modern machinery, and the use of such tools gives more power to the labourer, thereby increasing the quality and the quantity of his output. Given the scientific knowledge, the rate of

[9] *The Economic Development of Japan*, p. 192.
[10] *The Economics of Underdeveloped Countries*, p. 24.

economic progress strictly depends upon conditions which govern the accumulation of capital, for such knowledge without the means to turn it to practical use cannot contribute to material or economic progress. Thus economic progress hinges to a great extent on the availability of capital.

But how much capital does a country need for its economic growth? A wholly satisfactory answer to this question is very difficult to formulate, because so many factors will have to be taken into account in fixing the limit for capital requirements and capital formation. Even in the advanced countries, the normal periodic replacement of existing equipment—equipment that has been battered through use or has become obsolete through the passage of time—needs capital of the order of 3-4 per cent of the national income. Aside from this, there is the need to maintain at least the current standard of living in the context of a steady population increase; this must entail, as we saw earlier, a certain additional capital investment. Again, while a low rate of capital formation (say, 3 per cent of the national income) may be sufficient for the economically advanced countries, it is only in these countries that there is considerable scope for higher capital formation. A backward country with a 2 per cent annual increase in its population will need capital formation of about 8 per cent of its national income merely to sustain at present levels the increase in population. And a backward country can seldom save enough to achieve the capital formation necessary for both maintenance of the population that is being added year by year *and* a general forward swing of the economy as a whole.

INCOME AND INVESTMENT IN INDIA

Let us turn for a moment to India. Our difficulty is that it is only for the period since 1949 that we have reasonably accurate national income figures. Various national income estimates had been attempted before, but only for isolated years; and such estimates are therefore of little use for our purpose. As for the immediate past, it has been computed that the national income increased by 18 per cent during the five years between 1950-51 and 1955-56, and the per capita income by 11 per cent during the same period. During the next five years between 1956-57 and 1960-61, the national income increased by 20.4 per cent and the per capita income by 8.6 per cent. But during the first year (1961-62) of the third five year plan period, the national income increased only by 2.1 per cent, while the per capita income actually *decreased* by 30 naye paise per head[11]. Again, while in 1950-51, only 4.9 per cent of the national income was invested, the figure rose to 7.3 per cent in 1955-56. During the second five year plan period, investment seems to have risen gradually to 11 per cent of the national income, and it has been proposed that net investments as a proportion of the national income will have to rise still further "to 14-15, 17-18, and 19-20 per cent per annum by the end of the Third, Fourth and Fifth Plans". Whatever these distant possibilities, it is obvious that current rates are nowhere near the rates that prevailed in the advanced countries during their phases of rapid economic growth. Nevertheless, it is rather gratifying that the percentage of net Investment seems to be showing a definite upward trend.

A 'VICIOUS CIRCLE' IN THE UNDERDEVELOPED ECONOMIES

It is, of course, not very profitable to institute comparisons between country and country or between widely separated periods. Investment, expenditure, income, etc., are conditioned by a whole complex of factors—social, psychological and cultural—and hence one cannot say for certain what exact percentage of the national income should be invested in a given instance to produce a given result. All the same, some estimates, however apparently imprecise, are required, at least as the basis for planned action in the economic sphere. As the Planning Commission says, "it is fairly obvious that a doubling of per capita incomes within a generation or so (that is, 25-30 years) required in most of these countries a rate of net investment of the order of 12-15 per cent of the national income."[12] If a still higher and a more rapid rate of development is required, a higher than 12-15 per cent of the national income should be saved and invested. The Planning Commission has accordingly concluded that, in underdeveloped countries with low standards of living and a rapidly increasing population, a rate of growth commensurate with the pressing needs cannot be achieved

[11] See Annual White Paper on National Income released by the Central Statistical Organisation in February 1963. Also see *Third Five Year Plan*, 1961, p. 28.

[12] *First Five Year Plan*, p. 14.

until the rate of capital formation comes up to around 20 per cent of the national income.[13]

While admitting as above indicated that capital formation is an absolute necessity for the underdeveloped countries, it must nevertheless be conceded that such high rates of saving are far from easy, and there is almost a physical impossibility in saving under mere subsistence conditions. Saving, after all, is total income *minus* current consumption. But, as Kenneth Boulding pointedly remarks, "where the level of production is low, the insistent demand of the bare necessities of consumption presses continually against meagre outputs, and any accumulation is very difficult. There must be, in fact, in each type of society some level of output below which accumulation is impossible, for as soon as anything is produced, the urgent need for consumption swallows it up. This explains the great difficulty experienced by any poor society in making progress."[14] This is the vicious circle in which the underdeveloped economies are caught. Their need for economic progress is the most pressing, and it is for them that it is particularly difficult. A very low national income with little capital formation is the order of the day in underdeveloped economies, and even this modicum of capital investment is generally neutralised—or more than neutralised—by the pace of inexorable population increase.

THE PROBLEM OF INDUSTRIALISATION

So much for the overall capital requirements of the economy taken as a whole. We saw earlier that, on the one hand, there is a shortage of capital, and, on the other, the need for industrialisation which requires heavy capital investment. Without industrialisation rapid economic development cannot be achieved, and capital for such industrialisation is not easy to get. For backward or underdeveloped countries, then, industrialisation is both necessary and difficult. Besides, capital formation in the industries sector poses certain additional problems as well.

For one thing, in the underdeveloped countries, "land and trading stocks are always likely to attract a certain amount of capital away from uses which might be more socially productive."[15]

[13] Ibid., p. 14.   [14] *Economic Analysis* (1948 edition), pp. 654-5.
[15] *Processes and Problems of Industrialisation in Underdeveloped Countries*, p. 34.

It is true that all this is not conducive to the long-term well-being of the country, but it is also necessary to understand the psychology of the savers who prefer to invest in land and trading stocks rather than in industry. It cannot be denied that traditional investment, as in land and trading stocks, is not only liquid but also conspicuously secure from currency devaluation and price inflation. In the underdeveloped countries, it is inevitable that land-owners and traders should be the only classes that predominate in the higher income groups and that they should naturally invest their savings in land and trading stocks. Moreover, industrialisation means a higher capital : output ratio ; that is to say, the capital requirements tend to be much higher per unit of operation than those of the already existing agricultural and commercial activities of large sections of the people in the underdeveloped countries. Hence, also, some natural reluctance in investing in such high capital-absorbing ventures as modern industries. Above all, as pointed out by the U.N. Report on Processes and Problems of Industrialisation in Underdeveloped countries, these latter have no tradition of industrial development.[16] Both the industrial consciousness and the necesssary institutions to exploit the consciousness are lacking. Many external economic agencies that are available for entrepreneurs in advanced countries are simply not available to them in the underdeveloped countries.[17] There is a persistent climate of conservatism, and industrialisation by its very dynamism and novelty inspire fear and suspicion more than reassuring confidence or ready enthusiasm.

POLITICAL FREEDOM AND THE URGE TOWARDS
ECONOMIC DEVELOPMENT

We thus see that, owing to more than one reason, underdeveloped countries have a fatal tendency to remain backward. An apathetic or complacent reconcilement to existing conditions has ensured the continuance of a precarious hand-to-mouth economy

[16] For a discussion of the reasons for the factors of production not flowing to industry in the underdeveloped countries, see the above U.N. Report, pp. 11-47.

[17] See C. N. Vakil and P. R. Brahmananda, *Planning for an Expanding Economy*, p. 297. See also 'The Formation of Capital', in H. F. Williamson & J. A. Buttrick (Eds.), *Economic Development : Principles and Patterns*, p. 157.

over long periods of time. But recent decades have been witnessing a favourable change in the climate of the stagnant economies. Many of the backward and underdeveloped countries of Asia and Africa have become politically free, having at last shaken off colonial rule. The attention of these countries is now naturally diverted to the tasks of economic emancipation and economic progress. The ostensible goal of most modern governments is speedy economic development as a necessary condition of the larger goal of the Welfare State. Without security in the economic sphere, without opportunities for intellectual and spiritual growth, mere political freedom is only the freedom to starve and to suffer. The Indian Constitution has accordingly laid down that "the State shall, within the limits of its economic capacity and development, make effective provision for securing the right to work, to education and to public assistance in the case of unemployment, old age, sickness and disablement...." The State shall, in short, strive its uttermost to evolve into the Welfare State.

The goal of modern governments being the material (the material, that is, as the condition of all-round) advancement of the people, they cannot remain altogether passive, leaving the task of developing the country to the "enlightened self-interest" of the people concerned. A high rate of investment cannot be secured by merely allowing the market forces to function in the usual way. In addition to the police functions, the State must therefore willingly undertake the task of improving the economic condition of the people also. Most important of all, the State has to try to bring about an atmosphere that may be conducive to rapid economic progress. Such an atmosphere is chiefly promoted by what J. H. Adler calls the creation of external economies through the availability of social overhead capital;[18] and, as Vakil and Brahmanand affirm, "the main responsibility for this would naturally devolve upon the State".[19]

MIXED ECONOMY IN THE FREE UNDERDEVELOPED COUNTRIES

This necessity for enlarging and widening the functions of governments does not mean —at any rate, it should not mean—

[18] 'The Fiscal and Monetary Implementation of Development Programs', May 1952, p. 590. (*American Economic Review*)
[19] *Planning for an Expanding Economy*, p. 297.

serious curtailment of private initiative. A workable and satisfactory division of functions is possible. The State could undertake the types of investment which, owing to the enormity of the initial outlay required or the time-lag between investment and realisation, the private sector would normally be unwilling to undertake. It is indeed impossible for a mixed economy to function within an industrial framework largely controlled and coordinated through Government agencies. However, as R. N. Tripathy rightly says, the choice of economy—whether it is to be collectivist or mixed or free—is largely a political question.[20] As a matter of fact, in most of the present-day underdeveloped countries of the world (including India), there prevails only a mixed economy in which investment is made both by the private sector and the Government (otherwise known as the 'public') sector. Even so, the paucity of funds for investment continues to be a problem, whatever the type of economy; and if it is a mixed economy, the volume of savings being anyhow strictly limited in the underdeveloped countries, scarcity of investible resources poses a tough problem to public and private sector alike. On the other hand, the Government ('public') sector is generally in a position to mobilise the internal savings, such as they are; and should these prove insufficient, Government could try to procure foreign capital. It is the merest commonsense that internal resources should be exploited to the full before recourse is had to help from abroad, and since the principal methods of mobilising internal savings are borrowing, deficit financing, and taxation, the economic policy of the Government should first be directed to making good use of all these avenues towards capital formation and investment.

ROLE OF TAXATION

In this process of mobilising internal savings, underdeveloped countries are obliged increasingly to give a crucial role to taxation, for taxation is on the whole 'safer' than borrowing or deficit financing; these too may have to be resorted to, but taxation must come first. Underdeveloped countries usually lack good savings institutions, and hence borrowing as a method of savings mobilisation cannot be of much avail. As regards foreign capital, its

[20] *Fiscal Policy and Economic Development in India*, p. 6.

availability would be dependent upon many external factors, and thus cannot merely be taken for granted. Capital formation through deficit financing is a radical cure for radical ailments, and must not be resorted to in any cavalier spirit. It is pertinent in this connection to recall the warning given by Bauer and Yamey : "The general economic and social disadvantages of inflation should be set against the limited benefits (in terms of capital formation) which are possible in ideal conditions and wise management of currency".[21] Thus taxation alone remains, as the safest of the means of capital formation. Taxation means for the society a sort of compulsory saving, and if the revenue is gathered by development-conscious administrators, the savings—a considerable proportion of them, at any rate—would be utilised for socially productive proposes. At least, such is the hope entertained, the promise held out. It is not, of course, meant here that other methods like borrowing, etc. are unimportant ; but, certainly, if an intelligent tax policy were pursued, the other methods also could be then made to yield the best possible results.

Corporate Taxation and India's Economic Development

DIRECT AND INDIRECT TAXES

The use of taxation in inducing economic development, important as it admittedly is, nevertheless raises certain problems of its own. Indirect taxes on essentials and semi-luxuries are the more productive because they fall on the vast majority of the people ; but, for the same reason, they are also politically objectionable. In the underdeveloped countries, the number of people who pay direct taxes is small, and hence direct taxes are not as productive as indirect taxes. More often than not, it is this small group which represents the industrial class, and large amounts cannot be collected from them in the form of taxes without impinging on their incentive and impairing their ability to advance the economic development of the country. The result often is an adroit exhibition of tight-rope dancing by the Finance Ministers trying desperately to balance the direct and the indirect taxes. Among the direct taxes, corporation taxes—on account of the impersonal nature of

[21] *The Economics of Underdeveloped Countries*, pp. 207-8 ; see also pp. 204-8.

the corporations—cause the fewest, the least disturbing political repercussions, and hence the 'fatal fascination' (to use Carl Shoup's phrase) they have for the Finance Ministers who try to play endless variations on the exact burden of the taxes they impose on the corporations.

In a development-oriented economy, the tax proceeds (the bulk of them) are—or should be—spent on the economic development of the country. But corporate taxes should not be equated with other taxes because, whereas other taxes take out that part of the income which might be saved or consumed or invested, corporate taxes mostly (and certainly, in India they do) fall on that part of the income which is most likely to be invested again. In an underdeveloped country, saving and investment are as rare as they are vitally necessary, and hence they hold the real key to its economic progress. But where the savings are meagre, taxation should enable the community to save and invest that portion of its income which would otherwise be consumed. While this may be broadly true of other taxes, corporate taxation is on a somewhat different footing. Because it falls on the corporations and the class of people who generally save but to invest, and reap dividends only to re-invest, corporate taxation only transfers to the public (or Government) sector capital that would otherwise have been available to the private (or the individual) sector. If investment and economic development are the aims of taxation, corporate taxation would appear to achieve little; there may be a change of ownership and control of capital, but no positive spurt to the nation's economy. Thus there is some reason to believe that, for a developing economy, corporation taxes are not really as efficacious as other forms of taxation.

THE GROWTH AND ROLE OF THE CORPORATE SECTOR

The growth of the corporate sector in the economy reflects the shift from the primary agricultural stage to the secondary manufacturing stage in the economy—a shift which signifies the beginnings of rapid economic development. The continuous proliferation of the corporate type of business organisation is an indication of the increasing industrialisation and commercialisation of the economy. The reason for this is that the corporate form of organisation is comparatively rare in the agricultural sector, as may be inferred from TABLE 1.

TABLE I
PAID-UP CAPITAL OF INDIAN COMPANIES[22]
(Rs. in Crores)

Year	Agriculture & Allied Activities	Industrial Concerns	Commerce, Trade & Finance
1949-50	31.69	481.36	204.20
1950-51	32.10	508.55	221.38
1951-52	33.21	594.42	228.64
1952-53	34.90	625.26	237.41
1953-54	34.91	666.67	238.28
1954-55	39.50	584.36	247.23
1955-56	41.53	639.11	259.34
1956-57	42.33	698.39	266.95
1957-58	44.11	933.07	264.71
Increase of 1957-58 over 1949-50	12.42	451.71	60.51

The tell-tale figures in the table show how almost insignificant is the corporate capital engaged in agricultural and allied activities as against the capital engaged in industrial concerns and in commerce, trade and finance. As regards the increased capital engaged in 1957-58 over the 1949-50 figures, the ratio is steep, being about 1 : 36, which means that agriculture attracted only one-thirty-fifth the additional capital that flowed into industry, commerce, trade and finance. It is thus very clear indeed that agriculture has remained an individualist occupation, while industry, trade, finance and commerce are increasingly seeking expression through the corporate form of business organisation.

Towards the end of the second chapter we saw that corporate profits accounted only for a little over 2 per cent of the national income. But for a more realistic assessment of the part played by the corporate sector, we have to examine the share of corporations in the net national product. This is another area in which

[22] Source: Relevant issues of the *Monthly Blue Book of Joint-Stock Company* and *Statistical Abstract of India*, 1958-59.

paucity in statistical data makes it almost impossible for us to arrive at any valid conclusion. In its *First Report*, however, the National Income Committee estimated the domestic product of larger enterprises—which according to the Committee are really corporate establishments[23]—for the years 1948-49 to be 12 per cent of the net national product. Again, the Company Law Administration has recently estimated that the net product of the corporate sector was 8 per cent of the total net domestic product generated in the private sector and 7 per cent of the total domestic product generated in both private and public sectors put together in 1948-49. For 1956-57, the figures were 12 per cent and 11 per cent respectively. The 1957-58 figures were 13 per cent and 12 per cent. In other words, the estimated share of the corporate sector has risen from 1/15 in 1948-49 to 1/10 in 1956-57.[24]

There is another way also of looking at the role of the corporate sector in Indian economy. While it is no doubt true that the corporate sector now accounts for no more than about one-tenth of the national income, in the manufacturing field having factory organisation, however, the corporate sector really plays a much more prominent role and claims an overwhelming share of the industrial economy. For example, the *Census of Manufactures* for 1956, which covers 93 per cent of all factory establishments in India, reveals that the corporate sector controlled 92 per cent of the total productive capital (i.e. fixed assets + working capital) and produced 91 per cent of the net output. In other words, more than 9/10ths of the industrial potential and actual production would appear to be concentrated in the corporate sector.[25]

CORPORATE TAXATION IN AN UNDERDEVELOPED COUNTRY

We have seen already that corporate taxation is a major source of revenue in India. From the conclusion drawn in the above paragraph, it is legitimate to draw the further conclusion that the taxation of the corporate sector means, by and large, the taxation

[23] p. 30.

[24] Raj K. Nigam & N. D. Joshi, *Trends in Company Finances with Particular Reference to the First and Second Plan Periods*, pp. 36ff.

[25] After analysing various statistics, the Taxation Enquiry Commission (1953-54) concluded that "the company form of organisation is gaining importance as a major income-earning activity" (*Report*, Vol. II, p. 24).

of industries. It follows therefore that the capacity of the industry to pay taxes should be borne in mind while imposing direct and indirect taxes affecting it. India being now a developing economy any tax that affects the industrial sector has to be carefully weighed and considered.

The position in India today is that the Government itself is taking an active interest in the country's economic development. To put it differently, the basic philosophy underlying our economic policies is the continuance of a mixed type of economy in which both the private and public sectors are to grow simultaneously. Thus the prime objective of the economic policies of the Government is to promote investment in the public and the private sector alike, though also (in the long run) progressively more and more in the former than in the latter ; accordingly, taxation too, and more particularly corporate taxation, must have the same large aim. Corporate taxation, of course, has to discharge the twin duties of encouraging the reinvestment of profits in the private sector as well as securing a part of the profits for investment in the public sector. Such being the real position, the taxation structure in India cannot fully conform to the norms applicable to the taxation structures of the more advanced countries. As Ursula K. Hicks says, "Naturally the outlines of a tax structure tailored for development will look substantially different in a conventional underdeveloped country than in a highly sophisticated economy like ours".[26]

The two fundamental objectives of all taxation in an underdeveloped country are, quite obviously, (a) restraining or curtailing consumption, and (b) increasing the incentive to invest. Unlike other taxes (for example, income-tax, excise duties, etc.), the corporation tax has hardly any effect on the level of consumption in India. Dividends being sticky (as we saw in the previous chapter), corporate taxes only tend to reduce the amount of the retained profits. It is doubtless true that if resources are diverted into the hands of the Government, investment could be made to flow into channels judged to be the most desirable from the point of view of the community at large. On the other hand, as India is now

---

[26] 'Direct Taxation and Economic Growth' (*Oxford Economic Papers*, September 1956, p. 303) ; see also Raja J. Chellaiah, *Fiscal Policy in Underdeveloped Countries*, p. 60.

professedly a planned economy, the State could anyhow ensure that, even in the private sector, investments are made in accordance with the larger interest of the country's economic development.

TAXATION AS A MEANS OF REDUCING INEQUALITIES IN INCOME

While Government is not blind to this aspect of the matter (that is, the role of the corporate sector in an underdeveloped economy and the need to foster it by refraining from imposing too heavy a tax burden on it), it is none the less a fact that Finance Ministers find themselves unable to reduce appreciably the burden of taxation on the corporations. Besides, the socialistic ideal of reduction of inequalities of income, to which the ruling Party, the Congress, feels committed in a way, is apt to call the tune of taxation, and consequently Finance Ministers are obliged willy-nilly to maintain taxes, especially corporate taxes, at a high level. Desirable as such a course may seem to be from the 'ethical' point of view, if a fetish is to be made of this socio-political ideal of redistribution of income and wealth through high taxation, then the growth of national income is likely to be adversely affected so long as a professedly mixed economy prevails in the country. We are not, of course, advocating here gross inequalities of income as something very desirable or as a social virtue. There is no doubt that in India, as in many other underdeveloped countries, there is often a considerable concentration of wealth and income in the hands of people who perform few, if any, important economic functions. But, then, what is required in the present economic set-up in India is, in the words of Ursula K. Hicks, "much more functional inequality than we have at present in available incomes, if we are to get sufficient supplies of the skills and enterprise needed for rapid development. In increasing functional inequality and decreasing non-functional inequalities the tax structure can play an important part".[27] It is not as though our Planners are altogether blind to

[27] Ibid., pp. 307-8. It is, of course, easy to reduce through appropriate tax measures non-functional inequalities. But increasing functional inequalities present considerable difficulty because the line dividing functional from non-functional inequalities is very thin indeed. Moreover, the frequent changes rung in the social objectives and the increased governmental activities convert the many functional inequalities into non-functional ones, making them undesirable in their turn. (See also D. T. Lakdawala, *Taxation and the Plan*, pp. 79-80.)

such realities and imperatives of the national economy; but the usual pragmatic defence is, to take the words of J. J. Anjaria, Economic Adviser to the Ministry of Finance: "It is, however, virtually impossible to avoid hardships to some classes and the question ultimately becomes one of what priority the community attaches to development itself. Questions like... the desirability of redistributive taxation impinge on this wider issue and have, in fact, to be related to the basic decisions taken in regard to the size and content of the development plan itself."[28] But even granted that equality of incomes has to be achieved, the point could still be argued that, in a developing economy, corporation taxes are not really the correct weapons for achieving that end.

TAXATION AS A TOOL FOR ENCOURAGING INVESTMENT

Rather than making use of corporate taxation as an egalitarian hammer to tax the rich and bring about equality of incomes, it might be used to much greater advantage as a tool to encourage saving and investment and economic progress generally. In India today, the ownership of shareholding is showing a decided shift. Oversubscription has become a common feature in India especially after 1958.[29] It was seen earlier that still the corporate sector is dependent upon an insignificant minority for the new risk capital. But there is some evidence to show that even low income groups are participating in the purchase of shares. For instance, a special report in the *Hindustan Times* pointed out that even peons, waiters, and clerks are buying shares. A definite 'break from the past' has been noticed in that now people from all walks of life are investing in company shares. Most of them could buy only one or two at a time but they manage that much at least.[30] Again, in a recent floatation, Synthetics & Chemicals Ltd., the promoters claimed that most of the people who wanted to buy shares were lower middle class people like clerks, teachers, and small traders. In spite of these signs, the part played by corporate securities in the savings

[28] 'Problems of Economic Development' (*The Indian Economic Journal*, January 1960, p. 248).

[29] N.C.A.E.R., *Taxation and Private Investment*, p. 109.

[30] Issue dated 14 July 1961. The same tendency is found in Calcutta also. See *The Statesman* (Overseas Edition) May 19, 1962, for a special report.

of the household sector is very small. The only redeeming feature is that it has within its limits increased, as TABLE II shows.[31]

TABLE II

Year	Total Savings of Household Sector	Corporate & Cooperative Shares & Securities (Rs. Crores)
1950-51	509.88	12.22
1951-52	254.76	10.43
1952-53	492.61	10.34
1953-54	504.88	6.03
1954-55	561.64	12.85
1955-56	785.98	33.42
1956-57	810.36	61.15
1957-58	686.55	59.40
1958-59	837.57	35.98

While the shareholding habit has increased—though but slightly—still there is not much evidence to support the view of the late Lala Karamchand Thapar that in India the era of people's Capitalism has been ushered.[32] In fact, in a survey carried out by the National Council of Applied Economic Research, it was found that people with an income below Rs. 4,000 per annum, actually reduced their already meagre holdings of shares and bonds. In the same way the top income group invested much less relative to their income than the middle income groups.[33] Perhaps these savers are from what B. V. Krishnamurthy calls[34] the U-Sector, i. e. the rising class of salaried officials and top business executives. An analysis of the all India Income Tax Reports shows that the number of shareholders has been higher under salary earners from 1955-56 to 1958-59 (39 per cent) than under non-salary earner individuals (21 per cent).

[31] *RBI Bulletin*, August 1961.
[32] Presidential address before the 35th Session of Federation of Indian Chambers of Commerce and Industry on March 17, 1962.
[33] *Delhi Savings Survey*, Table No. 20, p. 121.
[34] *Economic Weekly*, September 24, 1960, p. 1439.

Besides this U-Sector, land ceilings and similar measures are breaking up large holdings of agricultural land, and property in excess of the ceiling is being sold or secured, and the capital and savings of the middle-classes are fleeing from the rural areas with the result that considerable past savings and the proceeds of present sales are seeking out suitable avenues of investment in the urban areas. While precise statistics relating to this drift are not available, there can be no doubt either about the prevalence of this tendency; he who runs can read the signs, and mark which way the wind is blowing. Zemindars on the one hand and the richer landlords affected by land-ceiling reforms on the other seem to be investing capital in urban property, in industry, in trade. Whoever may be the shareholders, it is good that the habit of shareholding is spreading.

This has to be viewed simultaneously with the declining part played by the Companies in holding shares of other companies. Till 1959 the share of the dividend income of individuals showed a decrease, but in 1959-60 once again the share of individuals went up at the cost of the companies' share which fell from 37.52 per cent in 1958-59 to 29.75 per cent in 1959-60.

TABLE III

SHARE OF DIVIDEND INCOME[35]

(per cent of total)

Year	Individuals	Companies	Jt. Families	Others
1955-56	58.23	32.30	6.83	2.64
1956-57	55.46	36.82	5.23	2.49
1957-58	56.73	34.04	6.46	2.77
1958-59	52.98	37.52	5.94	3.56
1959-60	60.25	29.75	6.45	3.55

The corporate securities held by the corporate sector had already begun to decline both absolutely and relatively as TABLE IV indicates.

[35] Calculated from Central Board of Revenue, *All India Income-tax Revenue Statistics* (relevant issues).

TABLE IV
OWNERSHIP OF CORPORATE SECURITIES[36]

Year	Total Paid-up Capital (1)	Securities Held by Corporate Sector (2)	(2) as % (1) (3)
1950-51	753.1	192.7	26
1951-52	812.3	206.3	25
1952-53	850.0	201.1	24
1953-54	889.5	221.8	25
1954-55	908.5	233.5	26
1955-56	960.4	240.5	25
1956-57	991.3	185.2	19
1957-58	1036.1	194.6	19

It is also not likely that the corporate sector will expand its shareholdings to any considerable extent because of the increasing difficulty in procuring working capital due to a variety of reasons. The corporate sector must of necessity look to the individual investors for venture capital. Evidently this is an opportune moment for corporate expansion. Now indeed is the time when the surplus in land and other odd savings could be diverted to industry. But encouragement needs to be given to the corporate sector if this trend, now no more than a trickle, should assume the proportions of a flood. Such encouragement should naturally imply a rational approach to the problems of corporate taxation.

A total abolition of corporate taxation is not advocated here, for it is outside the realm of realism or commonsense. For one thing, India is in a developing phase and large savings are required to push through the many schemes of expansion. In its search for revenues which in the given circumstances is bound to be ceaseless if not ruthless also, the Government must in the coming years resort increasingly to more and still more taxation. This has already been indicated by J. J. Anjaria, who on account of his present official position may be regarded as a Government spokesman: "There have been large increases in taxation in the

[36] N.C.A.E.R., *Taxation and Private Investment*, p. 109.

course of the Second Plan, and it cannot be said that the problem is easy of solution. Few would expect that the Third Plan could be seen through without a further tax effort of a sizeable order."[37] In this unpromising context, it is neither possible nor desirable wholly to abolish corporate taxation. Moreover, corporations too benefit from the various external economies generated by the Government participation in the economic development of the country, and it is reasonable that the corporate sector should bear these costs, in some measure at least. All that is suggested here is that, in the interests of the country's economic development as much as in the interests of the companies, there *is* a case for a lightening of the present burden of corporate taxation. Even dispassionate observers like I. M. D. Little have come to the conclusion that the present rate of direct company taxation (45 per cent) is 'fairly high' by international standards.[38] It is true that, as pointed out in the previous chapter, the corporate sector taken as a whole is paying only about 3 per cent of its gross receipts as taxes on income and profits—not, on the face of it, too much of a burden. Yet this doesn't reveal the correct picture. In recent years, due to considerable new investment in fixed assets, the tax provisioned is ultimately lessened on account of the tax holiday and the concession of accelerated depreciation added to the development rebate; but this fair weather cannot last; the tax burden must prove to be much heavier even with the existing rates after a period of about ten years.

There is another way also—perhaps a more satisfactory way—of evaluating the weight of taxation on the corporations. We might look at the ratio of taxes to the national income and try to draw valid inferences. Now the net domestic product of the private corporate sector is estimated by the Company Law Administration to be Rs. 1250 crores in 1956-57. During the same

[37] 'Problem of Economic Development' (*The Indian Economic Journal*, January 1960), p. 247.

[38] Paper presented at the Seminar on 'Tax Policy and the Third Plan' in the Institute of Economic Growth (attached to the Delhi School of Economics) in March 1959. See also his 'The Third Five Year Plan and the Strategy of Indian Development', *Economic Weekly* Special Number, 1960. According to him, in India only the corporation tax rates and personal Income Tax rates are high and even then the latter are not effective, p. 891.

year, the corporate sector paid in the form of direct taxes Rs. 118.50 crores, i.e. 9.5 per cent of the net domestic product generated by the private corporate sector; and this calculation does not take into account the indirect taxes. Further, also during the same year, the Government gathered 8.2 per cent of the private national income in the form of taxes. On the other hand, whereas the Government's draft on private income through direct taxes alone was only 2.5 per cent, the draft on the corporations through direct taxes was 9.5 per cent—almost a four-fold share. These are but pointers, but the conclusion is unescapable that the corporate sector is being made to contribute to the national exchequer proportionately much more than all the other sectors put together relative to income received. It is therefore not unreasonable to make out the plea that the Finance Minister should in future consider the possibility of tapping other sectors of the economy like agriculture, 'public sector' enterprises, etc. instead of heaping more and more burdens on the already burdened back of the corporate sector.

We are not concerned with the effects of the personal income taxation. Although very few claim that high personal taxes dull the incentive to invest in company shares, the common complaint is that "high personal taxes made it extremely difficult, if not impossible, for entrepreneurs in the high income brackets to save and invest funds in new enterprises".[39] It is very important because in India buyers of shares still decide mostly on the fame of the promoters,[40] and it is wrong "to overlook the key role of the promoter behind large-scale business ventures".[41] If high personal taxes really result in less investible funds in the hands of these promoters, it is a problem that requires serious attention.

THE CASE FOR A REDUCTION OF CORPORATION TAXES

One may, indeed, go further and say that, not only corporation taxes should not be enhanced yet further, but even that an attempt should also be made to effect a reduction of the rates. The case for such reduction would be strengthened if we examined (as we did in the fourth chapter) the phenomenal rise in the receipts from

[39] N.C.A.E.R., *Taxation and Private Investment*, p. 39.
[40] *Economic Weekly*, November 5, 1960, p. 1625.
[41] N.C.A.E.R., *Taxation and Private Investment*, p. 31.

the various indirect taxes of the Union Government. Call them direct or indirect taxes, both are, after all, paid by the corporations themselves. It is far more difficult for the corporations to avoid these taxes than for individuals in business, and therefore there can be hardly any question of evasion on the part of the corporations. Now indirect taxes are usually levied either on the *volume* or on the *value* of the output. These taxes, of course, are meant to be shifted to the consumer, but it is not always possible because indirect taxes (whether they take the shape of excise duties, customs, or sales taxes) increase the cost of production or distribution, thereby determining the quantity of the goods that could be sold. Among the important Central indirect taxes that affect the corporate sector are the import duties, the export duties, and the excise duties. Import duties affect the corporate sector only to the extent of increasing the prices of the machinery and raw materials imported. And, in the present Indian context, import duties do not present a serious problem. As for export duties, they are falling steadily owing to the Government's policy of encouraging exports. It is only the export duty on Tea, which is predominantly controlled by the corporate sector, that has increased considerably from a yield of Rs. 11.24 crores in 1950-51 to Rs. 20.47 crores in 1956-57. However, receipts from this source are again on the decrease, owing mainly to a fall in the exports.

The most important problem from the point of view of the corporate sector is therefore the rise in the yield of excise duties. Throughout the period of the first and second Five Year Plans there has been a progressive rise in the contribution of excise to the public fisc. From Rs. 67.54 crores in 1950-51, the contribution from excise duties has shot up to Rs. 312.94 crores in 1958-59, and the budgeted revenue for 1960-61 is nearly Rs. 380 crores, almost a six-fold increase in the course of a mere decade. Till 1954-55, excise duties were mainly concentrated on items like tobacco and matches, etc., and there the part played by the corporate sector was very small. But after the reversal of policy in 1955-56 (already referred to in the previous chapter) which involved a shift in emphasis from direct to indirect taxes, the base was broadened by the inclusion of new items like motor spirit, cement, etc., where almost all the production was in the hands of corporations, and the rates too were heightened on goods like steel ingots, electric bulbs, rayon, tyres, tubes and paper, where again production in the corporate sector predominated.[42] As the corporate sector produces (as we have seen already) about 90 per cent of the industrial output in India, it will not be far wrong if we hazarded the conclusion that nearly 90 per cent of the excise duties is really taken, by sleight of hand as it were, from the corporate sector.

Nor is it the mere increase in production that has resulted in this phenomenal increased yield in excise duties. Production has increased no doubt, but the tax yields have increased at an even faster rate as may be seen from TABLE V:

TABLE V

INDUSTRIAL PRODUCTION AND EXCISE DUTY [43]

Year	Index of Industrial Production	Index of Excise Duty Paid by 1,001 Companies
1955	100	100
1956	109	125.6
1957	112	179.1
1958	114	222.0
1959	124	236.7

Whereas production increased by 12 per cent in the course of two years, the yield from excise seems to have increased at a rate five or six times that of the increase in production. It is no less interesting to examine the part played by excise duties in company finances (TABLE VI).

As the excise duty is included in the cost of production, it sometimes tends to inflate the prices; in the Indian Textile industry, for example, this inflation in prices has had deleterious consequences. As the *Hindu* editorially remarked, "what was gained on the swings is lost on the sides".[44] Increased cost inevitably encounters corresponding consumer resistance. Consequently, if larger sums are collected by way of excise duties, the receipts

[42] See *Census of Manufactures* (1956).
[43] *RBI Bulletin*, September 1961.
[44] Issue dated 22 April 1958.

TABLE VI
EXCISE DUTIES AND DIRECT TAXES AS PERCENTAGE OF TOTAL RECEIPTS[45]

Year	Public Limited Companies (1,001 Companies)		Private Limited Companies (333 Companies)	
	Excise Duties as % of Total Receipts	Direct Taxes as % of Total Receipts	Excise Duties as % of Total Receipts	Direct Taxes as % of Total Receipts
1955	4.7	3.5	2.2	3.0
1956	5.3	3.6	2.6	3.0
1957	6.8	2.9	3.0	3.2
1958	8.0	3.0	3.8	3.7
1959	7.8	2.9	3.8	3.4

from other direct taxes are adversely affected. For instance, in the 1,001 public companies (for which figures are given in the table) we see that, while the excise duties have increased from 4.7 per cent to 7.8 per cent, the direct taxes have registered a fall from 3.5 per cent to 2.9 per cent during the same period (1955-59). The position is otherwise with regard to the private limited companies, as the above table clearly shows; they were, perhaps, more successful in shifting the indirect taxes without jeopardising their own well-being. All these considerations lead to the conclusion that, since the Government is now placing the main accent on excise duties and other indirect taxes, it can afford to reduce the rates of corporate taxation without seriously affecting the total yield of the taxes.

INCENTIVE TAXATION

The Indian tax system has certain features which are intended to provide incentives for increased saving and investment. We have already examined in the third chapter the various incentive measures like the tax holiday, the differential corporation tax, and the development rebate. It is claimed by the Government that

[45] *RBI Bulletin*, September 1961.

these incentive tax measures lead to increased production and a larger volume of capital formation. But, then, how far the rise in capital formation and increase in production are really due to the incentive tax measures is anybody's guess. As we saw at the end of the last chapter, taxation represents but one of the various factors that determine the quantum and nature of capital formation. It need not also be taken for granted that in the past tax concessions have greatly increased the incentive to save and to invest. Regarding the pre-Plan period, for example, R. N. Bhargava says: "The tax measures announced in 1946 failed to increase production to any considerable extent. The bottleneck to production is shortage of capital equipment, raw materials and technical skill. No tinkering with the taxation policy can automatically remove these hurdles."[46] A mere *tinkering* with the tax policy may not be of much use; but an imaginative handling of the tax policy may yield—indeed, cannot but yield—far better results.

The differential corporation tax which discriminated in favour of retained profits was abolished in the 1959-60 Budget. This tax was supposed to encourage an increase in the profit retentions of the corporations. On the other hand, even though the tax may reduce the dividends, it does not follow that such retention will be necessarily conducive to capital formation. The retained profits must be kept simply as reserves. One cannot therefore say definitely whether the policy of encouraging profit retentions can automatically increase the savings available for investment in the economy.

The Tax Holiday is yet another measure intended for providing incentives to invest, but this too has no more than a limited use. When a new company is promoted, it is seldom that taxation plays any vital part in its decisions except in so far as the taxes are also taken into account in calculating the probable level of the profits that may accrue.[47] Moreover, very few enterprises begin to earn substantial profits in the early years of their career to be

---

[46] 'Taxation of Business Profits' (*Commerce*, 3 May 1947, p. 693). See also Nanda K. Choudhry, 'Indian Taxation Policy: 1946-51' in the *Indian Economic Journal*, July 1955, p. 61.

[47] See article on 'Effects of Taxes on Concentration' by J. Lintner and J. K. Butters, in the Symposium, *Business Concentration and Price*

able to avail themselves of this scheme. The Taxation Enquiry Commission, after analysing the causes of the ineffectiveness of this measure, says: "The main reason for the ineffectiveness of Section 15C is the grant of initial and additional depreciation allowances which, together with normal depreciation allowances, make up nearly 80 to 85 per cent of the cost of fixed assets in the form of plant and machinery within the first five years of the life of the concern. As these depreciation allowances have to be deducted first before computing profits for purposes of income-tax, it has been difficult for any appreciable number of new concerns to claim the benefit conferred under Section 15C. Moreover, as the concession applied to all industrial concerns, it loses some of its effectiveness as a stimulus to capital formation."[48] In spite of all that we have seen, the income exempted owing to Section 15C has increased considerably i.e. from 14.02 lakhs in 1953-54 to 158.77 lakhs in 1959-60. But the number of recipients has not appreciably increased.[49] Nevertheless, as the principle underlying this scheme is doubtless salutary, a few modifications might make this measure serve its purpose better than at present. Now, the main objection to the measure as it stands is that the benefits offered in the early years are really superfluous for the new companies; for they are unlikely to make profits anyway, and the holiday is thus merely notional than otherwise. But if Section 15C, relating to the tax holiday, could be modified or improved upon through the provision under this scheme of carry-forward facilities for exemptions which the company has not been able to set off against operating profit, it might prove much more of a real incentive to the new companies.

The trouble with the various concessional measures like the development rebate, liberal depreciation provisions and the tax holiday in the corporate tax structure is that the more advantage is taken of them, the nearer is the period of full-fledged taxation. This can hit the corporate sector hard. From being completely

---

Policy, pp. 243, 246. Lintner and Butters rightly feel that taxes have little adverse effect on incentives to start new enterprises. Although people are interested in profits, they do not take note of taxes unless, of course, "tax rates approach confiscatory levels and are expected to remain there" (p. 243).

[48] *Report*, Vol. II, p. 101.

[49] Source: Relevant issues of the *All India Income Tax Revenue Statistics*.

free for a time from the attentions of the tax-gatherer, it could be embarrassing or worse to be called upon suddenly to pay a sizeable chunk of the profits. More than the pleasure and the relief that the holiday gives is the fear or anxiety that the holiday is soon going to end and that the full reckoning can be delayed no more! Moreover, the recent tendency has been to raise the tax rates almost in every budget, and the result may very well be that the companies that have enjoyed tax relief through concessional measures in days of relatively light taxation will be required to face full assessments at higher rates in the years to come.

One reform is worth trying. If, instead of a complete tax-free period of five years (as under Section 15C of the Indian Income-tax Act), the tax holiday were turned into a partial 'working day' involving the payment of, say, 30 per cent of the tax liabilities, and if concessional taxation were spaced and spread over many years, the tax rising by stages from 30 per cent to the full complement in the course of ten or more years, would it not be productive of better results? This should entail no loss to the exchequer, but, on the contrary, it may prove far more acceptable to the companies themselves. This extended tax holiday scheme, coupled with carry-forward facilities, may go far in providing real incentives to the companies.

It must, however, be candidly admitted that special tax incentives do not—and perhaps cannot—on the whole provide *any special encouragement* to the private sector to increase the capital investment. Rightly does the U. N. Report call tax measures as at best "blunt instruments for the specific channelling" of trade and investment.[50] Incentive taxation thus presents considerable difficulties, since it must necessarily be predicted on the estimates and expectations of the decisions of traders and investors which they might be expected to take as a result of the tax concessions. Even so, underdeveloped countries cannot quite afford to adopt the attitude of Benjamin Anderson that "taxation should be *neutral* as far as possible with respect to human decisions, which must rest on the individual circumstances".[51] Tax incentives are

[50] *The Effects of Taxation on Foreign Trade and Investment*, p. 6. See also U.N. *ECAFE Bulletin*, Vol. VII, No. 3, November 1956 (Bangkok), p. 49.

[51] *Financing American Prosperity : A Symposium*, pp. 54-55.

CORPORATE TAXATION AND ECONOMIC DEVELOPMENT 287

useful in theory, but theory often lags behind actuality ; in practice, investment depends, not on incentive taxation alone or on it particularly, but on investment opportunities and also on the interest rate. Many of these incentive taxation measures considered individually are efficient tools in attracting capital for the desired lines of investment. But the potency in them is considerably lessened by using all the methods at the same time. On the other hand, it must be conceded that tax concessions in the underdeveloped countries, while they may not have decisively favourable effects, do nevertheless create a favourable economic climate for the investors. Besides, the direct effect of tax concessions on the liquidity position of the company is important.

From what is said above it is not to be concluded that no improvements in the tax structure can increase the capital formation : this would be too pessimistic a view of the situation. Even if tax measures do no more than create a good climate, that is itself a consummation that is most desirable. All that is implied in our argument is that specific tax measures cannot by themselves solve the problem of capital formation. Actually, the problem is one of designing a complete structure of taxation that will be conducive to the accomplishment of rapid economic development, instead of the current piecemeal attempts—which by their very nature are apt to prove largely ineffective—at providing incentives to ampler capital formation.

Tax Reform

IMPROVEMENT IN ADMINISTRATION

The very first need in our tax system is a thorough tightening up of the administration and a corresponding increase in the efficiency of tax collection. A look at the increase in the cost of collection of corporation taxes will convince us that the efficiency—never very high—is now steadily on the decrease rather than otherwise. TABLE VII shows the cost of collections and the actual collections and the number of assessees for the ten year period from 1949 to 1959.[52]

[52] Source : *Combined Revenue and Finance Accounts* and *All India Income Tax Revenue Statistics* (relevant issues).

TABLE VII

Year	Cost of Collections (Rs. Lakhs)	No. of Assessees	Actual Tax Collections (Rs. Crores)
1949-50	46.8	7349	37.16
1950-51	55.4	8519	39.33
1951-52	58.7	10761	40.75
1952-53	70.1	9700	42.98
1953-54	79.0	9933	40.19
1954-55	78.4	9455	36.45
1955-56	81.7	10261	36.52
1956-57	105.4	10780	50.40
1957-58	112.8	10989	55.66
1958-59	111.9	10777	53.52

For an increase of 44 per cent in the total collections and an increase of 47 per cent in the assessees the cost of collection has increased by nearly 239 per cent. Obviously something is wrong somewhere which calls for a complete probe (not the partial enquiry conducted by the Mahavir Tyagi Committee) and the prompt institution of remedial measures.

PREVENTION OF EVASION

Directly flowing from this is the persistence of considerable tax evasion. There are no two opinions about this evil, though differing estimates are being given regarding the volume of tax evasion in the country. Nicholas Kaldor, for example, has estimated that the amount of revenues lost through the evasion of income and other direct taxes of the Union Government is of the order of Rs. 200-300 crores.[53] But the Central Board of Revenue puts the figure at about Rs. 50 crores.[54] It is quite possible that the CBR figure has underestimated the extent of the evil, but on the whole

---

[53] *Indian Tax Reform*, p. 105. Kaldor in his evidence before the Direct Taxes Administration Enquiry Committee said that he had included within this figure, not only tax-evasion, but also tax-avoidance. (*The Hindu*, 3 December 1959).

[54] See D. T. Lakdawala, *Taxation and the Plan*, p. 202.

this lower figure is likely to be nearer the truth than Kaldor's, because the latter has based his calculations on the national income estimates which, in their turn, "are based on very slender material". Nevertheless, even the CBR figure of Rs. 50 crores is no negligible amount to be allowed to be lost through mere evasion. Analysing the reasons for this apparently large-scale tax evasion, the *First Five Year Plan* rightly remarked : "The fact that the corporate form of organisation is confined to a limited sector of business renders the problem of checking evasion difficult, particularly in regard to trading operations. Even where the corporate form exists, the close inter-locking of managerial and other controlling interests in industry, trade and finance offers to the unscrupulous opportunities for evasion."[55] A widening of the corporate sector will certainly reduce evasion because of the strict watch now kept over its activities by the Company Law Administration and also because corporations themselves are in the felicitous phrasing of Louis Eisenstein, "a sturdy refuge from the discomforts of progression".[56]

KALDOR'S REFORM PROPOSALS

Kaldor, on being summoned by the Government of India as the physician of our tax system, suggested a thorough change in our tax structure so as to render tax evasion practically impossible. According to him, "it is far better to have a fool-proof system of taxation with a moderate schedule, than a system which has the appearance of high progressivity, but which cannot be effectively or impartially administered".[57] Kaldor's proposals accordingly aimed at broadening the tax base through the introduction of (1) an annual tax on wealth ; (2) the taxation of capital gains ; (3) a general gift tax ; and (4) a personal expenditure tax, in addition to the usual income-tax. The simultaneous operation of all these taxes, aided by the introduction of a "comprehensive return" and a "comprehensive reporting system on all property transfers and other transactions of a capital nature" were confidently expected to reduce evasion considerably, if not eliminate it altogether. Again, because all these varied taxes were to be

[55] p. 51.
[56] *The Ideologies of Taxation*, pp. 178-79.
[57] *Indian Tax Reform*, p. 2.

assessed on the basis of a single "comprehensive return", they would have an automatic self-checking feature in a double-sense, that is, "both in the sense that concealment or understatement of items in order to minimise liability with regard to others, and in the sense that the information furnished by a tax payer in the interest of preventing over-assessment with regard to his own liabilities automatically brings to light the receipts and gains made by other tax payers".[58]

However theoretically efficient Kaldor's system may be, it has to be admitted that it cannot be expected to work perfectly under Indian conditions. For one thing, if we must have Kaldor, then we must have him wholesale; only then can his proposals have a real chance of proving effective. But such a wholesale acceptance of the Kaldorian dispensation is not possible, for certain suggestions of his are likely to cause very adverse psychological reactions. India neither possesses a very efficient tax administration as is to be found in, say, Sweden; nor has it a majority of honest tax payers, and therefore considerable tax resistance has to be accepted as a continuing fact of our life owing to the operation of various factors.[59] If, in D. T. Lakdawala's words, "the taxed sector is not a world sufficient unto itself, or where different units of the sector are liable at different rates of taxation",[60] evasion cannot be controlled, much less eliminated, even with the introduction of Kaldor's scheme; and in India, the taxable units are few and the economy is not properly organised, and hence even Kaldor's system cannot prevent large-scale evasion here. The foremost objection to Kaldor's proposals, however, is that they have, in their totality, never before been experimented with anywhere so as to create confidence in their efficacy. It would indeed be hazardous to start and experiment with such new techniques of taxation, particularly at this anxious stage of economic development in India.

[58] Ibid., p. 2. But the Direct Taxes Administration Enquiry Committee (1958-59) came to the conclusion that this will not be worthwhile and "no additional benefit might accrue merely from the introduction of a comprehensive return". *Report*, p. 2.

[59] See R. N. Tripathy, *Fiscal Policy and Economic Development in India*, p. 143. See for an interesting list of the factors that are responsible for a low degree of tax tolerance, R. N. Bhargava, *Indian Public Finances*, pp. 49-50. [60] *Taxation and the Plan*, p. 203.

Even though Kaldor's proposals were not adopted in full by the Government of India, many features of his system (for example, the Wealth Tax and the Expenditure Tax) were blindly superimposed on the existing tax structure. But, as discussed earlier, the results have been far from satisfactory. The Kaldorian system, let us repeat, should be implemented all in all or not at all. To do the former would be hazardous in a country of the size and with the problems of India, but piecemeal experimentation may produce effects contrary to those intended. We shall be only achieving an additional twist of complication in the tax structure without reaping any proportionate advantage.

NEED FOR SIMPLICITY IN THE TAX STRUCTURE

Already, in some of the previous chapters, we have drawn attention to the complex nature of our tax laws and the mutually contradictory clauses to be found in the corporate tax structure in India. Any improvement in the tax structure should therefore first assume the form of a reduction in the complexities of the present system. An important first step was taken in this direction in the Budget for 1959-60, when the old system of 'grossing' was abolished and the total combined rate of corporate taxation was reduced from 51.5 per cent to 45 per cent to offset any increased burden that might occur as a result of the abolition of 'grossing'. But, as R. J. Taraporevala's recent study has clearly demonstrated,[61] this decrease is obviously not sufficient to neutralise the additional burden. It would be more in keeping with the capacity of the corporate sector if the total rate were reduced from the present 45 per cent to about 40 per cent of the profits.

However, the corporation executives and entrepreneurs seem to feel that even 45 per cent is 'fairly reasonable' and they are sore only about the taxation of bonus shares and a 'rigid' 23A Section.[62]

[61] *The New Scheme of Company Taxation* (Bombay, 1960). The Federation of Indian Chambers of Commerce and Industry and the Associated Chamber of Commerce have also published similar studies. However, the Indian Institute of Public Opinion has come to the conclusion that the new system of taxation has hit rather adversely all industrial sub-groups, except mining and quarrying. (See *Monthly Political Commentary*, November 1960).

[62] N.C.A.E.R., *Taxation and Private Investment*, p. 57. (Opinion expressed during the interviews).

In spite of such an expression of opinion, it doesn't seem to be a wise policy to increase the rate from 45 per cent to 50 per cent as the 1962-63 Budget has done.

The 1963-64 Budget—the first 'Emergency' Budget—goes even further, and a 'super-profits tax' is proposed to be levied on companies. After leaving out of the nett profits (i.e. profits *after* corporation tax at 50 per cent has been already paid) some 6 per cent of the company's capital and admissible reserves, on the rest of the nett profits the 'super-profits tax' would operate at 50-60%. It is needless to say that the tax hasn't at all found favour with those connected with the industrial sector, and the fear has been expressed that this additional tax would seriously interfere with capital formation.

In order to simplify the corporate tax structure in India, the special tax concessions given to corporations with incomes below Rs. 25,000 per year may be abolished. For one thing the incomes below Rs. 25,000 make but a poor total. For instance 5,567 companies with incomes less than Rs. 25,000 made Rs. 6.67 crores, while 4,224 companies with incomes above Rs. 25,000 earned Rs. 213.77 crores in 1959-60 (Income-tax figures). Apart from this, in the Indian context the profitability of the firm rises as the firms grow in size. TABLE VIII gives some comparative ratios for 1,001 large companies and 668 small companies which lead to the unmistakable conclusion that the larger companies are more profitable.[63]

TABLE VIII

	1957 Large	1957 Small	1958 Large	1958 Small	1959 Large	1959 Small
Gross profits as % of total capital employed	7.5	5.2	8.0	6.1	9.8	7.0
Profits after tax as % of net income	6.5	1.9	7.1	4.1	10.5	5.5

[63] *RBI Bulletin*, December 1960, February 1962, March 1962.

In a different study again, the Reserve Bank of India[64] has concluded that the profitability of companies in the sugar industry shows an upward tendency with the growth in the size of the companies. We have earlier seen that large companies have more capacity for auto-financing than small companies. Thus there is plenty of scope for economies of scale in the Indian Corporate Sector. Hence no premium should be placed on the smallness of the concern through tax concessions.

ELIMINATION OF 'NUISANCE' TAXES

Apart from such reduction in the combined rate of the income and corporation taxes, it is also necessary that certain 'nuisance' taxes should be abolished, because of their low collection and adverse effects on the psychology of the investor. Recently, A. D. Gorwala, an eminent administrator, caustically remarked : "Of Governments in India it may be rightly said as a general rule that they irritate more than they tax, tax more than they collect, and collect more than they wisely spend".[65] Foremost among these irritating taxes is the tax on bonus shares. As a tax it brings in very little revenue, when it is balanced against the psychological reactions it causes to corporations (i.e. corporate managements) and shareholders. For instance, in 1956-57, the withdrawal of the tax rebate in respect of the undistributed profits of companies, the supertax on dividends declared in excess of 6 per cent, the tax on bonus shares, and the other minor changes introduced in the corporation tax structure, all brought in just a paltry sum of Rs. 7.6 crores. The inequitable nature of the Indian tax on bonus shares has, besides, been adversely commented on by many authorities.[66]

The Wealth Tax on companies was another tax that caused considerable annoyance to the business community, till it was wisely abolished in 1959.[67] There is another tax, namely the Ex-

[64] Ibid., July 1961.
[65] *Of Matters Administrative*, p. 28.
[66] R. J. Taraporevala, 'The Unbalanced Structure of Company Taxation' (*Capital*, 18 December 1958). See also National Council of Applied Economic Research, *Taxation and Foreign Investment*, pp. 56-7, 116 ; and Taxation Enquiry Commission, *Report*, Vol. II, pp. 161-4.
[67] Actually the taxes on wealth and on bonus shares encourage the distribution of dividends. Most of the businessmen who were interviewed

penditure Tax, which, even though it does not affect companies directly, nevertheless influences investment indirectly by impinging on the high income brackets on the one hand and, on the other, making it difficult to import foreign technicians. The main objective in having the tax is to provide an incentive for saving and to stop excessive and wasteful consumption. But it is highly doubtful if the objective will be—or can be—achieved under Indian conditions.[68] In underdeveloped countries, the inflationary pressure is likely to be considerable when the development programme is large relatively to the size of the economy. As incomes rise, the marginal incomes will only go to raise the consumption level rather than augment the voluntary savings. Taxation is perhaps the only effective instrument to reduce such inflationary pressures generated by the momentum of economic development. Thus, as Ursula K. Hicks says, "expenditure taxes have an important part to play in curbing inflation in primitive conditions, but to be effective they must be assessed on things of which people buy more as they get richer, and must cover the purchases of as large a section of the population as possible".[69] But the expenditure tax, as applied to India, is not likely to influence the behaviour of 98.5 per cent of the tax-payers who, between them, account for more than 84 per cent of the assessed income, and thus this tax cannot serve the purpose it is apparently intended for. P. S. Lokanathan by the Indian Institute of Public Opinion were of the view that these taxes in practice encouraged higher distribution of dividends in general (See *Quarterly Economic Report*, June-July 1957). It is surprising that, at a time when the private sector is in need of capital for expansion, it is being forced by our fiscal policy to raise dividends instead of encouraging it to retain profits and reinvest them.

[68] A. R. Prest has questioned even the theoretical superiority of the expenditure taxes over income taxes in the matter of encouraging savings. See his 'The Expenditure Tax and Saving', *Economic Journal*, September 1959 and 'A Tax on Expenditure', *Lloyds Bank Review*, October 1956. See also Om Prakash, 'An Indian View of the Expenditure Tax', *The Manchester School*, January 1958, pp. 59, 66. In the Indian Expenditure Tax Act, many of Kaldor's important objectives were scuttled and Kaldor himself said that they were "little more than show pieces" and bear only a "superficial resemblance" to the taxes originally proposed by him. 'Tax Reform in India', *Economic Weekly*, Special Number, January 1959, p. 195.

[69] 'Direct Taxation and Economic Growth', *Oxford Economic Papers*, September 1956, p. 304.

says rightly that "it is a relatively ineffective weapon from the point of view of curbing unnecessary consumption and the administrative burdens and complexities which it imposes are out of proportion to its revenue yield".[70] There are thus strong reasons why this expenditure tax should be scrapped.[71]

The Capital Gains Tax is one more tax which also could be profitably abolished in the interests of higher capital formation in the private sector.[72] Many capitalists invest in new companies mainly because of the possible accrual of future capital gains. 70 per cent of the replies received from investors (with incomes over Rs. 20,000) indicated that they invested in shares with the objective of capital appreciation rather than earning secure or high incomes.[73] Thus capital gains—should there be any such at all—are merely the reward for the assumption of risk and initiative.[74] A tax on capital gains therefore acts as a deterrent on such risk investments and makes people play 'safe'. Moreover, the collection of capital gains can be a very uncertain affair. Taking all these circumstances into consideration, the State might boldly abolish this tax since, after all, taxes on capital gains must result ultimately in a reduction of the yield of estate duty, for what is gained immediately as capital gains tax is only at the expense of what will otherwise accrue later on as estate duty. As estate duties also from part of our tax system, little would be lost if the capital gains tax were now abolished. It would indeed be more conducive to the economic development of the country if, in the place of the capital gains tax, only the estate duty were retained and collection thereunder tightened in such a way that evasion is effectively eliminated.[75] The main reason

[70] From his Foreword to Raja J. Chellaiah's *Fiscal Policy in Underdeveloped Countries*.

[71] This tax has been abolished in the 1962-63 Budget.

[72] R. Balakrishna thinks that the tax is "certainly not appropriate for an underdeveloped country like India" (*Studies in Indian Economic Problems*, p. 42.)

[73] N.C.A.E.R., *Taxation and Private Investment*, p. 75.

[74] Ursula K. Hicks says: "I would maintain that the prospect of appreciation is something to be encouraged rather than taxed, since it is a powerful stimulus to risk-taking, and hence indirectly of hard work". ('Direct Taxation and Economic Growth', *Oxford Economic Papers*, September 1956, p. 315).

[75] The capital gains tax also acts as a deterrent to potential foreign investors because there is no capital gains tax in many other under-

given by the Finance Minister for the capital gains tax is equity. But it could be legitimately asked how far the equity considerations are justified if only the realised capital gains are taxed, since it is well known that not all the capital gains are realised. For instance, in the United States of America, large amounts of capital gains (66-75 per cent) are not realised and consequently not taxed.[76]

Finally, besides reforms in the rates and the number of the taxes, some real improvement is also called for with regard to the method of computing income for purposes of taxation. Generally speaking, the current Indian method does not militate seriously against the corporate sector; but there is still considerable scope for improvement, so that many procedural uncertainties and delays may be eliminated.

SECURITY FOR INVESTORS

It would not be out of place if one point were reiterated here: the tax system should give reasonable security to investors against the erosion of capital through inflation. Owners of capital are apt in times of inflation to lose heavily if the historical method is used in calculating depreciation allowances. During the developing phase of an economy, it is more or less inevitable that prices should rise—as is being witnessed in India today. Since it should be possible to anticipate with reasonable accuracy such rises in a planned economy, the Government could see its way to granting sufficient immunity to the investors against such anticipated capital erosion. At present the development rebate, which is the safety valve provided, amounts to 125 per cent of the original cost—which gives a bare margin of 25 per cent. But this is too small a margin for machinery with a long life. Hence, the development rebate might be given at considerably higher rates to the needed sectors of the industry, depending upon the anticipated rises and the probable "life" of the machinery concerned. The whole point is this: when price-stability is not possible because of the expand-

developed countries, especially in Asia. This aspect is very important because at present foreign capital is playing a significant part in the economic development of India. (See N.C.A.E.R., *Taxation and Foreign Investment*, p. 87.)

[76] See L. H. Seltzer, *The Nature and Tax Treatment of Capital Gains and Losses*, p. 110 and also *Economic Weekly*, December 15, 1956, p. 1469.

ing nature of the economy, the corporate sector should at least be adequately protected against the erosion of its capital as a result of inflation. It is, of course, not meant here that the State should take care of the expansion schemes of the companies by giving up its share of the profits altogether. Capital expansion may be entirely the companies' affair. But surely the State may at least be expected to take steps to safeguard the capital of the corporate sector. And this is necessary because the Indian Government exercises the right to fix the prices of many goods like cement, paper, iron and steel, sugar, etc., on the basis of only a reasonable —not an exorbitant—return for the industry. For example, in 1958, the cement industry was allowed only 12 per cent of the capital employed as the 'reasonable' return; in 1955, the rubber industry's 'reasonable' return was fixed at 10 per cent of the capital employed; and so on. The price being thus fixed for the products of vital areas of the corporate sector, the profits of the corporate sector are artificially contained; the corporate sector is not only denied the 'advantages' of the rising prices, but at the same time it is also beset with the 'disadvantages' of a rising price level with regard to the replacement of capital assets. The corporate sector —the bulk of it, at any rate—thus finds itself getting the worst of both worlds. A more liberal development rebate to safeguard the erosion of capital would therefore be a very desirable move and would help to give a real measure of security to the investors in the corporate sector.

NEED FOR CONTINUITY

We have seen in the preceding pages how certain modifications in the tax structure are urgently called for and how such reforms would make the tax structure more adapted to a climate of economic development than the present one. On the other hand, there is need also for 'continuity' in the tax system, for flexibility, although desirable within limits, could easily be overdone. Without sacrificing the principle of inner flexibility, the structure as a whole should be retained in its broad outlines for reasonable lengths of time. Too frequent changes in taxes and tax rates have adverse effects on the behaviour of the investors and of stock markets, and consequently on the pattern of investment also. During the developing stage of the economy, most of the corporations will have the continuing problem of 'decision' regarding projects involving considerable capital outlay. Imposition of fresh corporation taxes or an increase in the existing tax rates must appropriately influence the corporation management on this vital matter of decision regarding the new projects to be undertaken. Shoup has demonstrated, with the help of an interesting hypothetical case, how the business 'decision' is being constantly affected by corporation taxes: "The board of directors or the executive officers to whom they have delegated the power of decision making with respect to large outlays on capital goods come under pressure to review the cutoff point on the cost of projects available. If the firm has been embarking on capital outlays only when its engineers convince the board that a pre-tax profit of, say, somewhere near 15 per cent will be earned on the outlay, and if a corporation profits tax is raised from 30 per cent to 50 per cent, the board must decide whether the cutoff point, which had hitherto been at 21.4 per cent in terms of pretax return, must now be mounted up to 30 per cent."[77] This must give a violent twist of uncertainty to the 'decision' takers, and consequently much corporate expansion may not materialise after all. Hence the paramount need for reasonable continuity in corporate tax rates.

This however doesn't mean that the various aspects of the tax structure should not be reviewed and reassessed periodically with a view to getting the maximum for promoting the economic development of the country.

Conclusion : *The Future of the Corporate Sector in India*

The future of the corporate sector in India is obviously dependent upon the future scope given to the private sector. Today the private sector, in spite of the inroads made into its scope and activity by the State, continues to hold an important place in the national economy. A look at the targets decided upon for the fixed capital investment in the various Five Year Plans proves that the private sector is still growing. The first Plan envisaged fixed capital investment in the corporate sector of the order of Rs. 463 crores. As against this, the second Plan envisaged a total invest-

[77] 'Some Problems in the Incidence of the Corporation Income Tax' (*A.E.R.*, May 1960, p. 461).

CORPORATE TAXATION AND ECONOMIC DEVELOPMENT   299

ment of Rs. 685 crores, which was later increased to Rs. 840 crores.[78] In the Third Five Year Plan the net investment in the private industrial sector is to be of the order of over Rs. 1100 crores. And the corporate sector is expected to cover about 50 per cent of the total private investment and nearly 20 per cent of the total Plan outlay. Thus there is no ground for fear that the private sector will have no future in India. But it is doubtless natural for an underdeveloped country like India to make the public sector gradually stronger and stronger—as it is, in fact, now being done.

One of the distinct developments of the last few years is the tremendous growth of Government companies (that is, corporations in which all, or almost all, the shares are owned by the State), as TABLE IX clearly shows[79]:

TABLE IX

Year Ending on 31st March	Government Companies		Total Number of Companies	
	Number	Paid-up Capital (Rs. in crores)	Number	Paid-up Capital (Rs. in crores)
1956	61	66.0	29,874	1024.0
1957	74	72.6	29,357	1077.6
1958	91	256.8	28,283	1300.1
1959	103	424.2	27,479	1509.8
1960	125	468.4	26,921	1593.1 (Provisional)

In 1956-57, the increase in the paid-up capital of the Government companies was Rs. 6.6 crores, as against Rs. 47.0 crores in the private sector; in 1957-58, the figures were Rs. 184.2 crores for the Government companies as against Rs. 38.3 crores for the companies in the private sector; and in 1958-59, the corresponding

[78] The Planning Commission, *Appraisal and Prospects of the Second Five Year Plan*, p. 64.
[79] Source: *The Eastern Economist*, 1 April 1960. Nigam & Chaudhuri, *The Corporate Sector in India*, p. 12.

figures were Rs. 167.4 crores as against Rs. 42.3 crores. This pronounced gravitation of new paid-up capital towards the Government companies is understandable because Steel, Shipyard, Fertilisers, and similar gigantic projects in the public sector require very heavy initial investment, and in an underdeveloped economy the Government is easier likely to find the necessary funds than the private sector. On the whole, then, this trend is welcome because it will promote a healthy spirit of competition between the private and the public sectors. Of course, any extension of the public sector through departmentally run concerns is always liable to be viewed with suspicion as promoting inefficiency and waste. But there is also another way of looking at this matter. Whether it is stray individuals who provide the funds for a company or it is the State itself that starts a public corporation, after some time it tends—be it a company in the private sector or a corporation in the public sector—to acquire a distinct personality of its own. As H. T. Parekh points out, "its entity as a corporation gives to joint-stock enterprise its permanence of character with the result that, provided it survives an early period of stabilisation, it is capable of moving by its own momentum and unlike an individual does not wither away from age but on the contrary gathers strength. In short, it transforms industrial life from an individual to an institutional basis, thereby facilitating economic expansion".[80]

Thus the institution of joint-stock companies provides both the public and the private sectors a method of promoting the economic development of the country without giving any undue advantage for one over the other. It should, therefore, be one of the prime objectives of the Government of India to enable this form of industrial and business organisation to grow from strength to strength, both by removing as suggested above existing obstacles to its growth and by carefully refraining from raising new ones.

[80] *The Future of Joint-Stock Enterprise in India*, pp. 1-2.

APPENDIX

A COMPARATIVE NOTE ON CORPORATE TAXATION

THAT the corporate sector and the taxation of corporate income occupy a very prominent position in the advanced countries of the present-day world is common knowledge. We saw in the concluding pages of the second chapter that the share of the corporate profits in India's national income is barely 2 per cent; moreover, the corporate taxes account for no more than a 1 per cent share in the national income. This is clearly indicative of the very minor position held as yet by the industrial sector (and, consequently, by the corporate sector) in the Indian economy. We have only to compare the relative importance of dividends, savings of corporations, and direct taxes on corporations in India and in some of the advanced countries to realise how very much India lags behind them:

PERCENTAGE SHARE IN NATIONAL INCOME[1]
(average for 1950-59)

Country	Direct Taxes on Corporate Sector	Disposable Corporate Income	Net Savings of Corporations	Dividends
U.K.	5.1	7.9	4.3	3.6
Australia	3.5	7.9	4.8	3.1
U.S.A.	5.3	5.4	3.1	2.3
Canada	4.8	5.6	2.9	2.7
New Zealand	4.9	5.1	2.7	2.4
Japan	3.5	5.1	5.0	0.1
Norway	3.9	4.6	4.0	0.6
France	2.1	4.0	1.9	2.1
West Germany	3.1	3.7	1.8	1.9
India (1956-57)	1.0	1.0	0.5	0.5

India being a predominantly agricultural country, it is but natural that these variables should play as yet only a very minor part in our economic system. On the other hand, though in mere size the corporate sector in India is much less impressive than that in some

[1] Source: Except for India, U.N., *World Economic Survey* 1960, p. 30.

of the advanced countries, the corporate tax rate structure in India as such could be compared meaningfully with the rates ruling in the other countries. The purpose of such comparison is merely to see whether or not Indian corporations are being heavily taxed by international standards.

But comparing taxes in existence or tax rates in force is not easy and is really fraught with many difficulties. Mere comparisons of the tax rates will not give a correct picture because, if one traces the details of the same tax in different countries, one finds significant differences in the exemptions, deductions, concessions and the formulae adopted for arriving at the assessable amounts.[2] Also, it is next to impossible to bring all these variations into the comparative picture with a single norm. We have accordingly to compare only the rates as such, though we have also to bear in mind the other limiting factors before coming to any firm conclusion for policy purposes. The following table gives the corporate tax rates in selected countries :

PERCENTAGE OF INCOME PAID BY CORPORATIONS AS DIRECT TAXES (1956)

Income	India	Japan	U.S.A.	Canada	Sweden	United Kingdom
5,000	51.1	35	25	20	56	51.6
10,000	51.1	40	25	20	56	51.6
25,000	51.1	40	25	20	56	51.6
50,000	56.0	40	25	20	56	51.6
75,000	56.0	40	25	20	56	51.6
100,000	56.0	40	25	23	56	51.6
150,000	56.0	40	52	23	56	51.6
200,000	56.0	40	52	35	56	51.6
250,000	56.0	40	52	37	56	51.6
500,000	56.0	40	52	42	56	51.6[3]

In the above table, credit given to the shareholders has not been taken into account ; and there are other qualifications, too, to be

[2] See for a full discussion of the pitfalls in any bland comparison of tax rates in various countries, R. C. Gates's 'The Weight of Taxation in Five Countries' (*Economic Record*, November 1952).

[3] Sources : *A Key to Swedish Taxes* (with 1956 Supplement) ; *Outlines of National Tax in Japan*, 1957 ; *The Case of Relief in Direct Taxation* (Association of Indian Trade & Industry) ; *Quarterly Economic Report* (January 1958) ; Brudno & Bower, *Taxation in the United Kingdom* ; and G. C. Sharma, *Taxation of Companies*.

borne in mind. For example, in Japan, an extra Enterprise Tax is levied at rates ranging from 8 to 12 per cent—for the first Rs. 6,579, 8 per cent; for the second Rs. 6,579, 10 per cent; over Rs. 13,158, at 12 per cent. In the United Kingdom, the tax is calculated thus : the income-tax is @ 42.5 per cent (the standard rate of 8s.6d. in the pound); of the amount of profit remaining after the deduction of the income-tax, one-half (assumed to be distributed) is further taxed @ 30 per cent and one-fourth (assumed to be kept as reserves) @3 per cent. The tax in India includes the Wealth-Tax also, and the tax calculation is based on the results of the Reserve Bank of India studies regarding the net worth of the corporations, percentage of profits distributed, etc.

The limitations readily admitted, the above table nevertheless reveals clearly enough how India occupies the top place (sharing the honour with Sweden) in the matter of corporate taxation. (As regards the taxation of foreign companies, India indeed stands first, with the rate of taxation standing at 61.5 per cent). But Sweden being a fully developed economy, such high rates are unlikely to have as much adverse effect on her economy as such high rates must have in an underdeveloped economy like India. Actually, Swedish corporate taxation has devices like 'tax-free investment reserves' and 'flexibility of depreciation allowances' which help the economy to struggle effectively against the effects of the business cycle.[4] In order to reduce fluctuations in capital expenditure, the Swedish tax structure encourages corporate saving in times of boom and encourages corporate investment in times of recession. But in an underdeveloped economy like India, a stabilising fiscal policy would only perpetuate the existing backward conditions. What is necessary in the context is a positive policy to encourage capital formation. We saw in the third chapter how the Indian Government has provided many incentive schemes like the development rebate, the Tax Holiday, etc. But India is not the only country to have such measures as the Tax Holiday which exempt the corporations from paying taxes during the first few years of their existence. For instance, Bolivia, Mexico, Panama, Puerto Rico, El Salvador, Iraq and the Philippines are some of the countries that have similar measures to encourage investment in corporate ventures.[5] On a general view, then, it would appear that Indian corporation tax rates are very high compared to those even in many underdeveloped countries, and it is here that tax reform is called for most urgently.

[4] See M. Norr, 'Taxation and Stability' (*Harvard Business Review*, January-February, 1960).

[5] For fuller details see N.C.A.E.R., *Taxation and Foreign Investment*, p. 49.

SELECT BIBLIOGRAPHY

ADELMAN, M. A. : 'The Corporation Income Tax in the Longrun' (*J. P. E.*, April 1957).
AGARWAL, R. G. : *Price Controls in India* (New Delhi, 1956).
AHMAD, Z. A. : *Public Revenue and Expenditure in India* (Allahabad, 1938).
AMBIRAJAN, S. : *A Grammar of Indian Planning* (Bombay, 1959).
AMERICAN ECONOMIC ASSOCIATION : *Readings in Fiscal Policy* (London, 1955).
AMOS, J. ELLWOOD : *The Economics of Corporate Saving* (Urbana, 1937).
ANDERSON, WILLIAM H. : *Taxation and the American Economy* (New York, 1951).
ANJARIA, J. J. : 'Problems of Economic Development' (*The Indian Economic Journal*, January 1960).
ARORA, G. N. : *Taxation of Industry in India* (Bombay, 1956).
ASSOCIATION OF INDIAN TRADE AND INDUSTRY : *Financial Trends in Cement Industry* (Bombay, 1954).
———*Financial Trends in Iron & Steel Industry* (Bombay, 1954).
———*Income-tax Rates Compared* (Bombay, 1955).
———*Financial Trends in Paper Industry* (Bombay, 1957).
———*Financial Trends in Sugar Industry* (Bombay, 1957).
BALAKRISHNA, R. : *Studies in Indian Economic Problems* (Bangalore, 1954).
———*Recent Trends in Indian Finance* (Madras, 1955).
BALAKRISHNAN, G. : *Financing Small-scale Industries in India*, 1950-1952 (Bombay, 1962).
BASU, S. K. : *The Managing Agency System in India* (Calcutta, 1958).
BECK, MORRIS : 'British Anti-inflationary Tax on Distributed Corporate Profits' (*National Tax Journal*, September 1948).
BERLE, A. A. & G. C. MEANS : *The Modern Corporation and Private Property* (New York, 1940).
BERNSTEIN, E. M. & OTHERS : *Economic Development with Stability* (IMF Report : New Delhi, 1954).
BHARGAVA, R. N. : *The Theory and Working of Union Finance in India* (London, 1956).
———*Indian Public Finances* (London, 1962).
BHATT, MAHESH : 'Case for non-differential Corporation Tax' (*Economic Weekly*, 17 October 1959).
BLACK, DUNCAN : *The Incidence of Income Taxes* (London, 1939).
BLUM, WATER J. & HARRY J. KALVEN : *The Uneasy Case for Progressive Taxation* (Illinois, 1953).

SELECT BIBLIOGRAPHY

BODENHORN, DIRAN : 'The Shifting of the Corporation Income Tax in a Growing Economy' (*Q. J. E.*, November 1956).
BREAK, GEORGE F. : 'Income Taxes and Incentives to Work : An Empirical Study' (*A. E. R.*, September 1957).
BROWN, A. J. : *The Great Inflation* : 1939-51 (London, 1955).
BROWN, E. CARY : *Effects of Taxation : Depreciation Adjustments for Price Changes* (Boston, 1952).
BROZEN, YALE : 'Invention, Innovation and Imitation' (*A. E. R.*, May 1951).
BROUDNO, WALTER & FRANK BOWER. : *Taxation in the United Kingdom* (Harvard, 1957).
BUCHANAN, N. S. : *The Economics of Corporate Enterprise* (New York, 1940).
BUEHLER, ALFRED G. : *The Undistributed Profits Tax* (New York, 1937).
BUTTERS, J. K. : 'Discriminating Effects of the Annual Computation of the Income Tax' (*Q. J. E.*, November 1939).
────── 'Taxation, Incentives and Financial Capacity' (*A. E. R.*, May 1954).
BUTTERS, J. K. & JOHN LINTNER : *Effects of Federal Taxes on Growing Enterprises* (Boston, 1944).
BUTTERS, J. K. & OTHERS : *Effects of Taxation : Investment by Individuals* (Boston, 1953).
CENTRAL BOARD OF REVENUE : *Income-tax Manual* (New Delhi, 1957).
────── *Income-tax for the Layman* (New Delhi, 1954).
CHELLAIAH, RAJA J. : *Fiscal Policy in Underdeveloped Countries* (London, 1960).
CHOUDHRY, N. K. : 'Indian Taxation Policy 1946-51 and Private Investment' (*Indian Economic Journal*, July 1955).
CIRVANTE, C. R. : *The Indian Capital Market* (Bombay, 1956).
COLLIER, ROBERT P. : 'The Empirical Evidence of Tax Incidence' (*National Tax Journal*, March 1948).
COLM, GERHARD : 'The Corporation and the Corporation Income Tax in the American Economy' (*A. E. R.*, May 1954).
COMMITTEE ON NATIONAL DEBT AND TAXATION : *Report* (of the Colwyn Committee), London, 1927.
COMPANY LAW ADMINISTRATION : *Progress of Joint-Stock Companies in India* (New Delhi, 1955).
COSCIANI, CESARE : *The Effects of Differential Tax Treatment of Corporate and Non-Corporate Enterprises* (Paris, 1959).
CRUM, W. L. : 'The Taxation of Shareholders' (*Q. J. E.*, February 1950).
DALAL, R. K. : *Business Profits Tax and Capital Gains Tax* (Bombay, 1948).
DALTON, HUGH : *Principles of Public Finance* (London, 1952).
DAS GUPTA, B. : *Our Plans and Our Public Finance* (Calcutta, 1960).

DAS, NABAGOPAL : *Industrial Enterprise in India* (Calcutta, 1956).
DATTA, BHABATOSH : *The Economics of Industrialisation* (Calcutta, 1957).
DESHMUKH, C. D. : *Economic Developments in India :* 1946-56 (Bombay, 1957).
DE VITI DE MARCO, ANTONIO : *First Principles of Public Finance*, translated by Edith Pablo Marget (London, 1950).
DIRECTORATE OF INDUSTRIAL STATISTICS : *Census of Manufactures*, 1956 (Calcutta, 1958).
———*Ten Years of Indian Manufactures* (Calcutta, 1958).
DOBROVOLSKY, S. P. : *Corporate Income Retention :* 1915-43 (New York, 1951).
DOMAR, EVSEY D. : *Essays in the Theory of Economic Growth* (New York, 1957).
ECONOMIC ADVISER (GOVERNMENT OF INDIA) : *Governmental Measures Affecting Investment in India* (New Delhi, 1950).
EMPLOYERS' ASSOCIATION : *Are Our Taxes Realistic or Rational?* (Calcutta, 1950).
——— *Depreciation Allowances and Replacement Costs* (Calcutta, 1952).
——— *Five Year Plans and Personal Taxation* (Calcutta, 1952).
——— *Objectives of Taxation Policy* (Calcutta, 1953).
FEDERATION OF INDIAN CHAMBERS OF COMMERCE AND INDUSTRY : *Direct Taxes* (New Delhi, 1958).
FINANCE COMMISSION (INDIA) : *Report*, 1952 (New Delhi, 1953).
——— *Report* (New Delhi, 1957).
FORD, ROBERT S. : 'Some Economic Aspects of the Present Corporate Income Tax' (*Proceedings of the National Tax Association*, 1947).
FORUM OF FREE ENTERPRISE : *The Role of Joint-Stock Companies* (Bombay, 1959).
FRANKEL, S. HERBERT : *The Economic Impact of Underdeveloped Societies* (Oxford, 1953).
FURTADO, CELSO : 'Capital Formation and Economic Development' *International Economic Papers*, No. 4, 1954).
GAA, C. J. : *The Taxation of Corporate Income* (Illinois, 1944).
GADGIL, D. R. & N. V. SOVANI : *War and Indian Economic Policy* (Poona, 1943).
GATES, R. C. : 'The Weight of Taxation in Five Countries' (*Economic Record*, November 1952).
GIERKE, OTTO VON : *Political Theories of the Middle Ages*, edited by F. W. Maitland (Cambridge, 1927).
GOODE, RICHARD : *The Corporation Income Tax* (New York, 1951).
——— 'Accelerated Depreciation as a Stimulus to Investment' (*Q. J. E.*, May 1955).
GOPAL, M. H. : 'Industrial Profits in India' (*Eastern Economist*, 12 May 1944).

SELECT BIBLIOGRAPHY

———— *The Theory of Excess Profits Taxation* (Mysore, 1947).
———— *Financial Policy of the Indian Union*: 1947-53 (New Delhi, 1955).
———— 'Taxation in a Developing Economy' (*Indian Economic Journal*, July 1958).
GORWALA, A. D.: *Of Matters Administrative* (Bombay, 1958).
GOVERNMENT OF INDIA: *Report of the Indian Taxation Enquiry Committee*: 1924-25.
———— *Report of the Fiscal Commission*: 1949-50, Vol. I.
———— *Report of the Taxation Enquiry Commission*: 1953-54, 3 Vols.
GROVES, HAROLD M.: *Postwar Taxation and Economic Progress* (New York, 1946).
———— 'Neutrality in Taxation' (*National Tax Journal*, March 1948).
———— *Trouble Spots in Taxation* (Princeton, 1948).
GULATI, I. S.: *Capital Taxation in a Developing Economy* (*India*) (Bombay, 1957).
HALEY, B. F. (Ed.): *A Survey of Contemporary Economics*, Vol. II (Illinois, 1952).
HANSEN, ALVIN H.: *Fiscal Policy and Business Cycles* (New York, 1941).
HICKS, J. R., U. K. HICKS & L. ROSTAS: *The Taxation of War Wealth* (London, 1942).
HICKS, URSULA K.: 'Direct Taxation and Economic Growth' (*Oxford Economic Papers*, September 1956).
HOUSTON, G. SIDNEY: 'Taxation and Corporate Enterprise' (*Annals of the American Academy of Political and Social Science*, November 1949).
ILERSIC, A. R.: *Government Finance and Fiscal Policy in Post-war Britain* (London, 1955).
INDIAN INSTITUTE OF PUBLIC OPINION: *Quarterly Economic Reports* (April 1954 onwards).
JAIN, P. C.: *India Builds Her War Economy* (Allahabad, 1943).
KALDOR, NICHOLAS: *An Expenditure Tax* (London, 1955).
———— *Indian Tax Reform: Report of a Survey* (New Delhi, 1956).
KEITH, E. GORDON: 'Tax Policy and Investment' (*Annals of the American Academy of Political and Social Science*, November 1949).
KIMMEL, LEWIS H.: *Postwar Tax Policy and Business Expansion* (New York, 1943).
———— 'Our Tax Burdens and Taxable Capacity' (*Annals of the American Academy of Political and Social Science*, November 1949).
———— *Taxes and Economic Incentives* (Washington, 1950).
KISHORE, B. R.: 'Risk of Investment in Corporate Ventures in India' (*Indian Economic Review*, February 1952).

KRISHNAMACHARI, T. T.: *Speeches* (New Delhi, 1957).
KUCHHAL, S. C.: *Corporation Finance* (Allahabad, 1958).
LAKDAWALA, D. T.: *Taxation and the Plan* (Bombay, 1956).
——————*Justice in Taxation in India* (Bombay, 1946).
LANKA SUNDARAM & VITTAL BABU: *Union Finances* (Bombay, 1947).
LERNER, ABBA P.: *The Economics of Control* (New York, 1946).
LEVY, A. B.: *Private Corporations and Their Control* (London, 1950).
LINDGREN, G.: 'How Long does a Company Live?' (*Oxford Economic Papers*, September 1953).
LINDHOLM, RICHARD W.: *Introduction to Fiscal Policy* (New York, 1948).
LOKANATHAN, P. S.: *Industrialisation* (Bombay, 1943).
LURIE, SAMUEL: *Private Investment in a Controlled Economy* (New York, 1947).
MACGREGOR, D. H.: *Enterprise, Purpose and Profit* (Oxford, 1934).
MAGEE, JAMES D.: *Taxation and Capital Investment* (Washington, 1939).
MAGILL, ROSEWALL: *Taxable Income* (New York, 1945).
MAZUMDAR, H.: *Business Saving in India* (Holland, 1959).
MEHTA, S. D.: *The Indian Cotton Textile Industry* (Bombay, 1953).
MERING, OTTO VON: *The Shifting and Incidence of Taxation* (Philadelphia, 1942).
MICHIGAN LAW SCHOOL: *Lectures on Taxation of Business Enterprise* (Michigan, 1952).
MILLER, DONALD C.: *Taxes, the Public Debt and Transfers of Income* (Urbana, 1950).
——————'Corporate Taxation and Methods of Corporate Financing' (*A. E. R.*, December 1952).
MILLIKAN, MAX F. (Ed.): *Income Stabilisation for a Developing Democracy* (Yale, 1953).
MINISTRY OF FINANCE (GOVERNMENT OF INDIA): *Taxation of Corporate Income in India* (New Delhi, 1957).
MUNSHI, M. C.: *Industrial Profits in India: 1936-1944* (New Delhi, 1948).
MUSGRAVE, RICHARD A. & OTHERS: *Public Finance and Full Employment* (Washington, 1945).
MUSGRAVE, RICHARD A.: *The Theory of Public Finance* (New York, 1959).
MUSGRAVE, RICHARD A. & CARL SHOUP: *Readings in the Economics of Taxation* (London, 1959).
MYRDAL, GUNNAR: *The Political Element in the Development of Economic Theory*, translated by Paul Streetan (London, 1953).

SELECT BIBLIOGRAPHY

NATIONAL BUREAU OF ECONOMIC RESEARCH : *Business Concentration and Price Policy* (Princeton, 1955).
―――――*Policies to Combat Depression* (Princeton, 1956).
NATIONAL COUNCIL OF APPLIED ECONOMIC RESEARCH : *Taxation and Foreign Investment* (New Delhi, 1958).
―――――*The Managing Agency System* (New Delhi, 1959).
―――――*Taxation and Private Investment* (Delhi, 1961).
NATIONAL INCOME COMMITTEE (INDIA) : *Final Report* (New Delhi, 1954).
NICHOLLS, WILLIAM H. : 'Accommodating Economic Change in Underdeveloped Countries' (*A. E. R.*, May 1959).
NIGAM, RAJ K. & N. D. JOSHI : *Trends in Company Finances with Particular Reference to the First and Second Plan Periods* (New Delhi, 1960).
NORR, MARTIN : 'Taxation and Stability' (*Harvard Business Review*, January-February 1960).
OJHA, P. D. : *A Study of the Tax Structure of India* (Unpublished thesis : Bombay, 1955).
PANANDIKAR, S. G. : 'Taxes on Incomes in India' (*Commerce*, 2 April 1949).
PAREKH, H. T. : *The Future of Joint-Stock Enterprise in India* (Bombay, 1958).
PARKINSON, C. NORTHCOTE : *The Law and the Profits* (London, 1960).
PAUL, RANDOLPH E. : *Taxation and Prosperity* (New York, 1947).
PETRIE, J. RICHARDS : *The Taxation of Corporate Income in Canada* (Toronto, 1953).
PIGOU, A. C. : *A Study in Public Finance* (London, 1952).
PLACE, SIDDONS & GOUGH : *The Investor's Year Book* (Calcutta).
PLANNING COMMISSION (INDIA) : *Papers Relating to the Formulation of the Second Five Year Plan* (New Delhi, 1955).
―――――*The Problem of Economic Development* (New Delhi, 1954).
PODUVAL, R. N. : *Finance of the Government of India since 1935* (New Delhi, 1951).
POOLE, KENYON E. (Ed.) : *Fiscal Policies and the American Economy* (New York, 1953).
PRENTIS, Jr., H. W. : 'Taxation and Business Incentive' (*The Annals of the American Academy of Political and Social Science*, November 1949).
RAMESH, M. S. : 'Future of the Capital Gains Tax' (*The Indian Economic Journal*, October 1958).
RAO, V. K. R. V. : *Taxation of Income in India* (Bombay, 1931).
RHYS WILLIAMS, LADY : *Taxation and Incentives* (London, 1953).
RESERVE BANK OF INDIA : *Report of the Committee on Finance for the Private Sector* (Chairman : A. D. Shroff) (Bombay, 1954).
ROSEN, GEORGE : *Industrial Change in India* (Bombay, 1959).
―――――*Some Aspects of Industrial Finance in India* (London, 1962).

Rostow, W. W. : *The Process of Economic Growth* (2nd Edition, Oxford, 1960).
Sahota, G. S. : *Indian Tax Structure and Economic Development* (Bombay, 1961).
Sampath Iyengar, A. C. : *Role of Private Enterprise in India* (Calcutta, 1951).
———*The Indian Income-tax Act* (Madras, 1952).
Sarma, N. A. : *Taxation of Income* (Unpublished thesis : Bombay, 1947).
Schram, Emil : 'Taxation and Venture Capital' (*Annals of the American Academy of Political and Social Science*, November 1949).
Seligman, Edwin R. A. : *Progressive Taxation in Theory and Practice* (Princeton, 1908).
———*Essays in Taxation* (New York, 1923).
———*Studies in Public Finance* (New York, 1925).
Seltzer, Lawrence H. : *The Nature and Tax Treatment of Capital Gains and Losses* (New York, 1951).
Sen, Sunil K. : 'Government Purchases of Stores for India, 1858-1914' (*Bengal Past and Present*, Jan.-June 1961).
Shah, K. C. (Miss) : *Pattern of Corporate Savings and Investment in India* (Bombay, 1961).
Sharma, G. C. : *Taxation of Companies* (New Delhi, 1957).
Shirras, G. Findley : *The Science of Public Finance* (London, 1924).
The Shoup Mission : *Report on Japanese Taxation* (Tokyo, 1949).
Shoup, Carl S. : 'Some Problems in the Incidence of the Corporation Income Tax' (*A. E. R.*, May 1960).
Simha, S. L. N. & K. N. R. Ramanujam : 'The Present Price Situation in India' (*RBI Bulletin*, May 1948).
Simha, S. L. N. : *The Capital Market of India* (Bombay, 1960).
Simons, Henry C. : *Personal Income Taxation* (Chicago, 1938).
Singh, Baljit : *Federal Finance and Underdeveloped Economy* (Bombay, 1952).
Singh, D. Bright : *Inflationary Price Trends in India since 1939* (Bombay, 1957).
Smith, James G. : 'Economic Significance of the Undistributed Profits Tax' (*A. E. R.*, June 1938).
Smith, Dan Thorp : 'Business Profits During Inflation' (*Harvard Business Review*, March 1948).
———*Effects of Taxation : Corporate Financial Policy* (Boston, 1952).
Smith, D. T. & J. K. Butters : *Taxable and Business Income* (New York, 1949).
Somers, Harold M. : *Public Finance and National Income* (Philadelphia, 1949).
Srinivasan, M. S. : *Lectures in Income-Tax* (Madras, 1955).

STAMP, J. C.: *Studies in Current Problems in Finance and Government* (London, 1925).
———— *The Fundamental Principles of Taxation* (London, 1936).
STREETAN, PAUL: 'The Effect of Taxation on Risk-Taking' (*Oxford Economic Papers*, September 1953).
———— 'Some Problems Raised by the Report of the Royal Commission on the Taxation of Profits and Income' (*Bulletin of the Institute of Statistics*, November 1955).
STUDENSKI, PAUL: 'Towards a Theory of Business Taxation' (*J. P. E.*, October 1940).
SUNDARAM, V. S.: *The Law of Income-tax in India* (Madras, 1954).
SUR, A. K. (Ed.): *The Stock Exchange: A Symposium* (Calcutta, 1958).
TARAPOREVALA, R. J.: *The New Scheme of Company Taxation* (Bombay, 1960).
TARIFF COMMISSION, The: *Report on the Revision of Fair Prices Payable to Cement Producers* (Bombay, 1958).
TAX BUREAU (JAPAN): *Outline of National Tax in Japan* (Ministry of Finance, Japanese Government: Tokyo, 1958).
TAX INSTITUTE: *How Should Corporations be Taxed?* (New York, 1947).
———— *Taxation and Business Concentration* (New York, 1950).
TAYLOR, PHILIP E: *The Economics of Public Finance* (New York, 1948).
THOMAS, P. J.: *The Growth of Federal Finance in India* (Bombay, 1939).
TNEC: *Taxation of Corporate Enterprise* (Washington, 1941).
———— *Taxation, Recovery and Defense* (Washington, 1940).
———— *Saving, Investment and National Income* (Washington, 1941).
TRIPATHY, R. N.: *Fiscal Policy and Economic Development in India* (Calcutta, 1958).
TWENTIETH CENTURY FUND: *Financing American Prosperity* (New York, 1945).
UN DEPARTMENT OF ECONOMIC AFFAIRS: *The Effects of Taxation on Foreign Trade and Investment* (New York, 1950).
———— *Measures for the Economic Development of Underdeveloped Countries* (New York, 1951).
———— *India: Public Finance Survey* (New York, 1951).
UN DEPARTMENT OF ECONOMIC AND SOCIAL AFFAIRS: *Processes and Problems of Industrialisation in Underdeveloped Countries* (New York, 1955).
UN ECONOMIC AND SOCIAL COUNCIL: *Corporate Tax Problems with Special Consideration of the Problems of Underdeveloped Countries* (1952).
UN TECHNICAL ASSISTANCE ADMINISTRATION: *Taxes and Fiscal Policy in Underdeveloped Countries* (New York, 1954).

VACHHA, J. B. & OTHERS : *Income-tax Enquiry Report* (Delhi, 1936).
VAKIL, C. N. : 'Some Reflections on the Central Budget' (*Commerce*, 8 February 1947).
——————(Ed.) : *Papers in Economics* (Bombay, 1947).
VAKIL, C. N. & P. R. BRAHMANANDA : *Planning for an Expanding Economy* (Bombay, 1956).
VAN PHILIPS, PAUL A. M. : *Public Finance and Less Developed Economy* (The Hague, 1957).
VENKATASUBBAIAH, H. : *Indian Economy since Independence* (Bombay, 1958).
VICKREY, WILLIAM : *Agenda for Progressive Taxation* (New York, 1947).
WALKER, DAVID : 'Some Economic Aspects of the Taxation of Companies' (*The Manchester School*, January 1954).
WOLF Jr., CHARLES & C. SIDNEY SUFRIN : *Capital Formation and Foreign Investment in Underdeveloped Areas* (Syracuse, 1955).

Journals

All-India Income-tax Revenue Statistics (Annual : Central Board of Revenue, New Delhi).
Capital (Weekly : Calcutta).
Commerce (Weekly : Bombay).
Eastern Economist, The (Weekly : New Delhi).
Economist, The (Weekly, London).
Economic Weekly, The (Bombay).
Hindu, The (Daily : Madras).
Indian Finance (Weekly : Calcutta).
Indian Labour Gazette (Monthly : New Delhi).
Indian Taxation (Monthly, till 1956; now defunct : New Delhi).
Monthly Abstract of Statistics (New Delhi).
Monthly Bulletin of Statistics (U. N. O.).
Report on Currency and Finance (Annual : Bombay).
Reserve Bank of India Bulletin (Monthly : Bombay).
Tata Quarterly (Bombay).

INDEX

ADAMS, HENRY C., 15
Adelman, M. A., 50fn
Adler, J. H., 267
Ahmed, Z. A., 186fn
Amos, J. Ellwood, 100fn, 110
Anderson, William H., 42
Anjaria, J. J., 275, 278
Arora, G. N., 227fn

BALAKRISHNAN, G., 248fn
Balakrishna, R., 295fn
Baldwin, George B., 257fn
Barrel, George, 52fn, 205
Basu, S. K., 59
Bauer, 262, 269
Beaumont, Chief Justice, 127
Berle, Adolf, 3, 6
Bernstein, E. M., 260fn
Bhabha, C. H., 70
Bhargava, R. N., 136, 284, 290fn
Black, D., 47, 53
Blackstone, Sir William, 4fn, 5fn
Bollinger, 56fn, 252fn
Boulding, Kenneth, 265
Bowen, H. M., 35
Bower, Frank, 221, 302fn
Brahmananda, P. R., 266fn, 267
Brown, A. J., 227
Brown, E. Carry, 30
Brown, Ralph, 30
Brozen, Yale, 261
Brudno, 302fn
Buchanan, Norman S., 5, 6fn
Buehler, A. G., 34fn
Bullock, H. L., 26fn
Butters, J. K., 31, 36, 56fn, 202fn, 252fn, 284fn, 285fn
Buttrick, J. A., 266fn

CHAGLA, JUSTICE, 127
Chellaiah, Raja J., 273fn, 295fn
Chinai, Babubhai, 75
Choudhry, Nanda K., 284fn

Clark, Colin, 260fn
Coates, W. H., 47
Collier, Robert P., 50fn
Colm, Gerhard, 7, 201, 203fn
Colvin, A., 122
Cosciani, C., 56fn
Crum, W. L., 52, 53fn

DALAL, R. K., 175
Darrel, Norris, 31
Das, N., 252fn, 256fn, 257fn
Day, Mr. Justice, 9
Desai, Morarji, 179
Dewey, H., 238
Dewing, A. S., 34
Dobrovolsky, S. P., 103fn
Domar, E. D., 54
Dutta, B., 260fn

EISENSTEIN, LOUIS, 289

FISHER, IRVING, 26
Ford, Robert E., 47
Frankel, S. H., 259fn

GAA, CHARLES JOHN, 27, 38fn, 160
Gates, R. C., 302fn
Gillim, M. H., 48fn
Ginwalla, F. R., 62, 71fn
Goode, Richard, 4, 7, 9fn, 10, 12, 18, 28, 30fn, 35fn, 49, 54, 203, 255
Gopal, M. H., 90, 106, 107, 171, 203, 223fn
Gorwala, A. D., 90, 293
Groves, Harold M., 15, 16, 29, 31, 34fn, 40fn, 41, 44, 49, 50
Gulati, I. S., 23fn, 158fn
Gupta, L. C., 252fn

HABERLER, G. VON, 97
Haig, Robert Murray, 25
Hall, James K., 245fn
Hansen, Alvin, 53

INDEX

Harriss, C. Lowell, 50fn
Hatfield, 27
Hazari, R. K., 181fn
Hearne, W. L., 56fn
Hicks, J. R., 23, 24, 25-6, 33fn, 223fn
Hicks, Ursula K., 23, 24, 33fn, 51fn, 223fn, 273, 274, 294, 295fn
Hobson, 18

IYENGAR, A. C. SAMPATH, 182fn, 184fn
Iyer, K. V. N., 58fn

JOSHI, N. D., 248fn, 272fn

KALDOR, NICHOLAS, 26, 40, 41, 44, 53, 102, 137, 152fn, 156, 157, 163, 175ff, 180, 183, 204fn, 288ff, 294fn
Keynes, J. M., 170
Khan, Liaquat Ali, 173, 174, 176, 216
Kilachand, Tulsidas, 75
Kimmel, Lewis H., 15, 18, 50fn
Kishore, B. R., 249fn
Krishnamachari, T. T., 176, 177, 179, 180, 191, 245fn
Krishnamurthy, B. V., 276

LAKDAWALA, D. T., 274fn, 288fn, 290
Lerner, Abba P., 14, 20
Levy, A. B., 4
Lintner, 56fn, 284fn, 285fn
Little, I. M. D., 279
Lockwood, W. W., 261
Lokanathan, P. S., 184, 294

MACGREGOR, D. H., 248
Magill, Rosewell, 156fn
Maitland, F. W., 6fn
Masani, M. R., 172, 179
Matthai, John, 175
Meade, J. E., 53
Means, Gardner, 3, 6
Mering, Otto von, 53fn, 54fn
Miller, Donald C., 48fn
Millikan, M., 30fn
Mody, Homi, 75
Moult, Frank G., 170
Mulky, M. A., 66, 67

Munshi, M. C., 91fn
Musgrave, R. A., 30fn, 54, 229, 231
Myrdal, Gunnar, 51

NIGAM, RAJ K., 248fn, 272fn, 299fn
Niyogi, J. P., 120fn
Noel-Todd, G. N., 204
Noonan, Joseph D., 48
Norr, M., 303fn

PAGAR, S. M., 120fn
Palkhiwala, N. A., 182fn
Parekh, H. T., 99, 243, 300
Paul, Randolph, 37fn
Petrie, J. Richards, 15, 18fn, 19fn, 27, 49fn
Philips, Paul A. M. Van, 56fn
Pigou, A. C., 24fn, 47, 52fn
Prakash, Om, 294fn
Prest, A. R., 294fn

RAISMAN, SIR JEREMY, 139, 169
Ramanujam, K. N. R., 224fn
Rao, V. K. R. V., 123, 136fn
Reddi, Nagi, 179
Robbins, Lord, 53
Robertson, D. H., 48fn, 49
Robinson, Joan, 109fn
Rosen, George, 108, 248fn, 256fn
Rostas, L., 23, 24, 33fn, 223fn
Rowlands, Sir Archibald, 139, 172
Roy, A. K., 196fn
Ruttenberg, Stanley H., 57fn

SASTRI, A. V. VISVANATHA, 62, 72
Seligman, Edwin, 10, 11, 17, 19, 21, 22, 24, 39, 42, 45, 47
Seltzer, Lawrence H., 40fn, 296fn
Shah, K. C., 67, 115fn
Sharma, Girish Chandra, 150, 152, 302fn
Shirras, G. Findlay, 44
Shoup, Carl, 49fn, 270
Simha, S. L. N., 224fn
Simons, H. S., 35, 40, 52fn
Singh, D. Bright, 225
Smith, Dan Thorp, 55

Somani, G. D., 75, 179
Somers, Harold M., 202fn, 221
Srinivasan, M. S., 127fn
Srivastava, S. S., 157fn
Stamp, J. C., 18, 23, 53
Studenski, Paul, 9, 12fn, 18
Sumner, Lord, 156
Sundaram, V. S., 154fn, 156fn
Sur, A. K., 205fn, 216fn, 252fn

TARAPOREVALA, R. J., 291, 293fn
Tata, Dorabji, 78
Tata, J. N., 78
Tata, J. R. D., 241
Thapar, Lala Karamchand, 276

Thompson, 56fn, 252fn
Thorp, W. L., 15
Tripathy, R. N., 268, 290fn
Tyagi, Mahavir, 182, 288

VAKIL, C. N., 122fn, 266fn, 267
Venkatasubbaiah, H., 252fn
Vickrey, William, 19, 29, 40, 45
Von Gierke, Otto, 5

WAGNER, ADOLF, 14, 254
Walker, David, 201, 229
Williamson, H. F., 266fn
Woodcock, G., 26fn

YAMEY, 262, 269